BEYOND CUSTOMS
An Educator's Journey

BEYOND CUSTOMS
An Educator's Journey

Charity James

With a Foreword by
James Macdonald

AGATHON PRESS, NEW YORK

Distributed to the trade by
SCHOCKEN BOOKS, NEW YORK

For information regarding reproduction in any form, except for purposes of brief quotation, address:

AGATHON PRESS, INC.
150 Fifth Avenue
New York, N.Y. 10011

Distributed to the trade by
SCHOCKEN BOOKS INC.
200 Madison Avenue
New York, N.Y. 10016

Library of Congress Cataloging in Publication Data
James, Charity.
    Beyond customs: an educator's journey.

    Includes bibliographical references.
    1. Teaching. 2. Adolescence. I. Title
LB1025.2.J34   373.1'1020924   73-81795
ISBN 0-87586-042-7

ACKNOWLEDGMENTS: We are grateful to the following for permission to reprint previously published material: For Chapter 8, Ontario Institute of Education; for Chapter 9, *Learning for Living*, London; for Chapters 10 and 14, *Ideas*, a publication of University of London Goldsmiths' College; for Chapter 11, *Forum for the Discussion of New Trends in Education*, Leicester, England; for Chapter 15, University of London Institute of Education; for Chapter 16, Council for Education Advance, London; for Chapter 17, Penguin Books Ltd., London.

PRINTED IN UNITED STATES

Contents

Foreword

IT HAS BEEN my great good fortune to come to know Charity James over the past seven years. It all began with her invitation to me to be a visiting professor at the Curriculum Laboratory at Goldsmiths' College, University of London in 1967-68.

In some ways, at least on the surface, we were an "odd couple." On the one hand a somewhat theoretical and systematic American male dedicated to progressive ideals and to getting the job done. On the other hand a rather puzzling (to me) English lady exuding style and "class" with an almost irritating ability to move in circular intellectual patterns and uncover brilliant and incisive insights about education. In a real sense I was fascinated, attracted and constantly "off balance" during those early days of our friendship and collaboration.

The Curriculum Laboratory carried Charity James' "aura" throughout it, although in saying this I in no way mean to lessen the contribution of the other fine staff members there. She had chosen and sparked a collaborative team which created a dynamic, exciting, and unusual in-service center for educational change and innovation.

When I arrived, the Laboratory was beginning to have run its course. The signs of becoming institutionalized were beginning to emerge. It is indicative of Charity James' intuitive commitment to and the courage of her convictions about creative education that she, in a sense, let it die rather than killing it by bureaucratizing its function. She did so with the complete faith that constant renewal is necessary for individuals, groups, and societies if we are to maintain our personness.

The thoughts you will encounter in this book are integral to the person of Charity James. They come from a life full of unusual experiences, dedicated to the task of self-discovery and the encouragement of the development of other persons' potential, whether in schools, museums, communities, or wherever one might be.

Indeed it is the very breadth of concern and trans-national perspective, whether focused critically upon programs for early adolescents, or upon the aesthetic impulse and activity that can integrate our lives, that adds a unique way of speaking to our educational concerns in America.

Throughout Charity James' personal voyage such themes as youngsters' needs, enquiry, making, dialogue, and aesthetics are woven and rewoven in various patterns, integrated in the curriculum construct variously called Interdisciplinary Enquiry (IDE) or Interdisciplinary Enquiry and Making (IDE/M); and used as critical tools for appraising education and innovations.

It is my hope that you will encounter Charity James in her writing much as I did in my personal knowing and experience which I see reflected in her writing; that you also may feel the aura of her personality, follow the circular patterns of her intellect, and experience her insights with a sense of joy, as I have. In any case you will be in good hands when you make this voyage with Charity James.

JAMES B. MACDONALD
University of North Carolina, Greensboro

Crossing—A Personal Introduction

IN JUNE 1938 I sailed from Montreal to England. I stood on deck in the early morning and thought how easy it was going to be to come back to the United States. Two years before, I had spent several weeks visiting friends in New York City and the South, and now I had just finished a year as a graduate fellow at Radcliffe. America was like a second home. Of course I would soon be back. No problem.

Well, there were problems: bad problems like Munich and the war and my husband's illness and death; good problems like marriage, work, and family. So it was 29 years later, in March 1967, that I came back to America for the first time. I had been invited to talk to the Association for Supervision and Curriculum Development (ASCD) Conference in Dallas on innovations we had been promoting at the University of London Goldsmiths' College Curriculum Laboratory ("the Lab"), of which I was director. There we had been making a total reappraisal of adolescent education, in collaboration with groups of experienced teachers and administrators. It seemed that the policies we had developed had relevance for young people in America, and there was interest also in the fact that in less than two years our courses had led to substantial change in schools.

I enjoyed my visit so much, meeting new friends and old and revisiting places long remembered, that I failed to realize until I was back in England that I had gone into extreme culture-shock. I could not at the time fully analyze my fear and sense of doom. All I could do was to write three long poems about the end of the world; they were called "New King's Road" (which in London leads through

World's End) and were about the disaster which must follow man's overweening pride in power and grandeur.

The shock was valuable because it brought into salience for me the immense importance of the enterprise we engage in when we try to humanize education. We are apt to think of our innovations as a new growth of the human spirit, which indeed they are; but this aspect in isolation can make the whole work seem too exciting, too perishable, for its own good. We must see ourselves also in this period as holding the line, as helping to maintain, through our new relationships with students and our new hopes for their learning, an older humanism which the march of matter, the parade of power, would otherwise destroy. Looking back at my writing since that crossing in 1967, I see that the context of man's crisis has been a recurrent theme; and since then I have also found that when I work with teachers in these terms we discover a shared concern which makes some of our usual prejudices and arguments seem frivolous and strengthens our determination towards reform.

So despite the turmoil of my first return to the States, I was very happy to come back. I visited this country again a couple of times for conferences and lectures and in 1970 accepted a year's teaching of graduate students at Boston University's School of Education. This voyage to New York in 1970 marked the beginning of my final crossing, and appropriately it was almost a replay in reverse of that earlier departure, now more than 30 years past. We sailed into New York harbor in the dawn of a morning in high summer. The sky behind the skyline was a warm, smudged pink, and I remembered some lines I had written three years before:

> But when the pink hour comes, mouse-nosed, mole-pudded,
> The snows will be for melting in the quiet places.

As I watched that sky, I wondered whether these lines (which I had never understood) had been prophetic for my own life. For many years I had been aware of a kind of coolness which distanced me from people, even from ideas and actions. Perhaps in this dawning world that inner indifference might melt at last. A few weeks later, after wondering rather nervously how I might best meet with my first group of graduate students at Boston, I heard myself telling them of these thoughts. And so began a good course, in which each of us found some new growth-point in our working and personal lives. The course was called "Philosophy of Education," and since it was philosophy of experiential education, how could we reflect without first experiencing? We talked and read, of course, but we also danced, did theater improvisations with a visiting company, worked with favorite objects, introduced each other to movement, Japanese calligraphy, Nuffield math—anything we happened to know and enjoy.

It was during that first course that I realized that the marvelous warmth and generosity of the American temperament, the capacity for enjoyment and pride in each others' joys, which I first learned about 30 years earlier, hadn't been destroyed. In 1938 I had left a country that at times I could see only as grand-operetta. The corruption, even the social injustice, the despising of the poor by the fortunate, had for me a quality of gimcrack optimism, as if it really would be "all right on the night." When I returned in 1967 the night had come, and with it had come the seeping wound of war: men in uniform (a sight I hadn't seen for 20 years), little concern for the quality of public life, and a kind of coldness as well as fear in public places. Where before there had been almost excessive friendliness— I remember my father, for instance, being stopped in a hotel elevator and asked to recite the Gettysburg address on the way up, because of his accent (alas, he didn't know the words)—in 1967 the fabric of social relationships seemed dangerously thin. But as I have come to work in greater depth and intimacy with American colleagues and students, including teachers, artists, social workers, administrators, and businessmen, I have found that the generosity and warmth are still there. To be sure, they are being maintained privately and in isolation, and need tending if they are to survive and if they are to affect public as well as private life, but they have not disappeared.

So I realize one reason why it is good for me to be here. For although life in England is much less abrasive, much better supported, altogether cosier, there is also a kind of wryness there, a cutting of hopes to size, which is not so helpful to me personally in my work and my personal life at this time.

This recognition of mutual need has reinforced a belief which we developed at the Lab in relation to students and teachers in schools:

the concept of collaborative learning. We came to see teachers as co-learners, learning with and from their students and each other, and students as co-learners also. In similar fashion, as a transatlantic visitor, I learn from Americans' generosity and sense of scope. I have also learned important lessons here about truthfulness (though these have come about in private life, not in schools): English people are apt to be so mutually protective that we sometimes infantilize one another, hiding unpleasant truths which the other has a right to know and come to terms with. I respect the greater frankness that I meet in people here, even though it can cause greater pain. I respect too the struggle for personal authenticity which a less protective society requires, even though at times I do miss that English sense of humor, the other side of our wryness.

Similarly, in the collaborative learning of our nations, there is a good deal which English people can give. For example, we actively enjoy what the *I Ching* would call the "preponderance of the small." At the moment, when America is dominated by bigness—big industry, big unions, big universities, institutions heavily controlled from "above"—this is a timely quality. I find, for instance, that if someone tries to do down what I stand for, I immediately think of the Armada. I have a full-scale scenario at the ready, with Drake in person banging his drum on Plymouth Hoe, and the great ships aflame.

I can so well see that if your geography is dominated by a land-mass, with vast technical problems to be solved, "unfriendly" environments or indigenous peoples to be mastered, and always a new place to move on to if need be, this feeling for staying put, for holding the line, this tenaciousness, is more difficult to muster. Hence the sense of powerlessness which dominates so much educational thinking is more pervasive in America, and energy which in England is spent within the public school system goes here into creating new alternatives outside and is sometimes frittered away in rhetoric.

My feeling is that during this interim of our time powerlessness can be counteracted best by small friendship groups, people who trust one another and will take risks together but who do not split off into a pluralism of mutual contempt. Here again another English characteristic can be helpful. We are gradualists who do not demand the instantaneous, being more slow-moving and organic in our approach to change. Also, we find it easier than Americans do to feel real to ourselves even when we are not working, since we have roots that go deep into a past before the Puritan ethic and the rise of capitalism.

But it isn't only because of these and other aspects of give-and-take that I am glad to be here. I also believe that for the Western world America is where the action is. England and Western Europe are for the time being on the sidelines. That isn't to suggest a turning away from the rest of the world. Indeed, if the human race is to come through the present crisis, each of the great human systems should have its contribution to give: the ancient East, the modern East, the African heritage, the West. But because the dangers of the West are most visible in this country, the polarization most extreme, it will be here, I believe, that Western man's contribution must eventually emerge, however painfully. Further, whatever the future is to be—and I am one of those who believe we are at a crisis point in man's fever and possibly, hopefully, at a mutation point in his evolution—it is important that Americans, retreating from idyllism, do not drop into a slough of self-accusation. Both attitudes are equally romantic, equally impractical. Americans must go on dreaming; it is simply that the dream has to change. It is from this creative agony that I don't want to be cut off, just by the chance of having been born on the other side of the Atlantic.

Having decided to settle in for a long sojourn, I thought it sensible to send home for some baggage. I have contributed a good number of articles to English books and journals which are not easily available here. Some of these are contained in the last two sections of this book. Part I, "Beyond Customs," consists of previously unpublished material, mainly an adapted version of a report which I wrote for the Ford Foundation in the summer of 1972, as part of a study of the possible development of education for 11- to 16-year-olds in different areas of the United States, to which I have added comments from my more recent experiences as a consultant to schools. Part II, "Porpoises and Rainbows," is a selection from various speeches I made between 1967 and 1970 to international meetings, together with articles which develop some special themes that went rather beyond the limits of the work at the Goldsmiths'

Curriculum Laboratory. The final section, "Passport for the Journey," is a grateful acknowledgment of the opportunity I had to work with heads of schools and experienced teachers in a collaborative situation at the Lab from 1965 to 1970. If it had not been for those years, I would have had little to offer on my arrival here.

When I settled down to write this introduction I assumed that I would compose a sober professional beginning to what is, after all, a fairly sober collection of observations and reflections. Two or three hours later I found that I had written this very personal statement. I was surprised, but decided that if this was the kind of book my inner consciousness had decided on, so be it; and I went on to write the headnotes to each section in much the same mood. Subsequently, I wondered if this personal tone might prevent some readers from taking the contents seriously. I would be sorry if that were so because the book contains a great part of what I have learned about education over the last few years. But then I thought if that is how it is to be, again so be it. For years I've been writing and talking about the nature of personal knowledge, the importance of personal disclosure in teaching, the danger of being locked in an unreal customary role, the need to take risks. Now I seem to have learned my own lessons, and I must take the consequences.

This book covers a period of more than seven years. How can I tender thanks to all the people with whom I have shared years or moments of time? When I wrote my report for the Ford Foundation, the names of individuals and faculties who had helped me during one year alone came to more than 150. So I have to simplify and can mention in this country only my friends in the Middle Years Consortium, the group with which I have worked most closely for 18 months: Doris Dondis, Marie Genest, Dennis Littky, Jim Macdonald, Tom Minter, Mary Ann Penny, Dan Scheinfeld, and Florence Scroggie; Florence Roane, through whose suggestion I first returned in 1967; Gene Phillips, who brought me over here in 1970 for a rest; Mary Kohler, James Aldrich, Sam Black, and George Hein, who by their kindness and good advice have kept me going without one; Marjorie Martus of the Ford Foundation, to whose interest in open education I owe my work last year; Mary Caroline Richards, whose home has been my home and to whom I look for personal help and advice; Claire James and Jules Harris, who are my family; in the middle period, Geoffrey Caston, Renée Marcousé, and Seonaid Robertson, who encouraged me to a greater sense of scope; and back at the Lab—the *fons et origo* of this phase of a life in process—Edwin Mason, Leslie Smith, Mary Darby, Catherine Dais, Peter Mauger, Sam Mauger, Margaret Horne, Sonya Caston, and Mike Savage. Finally, I am grateful to Burton Lasky, who wanted to publish this book, and to Arthur Tobier, who has helped to put it all together.

Whatever my work may turn out to be in the future it will, I believe, be in North America. This time, hopefully, I have come back to stay.

New York City, March 1973

Part I
Beyond Customs

PASSING THROUGH A CUSTOMS BARRIER takes time. I have been
working at it for two and a half years now: first at Boston University;
then in 1971-72 on a Study and Travel Award from the Ford Foundation, which took me to visit and work with schools across the
United States; finally, in recent months, as a consultant to schools in
and around New York City. I have wanted to keep the freshness of
my earliest observations of American education, for I remember how
valuable to us in the Lab was the initial surprise of our American
visiting professors at many things they found in English schools,
things we had hardly questioned. Sometimes our English assumptions were different but equally valid; sometimes our visitors saw
failings we had never noticed. But while trying to hold on to some of
this freshness of outlook, I have tried also to come to a deeper understanding of our differences of custom, and especially to distinguish between those which are no more than alternative solutions
to similar problems and those which seem to represent alternative
viewpoints about human nature and human destiny. Here are two
examples, one of each kind.

The first example concerns the status of teachers vis-à-vis the lay
public. I must admit that it makes my gorge rise to find good
teachers in this country exposed to extreme pressure and threats
from the so-called "community," often from reactionary and self-
serving groups and not the larger community at all. But then I have
to remind myself that the sources of our national schooling are quite
different. In England, schools derive ultimately from the priestly
tradition and later, in the early nineteenth century, from a middle
class movement to improve (and control) the masses. So every

classroom teacher inherits some sense of self-determination and professional authority; and this is institutionalized in the head teacher's autonomy in running his or her school (not, by the way, as a "building principal" at the bottom rung of the administration, but as principal teacher, educational leader and guardian of the flock against intruders). Head teachers expect independence, even though if wise they build up a relationship of trust with parents and community.

The American school derives from the early need of individual communities across the land to educate their young. So the teacher starts off as a servant of the immediate community, in a sense which is quite alien to me; and since school districts are often so small and funding so local (another difference of custom), the pressure can be extremely direct and hard to counter. In both countries I have been working with sensitive and reflective teachers who are eager to move towards a notion of schooling which far outstrips the understanding of the general public, who find it hard to appreciate anything they themselves didn't experience in school. In this situation, the relative independence of the English teaching profession is an advantage. And even when the shoe is on the other foot, when parents are forward-looking and teachers laggardly, I don't think the possessive and rather driving style of intervention that I find here is the best way to help teachers to improve their ways and still retain some necessary degree of self-esteem. On the other hand, in England we have a tremendous amount to learn from the United States about the possibilities of positive involvement of parents and volunteers in school affairs. The American way is likely to be slow, because it gives so little chance to schools to move ahead and prove that the new ways are an improvement; but in the long haul it may be no less fruitful, since the fundamental problem in both countries is not just to improve schools but for the society as a whole to arrive at a more evolved and mature outlook on humanity and the social forms it needs. For this, the very frustrations and conflict of the American scene may have value, uncomfortable as they certainly are.

My second example of differences in customs is of a kind that I have found much more difficult to handle, for it represents a difference not of organization but of intention, a quite important divergence of viewpoint on children's behavior and hence of human behavior in general; in fact, it goes beyond customs. I have noticed that many innovative teachers in this country appear to accept without demur, even from the youngest children, two behaviors which experienced English teachers would not stand for (beginners often meet them, of course): one is a kind of brash ill manners towards the teacher, the other a grab-as-grab-can among themselves. I have tried to write off my discomfort as merely due to my being foreign. But after much soul-searching I have come to believe that it is quite simply bad for children to be allowed to be habitually rude, selfish and disruptive. For a child to blow up occasionally in an unforeseen volcano of genuine feeling, or to have a mood that he or she doesn't quite know how to handle, is of course a very different matter, and so is ordinary testing out of a teacher. I can sympathize when a teacher's permissiveness stems from uncertainty about his or her change of role in the classroom. But too often it seems to be based on a mistaken notion of "individualism" which sees the separate development of a child as outweighing his or her obligation to others. This must be mistaken, for we are social beings who will grow best as individuals in social circumstances where we can give and receive honest personal respect. In terms of the staying power of mankind, to help young people build a community based on respect and caring is perhaps the greatest contribution teachers have to make. It cannot be put aside, whatever the pressures of a possessive individualism. In fact, its importance is growing yearly, as children more and more tend to imitate the crazy behavior of the adult world. I have noticed recently how many teachers who are aware of this problem have agreed that it is increasing, and that it is partly imitation, but partly also an expression of the children's deep pain at the incoherence of the world they have come to live in.

Good English teachers have sometimes confused their American visitors because they work from implicit expectations of which they are not always consciously aware and which they may not see much need to explain to children. Good American teachers tend to be more explicit, to talk more with children about behavior rather than go about quietly creating a setting in which behaving well seems the natural way to be. Any visitor to this country from a less complex and more long-rooted society, must honor this difference of custom, as long as children are not submitted to compulsory amateur encounter-group sessions as occasionally happens. I must admit that I prefer the English style, for children of elementary school age at least. For one thing it leads to less moralizing, for another it implies that the adult is prepared to take responsibility for providing a coherent environment where children can make the choices they are ready to make and are not urged to carry a moral load they aren't yet mature enough to manage. In either case the procedures which liberate children to work with self-respect and mutual care seem to amount to roughly the same imperatives: acknowledge the different strengths and needs of different children; treat each youngster as partner in her or his learning; show that decisions are not arbitrary but are an outcome of reasonable expectations; ensure that as well as opportunities to work privately there are things to be done which cannot be achieved except communally.

In this section I have included most of the pieces I have written about American education. Chapter 1 is part of an article I wrote in the early summer of 1971 for a journal which was preparing an issue dealing with early and middle adolescence. In terms of my metaphor, the customs barrier, Chapter 1 might be described as the statement of what I had to declare, since it outlines the expectations for education in adolescence that I had arrived at as a result of working with English teachers and principals from 1965 to 1970. The rest of the section (Chapters 2-5) is an extended version of the report I wrote for the Ford Foundation at the end of my study period. I have added a good deal of material as a result of working with schools in 1972-73, but have retained the original shape of the public sections of my report. I am very glad to have this opportunity to thank the Ford Foundation for a generous personal grant; I think I learned most of all from having the chance to offer suggestions to schools in different parts of the country and to see with them how they worked out in practice—a much more fruitful way of studying than any more casual visiting could have provided.

During my study, I was concerned mainly with trying to introduce some exploratory and collaborative programs in a few schools and with identifying and making a personal assessment of some new trends in education which are influencing American schools. As I traveled, I began to guess at and categorize some educational needs of adolescents. My study concluded with comments about educational change in this country and a short description of the Middle Years Consortium, the small group of teachers and educators with whom I collaborated. Because of the provenance of this section, these aspects—intervention, needs, survey, and change—are its four main emphases also.

There are many questions about this level of education, questions much on American educators' minds today, such as busing or funding or drug education or bilingual programs, which I have kept away from because I don't know much about them. I've left out other problems, such as inhumane teachers or prison-like schools in the decaying centers of big cities, because my task was to concern myself with growth points rather than disaster areas. I am aware also of many hidden meanings—personal, societal, and spiritual—of much that goes on in schools; I have ignored these because I want to write about them at greater leisure. I hope that this section will be read for what it is: one person's observations based on 18 months' working with teachers who are interested in improving the education of American adolescents.

1. How English and American Schools Fail Adolescents

CAN TWELVE TO SIXTEEN be isolated as an age range with identifiable problems of its own, as the issue of this volume suggests? If aunts count as evidence, I have a formidable one to offer on behalf of this particular brief. When I was 14, mine looked at me and said, "People of your age ought to be put away for four years where none of us would have to see you." At that moment, if ever, I understood the doctrine of the Fall, for surely there was something ineradicably wrong with me and my kind. In terms of puberty, the ages 14 to 18 some forty years ago were equivalent to the ages 12 to 16 today, so presumably my aunt would have some understanding of the concept 12-to-16 which is denied to me. If I do think in terms of ages in education, it is more likely to be 9 to 12 or 13, 13 to 14, and 14 to 18, as roughly covering the varied onset and development of puberty and, respectively, referring to three phases in relation to adults: comfortable and relatively serene amity, a necessary and painful withdrawal, and then a more settled later adolescence. Ironically, I worked in England mainly with 11- to 16-year-olds, and in the United States I claim sixth to tenth grades as a special concern. The reasons are cogent yet paradoxical. In England (apart from school systems with middle schools), 11 to 15 is the age of transfer to secondary school and 16 is the end of compulsory schooling, so 11- to 16-year-olds are usually all together. In the States I deliberately chose this grade range because it spanned every kind of school from elementary through to high school.

About one thing my aunt was certainly prescient. In both English and American education, young people from around 12 to 16 are not seen, neither are they heard. One of the first things I noticed in com-

6

ing to teach in the United States in 1970 was that there is a ferment towards reform at the beginning and end of schooling, but the middle years are left very much as they were, except insofar as the introduction of middle schools for roughly ages 11 to 14 is causing some reconsideration in some school districts. Ask about innovative programs, funded research projects, parents or teachers on strike, community schools, home-based schools, open campus, free schools, alternative schools, even nongrading, and the chances are that they exist only for kindergarten through third grade or ninth through twelfth grades, with the emphasis in high school on juniors and seniors; the younger adolescent will be ignored.

In England the situation is different, but in its negative aspects it is similar. Sixteen has significance because it is the age at which the first public examinations take place. There has been only a certain queasiness felt about those 60 percent or so who are so unfortunate as to be "non-examinable." For these second-rate citizens a different kind of education is sometimes provided: a serious study of social and ethical problems, plenty of art and drama, an outgoing education beyond school boundaries; but the clear implication is that this is inferior and unworthy of anyone who is capable of proper scholarship. Meanwhile, the more talented are encouraged to continue along traditional lines, learning early to hide their sterility behind a fig leaf of paper qualifications. I do not, of course, suggest that all college-bound or similar youngsters in either country are intellectually or spiritually barren, but from the point of view of their traditional educators it does not seem to matter much whether they are barren or generative. The only requirement is that they should be able to stomach the sour apple of predetermined adult knowledge. The result of these stereotyped expectations of education in early and middle adolescence is that no one knows much about how young people of this age might be educated, an ignorance markedly in contrast with our increasing understanding of the educational needs of younger children.

Why at a phase which in our culture is perhaps uniquely vulnerable are the needs of young people so little considered? One reason must be that this is a stage of life when the young are least able to make a case in their own defense. They have not the charm and dependence of younger children, nor have they the power to explain themselves and their legitimate requirements for change, a power which enables some senior high school students to lead the way for others. For these same reasons many of the more inventive teachers have tended to work with younger or older pupils and there, being distressed by the carnage around them, have become urgent for reform.

These intervening years are also the period when parents are most ambivalent. The wise ones realize that the cord has to be cut, but even they may still be hurt to find their children slipping downstream, further and further away, so that they can call to each other only across an echoing distance. Baffled by moods that are unpredictable and seem irrational (even if often internally necessary), aware of how little the adolescent's powerful new sexuality is understood, fearful of the dangers of hard drugs and commercial exploitation which meet a short-term wish for excitement and extreme conformity, even the most understanding parents cannot offer good evidence of how school might best serve their children. And however wise parents or other adults may hope to be, most of us in fact have underlying jealousies and hidden agenda which do not help. It is difficult not to be jealous of the promise of youth; in an appetitive society it is difficult not to be jealous *for* one's own children, hoping they will match one's own success or compensate for one's failures.

While young people and their parents are confused and ambivalent, the claims of public society are at their most uncompromising. The fact that these claims are irrational does not reduce their emotive force. Stated unkindly, the underlying illogic seems something like this: childhood is all very well; we can just afford it, and children are not dangerous. But can we really afford time for these wild adolescents to grow into themselves and their futures? On the contrary, the demands of the economy require that we begin to sort out young people for the labor market; and *that*, therefore, will be good for them. At the same time, it is increasingly essential for the balancing of social forces in the economy to keep young people off the labor market, where they are certainly not needed. So how is society to do both—sort them out and keep them out? Well, for one thing, society can keep them learning; but it should be the kind of learning that is both boring and impersonal because that is what real life is. Learning must also be made to seem extremely difficult, because otherwise the whole process will be exposed as a confidence trick. We don't want to hear evidence that material seems less difficult if you want to learn it for intrinsic reasons or if teachers expect that you will be able to master it, and we certainly don't care for reminders of periods when economic needs were different, such as during World War II when women, no less, learned within a few months the skills that should have taken them years. There is no time for youth and there is nothing useful for youth to do, so let's keep their noses to the grindstone. Then they will not be dangerous to us.

The process of castration doesn't end at sixteen. Educative societies are not created by carrot and stick. Having seen how longer and longer education, on which I had set great hopes, can extend the feeling of disillusionment and the fact of dependence, I am not surprised by Ivar Berg's evidence that what he calls "the great training robbery" does not even work.[1] Even if the United States turns out to be rich in serious and thoughtful young people, it will be because the dogma of progress can no longer protect them from observing the unequivocal crisis of our species. Most of this understanding they will have learned from one another or from the media, not from formal education. So it ill becomes adults to turn on them and call them sentimental (even when this is a true charge), considering how little we have offered to their thinking.

In the long run, the education of 12- to 16-year-olds will be made good only within a very different concept of society from what we have today, one that is in the wings but has not yet emerged in recognizable form. In the meantime, people connected with educational reform will have the unenviable task of trying within the school to prefigure that more human society without having the public support for doing so. We have to accept the riskiness and pain of autonomy and mutuality if we are not to accept the certainty of self-destruction. We are right to have a sense of urgency because there is little time; but the changes that are required involve no less than a spiritual mutation, so that superficial changes based on fads and fashions and facile agreement may be less helpful than hard-held disagreement.

Fortunately, fundamental reform has advantages on its side. The same technology which may destroy us is in its short life already changing and expanding human intelligence, as tools do,[2] teaching us to be less simplistic, more aware of cues in many media, and more at ease with the obsolescence of knowledge. We are thereby ready to envisage and start bringing into being a culture that is less hierarchical, more sensitive, more exploratory, more creative. We are becoming better able to cope with complexity; we can be more open to the earthshaking implications of the instant. These kinds of values need to be reflected in our educational system. In trying to accomplish this, we need not be surprised at the increasing anxiety and rigidity we find among parents and teachers. These developments are inevitably very threatening to those who do not have the disposition or opportunity to mole away at them in their secret being.

SOME REQUIREMENTS PROPOSED

From this general belief stem certain essential requirements of education, whether the students are children, adolescents, or adults. The first requirement concerns our exploratory and creative gifts. The young need to explore and create not just in the labs or studios, nor even just throughout the learning curriculum, but through the whole way of life of the school, and this means that the school must not seek a bureaucratic rigidity. They should be encouraged to look at the world questioningly, to formulate questions that have meaning for them, and to refine these and make them operational. (This is not the same as much so-called inquiry education, which is inductive in technique only and not in intention.) They need to be able to make works of art or inventions or communications according to their inner vision, to make good guesses about human behavior and, for that matter, about the behaviors of newts or molecules or spacecraft. They also need to see that they can make a difference to their social environment. They need to learn how best to make lives that have meaning for them by sharing in the making of the social system in which they spend most of their day.

These living behaviors of inquiry and making are necessary but not sufficient. Over the last three or four years I have come to think that a third behavior which I have called "dialogue" is even more central and even less acknowledged. Indeed it looks all too possible that the epitaph, necessarily unwritten, of the human race may turn out to be: "This was an exploratory and creative species, but it did not learn to listen." As we begin to understand how the rapacity and exploitation of advanced societies may destroy the planet, it becomes clear how much we need many kinds of awareness—the sensuous competence of an animal, the sensitiveness of a social person, the syncretistic vision of an artist, the innocence of a lover, the trust of a spiritual being. Dialogue can find its place in many ways in a school: through role-playing and improvisation, through seriously maintained debate on personal values, through the feedback of film or videotape, through literature and creative writing, through multisensory work with objects and materials, through having time to contemplate objects, ideas, and people peacefully, through listening to music, and through aesthetic experience of the marvelous inevitability of mathematical forms. It is a value diffused throughout the humane school, a value evidenced in the collaborative work of groups, in being allowed time to discover one's own rhythms of engagement and withdrawal, in openness to hunches and intuitive responses, in listening to the inner voice of poetry, in having time to breathe.

A second requirement of education involves concerns. The minimum requirement we can make of a society is that it should pay attention to the matters that most touch its members. We have here the excellent evidence of Fantini and Weinstein[3] that younger disadvantaged children in the States are deeply concerned with their search for identity, their capacity to make relationships, and their ability to affect the environment. As adults we recognize the same concerns in ourselves, and we can take it that early and mid-adolescents are even more sharply aware of these problems, which are the stuff of their fantasies, the basis of their decisions, and also to a quite exceptional extent the theme of their conversation. These concerns should be the subject of their studies also.

Although their main concerns can ultimately be categorized under the three headings of identity, relationship and mastery, people's priorities change in the course of growing up. All in all, the situation of the 11 to 12-year old is usually not too bad. They have survived the early separation of self from surroundings and around 9 or so have become pretty conscious of individuality—and often expressed that consciousness in rather ruthless ways—but by 11 or 12 they have mastered childhood and are likely to be optimistically communal and on comfortable terms with reasonable adults. Then somewhere along the line comes the break with parents, the greater, inevitable lasting loneliness of the grown person in an individualized society, and with it the search to merge oneself with others in the same phase. At about 13 or 14 it seems that the whole task of entering a complex and anomic society is at its most difficult, fantasies most absorbing, moods most incomprehensible and extreme, ambivalence towards adults becoming most obvious. It is only in the middle teens as a rule that the majority begin to have assured access to complex abstract ways of thinking[4] which can help them to distance themselves from their problems and (surely no coincidence) in some cases begin to free themselves from quite rigid ethical and social assumptions.[5] It is then that interest in public affairs can be expected to grow alongside the earlier preoccupation with private experience.

A third requirement is diversity. One form that awareness and respect for concerns must take is for a school to recognize and delight in the fact that people are diverse, rather than to process them into conformity. Very practical results follow immediately. As a first step, the didactic technique of the class lesson is dethroned and is replaced for the most part by a ferment of small group work interspersed with individual self-direction. Rigid timetabling also goes, to be replaced not so much by modular scheduling of batches of students as by providing mutual access of teachers and students, arrived at in the least regimented way a school can devise.

Beyond this, awareness of diversity involves our being much more sensitive to the variety of individual interests and personal needs. Both may be very significant in young people's lives. Interests are not to be sidetracked into luncheon breaks and after-hour clubs. Nor are they to be shelved until they happen to coincide with teachers' or parents' plans: it is not good enough to ask to play the trumpet at 12 and three years later be allowed to learn the clarinet, as happened to a young friend of mine. Interests may express passing phases and even crazes, or they may be evidence of a lasting vocation; one can never know until one tries one's hand at them. Interests need acknowledgment because they always represent (even if at times in a superficial form) an underlying concern.

We also have the yet more difficult task of reshaping our notion of young people's personal needs for help in learning. Usually a student is regarded as having a special need if he does not come up to teachers' norms—does not read, for instance, or compute or punctuate according to expectations for his age or grade or according to extrapolation from his own previous performance. But as we change and grow, we all have changing needs. People do not develop all of a piece like predesigned, prefabricated buildings. The processes of assimilation and accommodation are much more complex, and growth is often seemingly haphazard to the outside observer. In adolescence, a time for gathering up new notions about one's future life, it is quite natural that young people should find themselves held back by weaknesses that didn't seem important before: lacking the basic mathematics or science, say, for an invention in the workshop, or the broader educational requirements that a profession will require. With our Parkinsonian attitude to learning we too often write young people off, when in fact with motivation running high it is possible for them to do a speedy rescue operation on themselves and possibly thereby revolutionize their self-concepts. It is here that diagnostic help is needed, and carefully individualized programs or assignments—dangerous if they are the main content of the curriculum—are justified by the fact that they are truly intended for the individual.

Fourth, there is open and closed learning. In a static society one can be pardoned for purveying the established culture neatly packaged and supposing one has done well. But today, it is essential to learn to use a broader canvas also. Young people need to ask questions of fundamental importance about our species, our environment, and our fellow-travelers on the planet, and at this age such studies should be not merely integrated in content but truly interdisciplinary in conception. (See "The Open Curriculum," Part III.) This in England I called Interdisciplinary Enquiry (IDE); and in the States, Open Inquiry. I see it as an activity of central importance for both students and teachers, providing an occasion for invaluable collaboration in groups of different specialisms or personal lines of interest. It is, of course, also important to have some narrowly focused learning, whether in long-term development within a subject discipline or in short-term electives, but to work always within narrow demarcations is ultimately to deny the young person's right to search for meaning and reduces his chances of finding any, now or later.

Finally, and above all, appropriate relationships are the necessary condition of good education, and also its expression. A center for education needs to be collegiate, in the sense that older and younger scholars work alongside each other rather than being locked in a series of confrontations. We should look to the small group, with its known effectiveness in promoting and sustaining change, as the basic learning cell. The big bureaucratic machine may perhaps have some future in keeping going the armies and industries of the world, but it is certainly inappropriate for a community concerned with growth, flux, and diversity.

With regard to relationships outside the school, in theory it may be necessary to affirm that a confidently unstable organism will not shut itself off from the surrounding world, but in practice opening up to the community just happens, since its members find that they need all the help they can get and are welcomed in interchange.

THE FAILURES OF TRADITIONAL SCHOOLING

How far does the traditional education for 12- to 16-year-olds match up to the requirements I have proposed? In inquiry, practically not at all. Questions are asked by teachers, not children, and then mainly to wake them up and check whether they have taken in the required information. On making, practically not at all. Students come into a ready-made school, and they have to take it or leave it, but of course are not allowed to leave it. As a colleague said to me once, the only kind of making they can do is to make a nuisance of themselves. The sense of pleasure and involvement you find in a good art studio, workshop, or home economics class is clear evidence of how much boys and girls relish creative work; but these places are usually thought to be inferior, and in the "academic classes" young people's ideas count for little or nothing except with an occasional enlightened teacher. So creativity and commitment, being un-rewarded, do not grow—or grow only outside the school curriculum. In school the young are being effectively prepared to be passive members of a consumer society. As for "dialogue," that is hard to find in the traditional curriculum because there is no stillness. If a student manages to cut out some of the noise in the system, it is more likely to be by cannabis than by curriculum. Traditional curriculum is akin to a much more dangerous drug, speed—one well suited to a culture that is greedy for experiences but will not stay to enjoy them.

Concerns are ignored, with one significant exception: when they coincide with public, economic interest, that is when young people are bothered about their working future. One should not write off this concern, for it is vitally significant to two different groups of students, those who have a lifelong vocation for some particular kind of work and those many members of underprivileged groups for whom job and paycheck are early recognized as the difference between penury and prosperity. But too often, with the schools' connivance, the basis of one's sense of identity is narrowed to identity through job; relationships, to marketing oneself; and effectiveness, to job potential. And as for the changing priorities of young people as they move from childhood into adult status, these are studiously ignored, so we have little knowledge of how they should be reflected in schooling.

As for diversity, in both the United States and England, individual differences are broadly the differences between "cans" and "can'ts" (apart from the influence of early specialization in English schools). If you can't do calculus, you can move to the other side of the tracks and concentrate on carpentry. If you can't read, you are recognized as a suitable case for treatment and probably kept at it until the very idea is increasingly abhorrent. If you can't keep up, you can repeat a grade or drop a stream or track. If you can keep going, you can keep on marching into the distance until the gates of the university close behind you.

Another aspect of diversity which in traditional education is usually at one and the same time overemphasized and undervalued is sex differences. The problem arises in the teens from the fact that girls are involved in puberty earlier than boys, and that with this earlier manifestation seems to come an earlier anxiety and also an earlier emotional maturity—these differences are ignored in the typical coeducational class. On the other hand, stereotyped sex divisions abound in the curriculum as a whole, with engineering for boys and home economics for girls, for instance, and with physical skill and challenge too often narrowed at junior high school and high school level to a crude athleticism and team idolatry for boys and hardly recognized in girls at all. It is, of course, important that adolescents be able to identify confidently with their sex, but this should not be confused with stereotyped roles. We are all bisexual, and the range of physical and temperamental differences within each sex is potentially more important throughout life than the differences between them.

Open learning as well as closed? Open interdisciplinary inquiry is unheard of; integrated studies of a didactic character are to be found occasionally, and sometimes they prove very rewarding to the teachers who plan them. But, in general, narrow studies dominate our traditional schools, as if the student's daily experience were deliberately made incoherent. (In England this rotary system of subject teaching is sometimes known as "bells and cells." Recently this was improved on by an audiotypist who wrote it as "bells and sells." So what are teachers then? Buskers for the corporate state?)

Finally, the traditional pattern of relationships is autocratic, although sometimes not unkindly. Students do not experience the satisfactory dynamic of working together, unless they are accomplished at cheating. Nor do teachers. Without this mutual support, and in an unfriendly or uncomprehending public climate, it is hardly surprising that teachers and students learn not to take risks, and lights of invention are so often doused.

Although the requirements I have listed may not seem too extreme, when viewed against actual practice they amount to a request for a total rethinking of schooling. The reformation of education in these middle years must not be long delayed. We are failing our adolescents—and they know it.

2. Some Educational Needs of Adolescents

I SUGGESTED IN THE FIRST CHAPTER that people connected with educational reform have the task of trying to prefigure within the school a more humane society which does not yet exist in the world. More recently I have come to see that this society will be based on a generous understanding of students' personal needs. (In *Young Lives at Stake* I argued that we should think of a person-centered rather than a child-centered school. In concentrating here on the needs of adolescents I am not recanting but merely taking a first necessary step. I only wish that more studies were undertaken of the needs experienced by teachers in their search for continuing personal and professional growth within a school.)

The need-polarities I have chosen came to my mind in the course of working in schools: I would notice, for instance, that fifth-graders seized on fairy stories although so little folklore was usually offered at that age, or I would observe the intense satisfaction of older adolescents when they had done some human service, or I would empathize with the febrile energy or flat lethargy of young people who were at their desks all day. From these clues I began to piece together tentative generalizations about needs that were not being met, such as a need to be needed, a need for myth, a need for physical activity, and a need to belong. Then I checked up on these quite informally or made suggestions which might work well if my hunches were correct. The result of this procedure is that the terms in which I have written are less general than the statements of psychologists and form a basis, I hope, of some quite specific educational guidelines.

No doubt all the needs I observed, and others also, could be set

17

well within Abraham Maslow's hierarchy[1] or other psychological classifications; I am certainly not hoping to supersede systematic studies of that kind. My observations are more impressionistic but also more closely directed towards education. For instance, self-discovery and self-actualization are undoubtedly central life-tasks for adolescents, but it is perhaps useful to suggest to teachers that they will be best achieved in a school which acknowledges a need to be needed, a need to need, a need for myth, a need for intensity, a need to relate with adults.

I do not suggest this list as in any way final. It is simply what I came up with in the course of my work with schools and felt competent to write about. In fact, I am conscious of other needs which I have left out because I am not able to formulate them adequately at present: I have in mind particularly the need through the arts to realize emerging inner forms in outer reality; I am well aware too that I have not tackled the question of the adolescent's overriding concern with his or her sexuality.

As I began to categorize educational needs, I found that they could be paired conveniently in what I have called "polarities." Colleagues planning to try out these needs in working with adolescents tell me that the polarities make a useful frame of reference for placing the requirements of individuals and groups.

I have found three ways of looking at educational needs that are helpful to me. The first is to distinguish between prevailing and countervailing activities. Sometimes it is important to move with the flow of students' needs, such as in accepting the fact that early and middle adolescents long to understand human behavior to guide their self-understanding and their grasp of relationships. On the other hand, sometimes we have to countervail a prevailing imbalance. For example, one day I described to a teacher in a sophisticated suburban area the studies of the future to which I refer in Chapter 3 (pg. 52), and she suggested that I might talk with her seventh-graders about them. I soon realized they had a great deal of half-baked information about the future and were almost totally unaware of the here-and-now. So instead we embarked on a study of their own education in relation to a new satellite school building which was being planned on an interesting woodland site. They considered what they themselves thought education was all about, and how they felt about it; they questioned specialist teachers and the principal on their aims and purposes; some contrasted education in their parents' and grandparents' time; many read a number of paperbacks on educational change; others examined designs for school buildings, surveyed the area to be used, discussed the ecological aspect of building there. Finally, they sent statements to the district task force and school board and gave evidence through elected representatives. Their feet were now on the ground—where they had needed to have them put—but the directions they chose to move in were varied and were their own. It is often important for suburban youngsters to ground their thinking in factual reality this way; whereas for inner-city children, who have far greater social realism, it can be much more important to extend their "need to need," helping them to engage in interests they see as beyond their reach, countervailing the narrow limitations of their real hopes (as against their sometimes unrealistic fantasies).

Secondly, I find it helpful to identify the sources of new educational needs. Some are emerging now because people have remained the same while societies have changed rapidly. A need to be needed, for instance, has a quite new intensity when societies are dedicated to a higher GNP, which as everyone should know does not signify the "Greater Needs and Purposes" of its members. Again, the need for myth is acute today in order to balance an often mechanistic science with older kinds of wisdom. A need for physical activity dominates when children no longer come to school exhausted from their work in the fields. A need to relate to adults other than parents, always important in adolescent development, becomes more salient for the suburban youngsters whose parents have (as one described it to me) reduced all relationships to administrative relationships, thereby creating a generation gap. On the other hand, there are also new positive needs which stem from our new crisis of human opportunity—for I believe that our species is at the beginning of a new transformation in its psychic and spiritual evolution. Now that we begin to leave behind many of our old standards and institutions, "as a snake leaves behind its old skin" which has become "too tight, and therefore not functional,"[2] we find youngsters engaged in a new search for meaning, seeking a new and more intimate relationship with the cosmos and with their inmost selves; and so a new need for stillness is created, as are new ways of belonging with peers and adults.

The needs I propose here, by the way, do not supersede the study needs in the "clinic" aspect of the fourfold curriculum (see page 82). That concept refers to one need I describe in this chapter, namely, learning by needing. It had to do with an individual child's need for coaching either when he is stuck in some learning problem or when there is some new advance he cannot make because some information or knowledge is lacking. Children do not grow all of a piece, nor do adults. Often we drop stitches which we need the chance to pick up; coaching to meet those individual needs is an important provision for any child. Similarly, in thinking about the need-polarities which follow, we have to think individually. One of the most important aspects of Open Inquiry is that within a shared area of investigation, different individual or group interests can be met and problems worked on, since then the student is able to choose an emphasis which meets his particular set of needs.

Finally, we should look at these need-polarities developmentally. All of them are true of all human beings to some extent; but some, I think, are of special significance in early and middle adolescence. I would doubt, for instance, if younger children have the same intense need as adolescents to be needed, to change the outer environment, to study human behavior, to forge new kinds of relationships with adults, to collaborate in large-scale achievements, to have peace and quiet. But I may be quite wrong: it may only be that the form the need takes is rather different, and in that case I hope that teachers of younger children will find these polarities useful. Within the needs of the age range 11-16 itself there are developmental changes, which I have briefly suggested (p. 26) but I do not want to impose very tentative generalizations on others. We have too little knowledge of young people's real educational biases at various ages because we have not thought about them or allowed youngsters to reveal them. Anyway, there are differences between boys and girls at these ages and between individuals. It seems better to acknowledge a likely range of needs, to consult the young or draw them on by one's own interest, and also to make broad and varied offers they can take up in a form that suits them best. What follows is a detailed description of some of the need-polarities I suggest.

A NEED TO BE NEEDED

My most outstanding realization I have arrived at during the past 18 months is of the damage that is done to young people growing up in a society where the needs of the economy take precedence over the needs of persons, as is the case in a modern consumer society. Throughout history, puberty has been the latest period at which the majority of younger members of societies have been accepted as contributing to the common good; indeed, in the past many children have been essential to the economy of their society or household at an age when today they would be in the primary grades of an elementary school. There has been a widespread claim to *machismo* or adult status at age 14 or so, which is totally denied by a society that finds it economically necessary to keep young people off the labor market into their late teens or their twenties. And where households are united as consumers and not as producers and much simple manual work is done by domestic appliances (especially in small families, in which the parents can do all the caring for their children they conceive as necessary), it is possible to go right through into late adolescence and beyond without having any experience of being needed, or being anything more than just one more consumer—whether the consumption consists of food, entertainment, or schooling.

In *Young Lives At Stake,* I stressed the importance in the curriculum of *making* of all kinds: making of ideas, of objects, of experiments, of visual expressions of abstract ideas, of contributions to the wider community, of the collaborative climate of the school. But I had envisaged this engagement mainly in terms of a creative curriculum which would give the young plenty of opportunity to contribute their own ideas, to create in the arts, to become involved in community projects of the school if that seemed attractive, and so on. I still think such things are essential. But now I realize that it is extraordinarily difficult to come through adolescence in good shape in a society that has as little use for the vibrant energies of the young as there is in this country. I realize, of course, that there are still some prosperous parents who are aware of the need to make demands on their children. I also realize that probably a majority of youngsters in grades 6 through 10 have had some experience of casual or regular out-of-school work. This helps, and when it is of economic importance to the home, as opposed to being just a source of pocket money, such work can bring self-esteem. I respect these facts, but I am concerned with urging a society to show greater public recognition of its need for its young.

At present, of course, consumerism is more a problem in America than elsewhere, partly because the economy is more advanced and has less use for the young worker, partly because the level of consumerism is higher, partly because in so highly individualized a society the collective fabric which should help young people to find an accepted place in family or neighborhood appears to be thinner than in less mobile, more traditional cultures. But since this *is* in the first instance an American problem, it is an opportunity for Americans to be socially inventive in ways which may be helpful in due course to less advanced countries. Indeed, of all the recommendations I would make as a result of my year's observations, the most urgent is that Americans make a concentrated effort to find ways in which the energy of the young can be made welcome.

Until a few decades ago, young people could expect to be out at work by 14, 15, or at the latest 16 if they wished, without being despised as dropouts. They could feel that they would be involved in "real life" and, in the case of boys, that they had escaped from what had traditionally been seen in the United States as the rather female, apron-stringed atmosphere of school, and could identify with older men at work. With regard to being needed, it is not appropriate to ask that such gratifications be deferred. To defer may be to destroy the self-esteem that comes from knowing that one contributes positively to the world around one. This means that the new proposals for career education which receive so much support from the Office of Education, although in many ways a sensible and important notion, are not enough for middle or older adolescents, since they involve only "salable skills" meant to be sold in the future.

I would suggest that it is at around the age of 14 years (say, 9th grade) that the need to be needed is most urgently felt. Before that time, a creative curriculum such as I refer to briefly in Chapter 3 (pg. 52) is possibly enough, although as I have already described one school reported how valuable it was for a group of alienated 12-year-old girls to work with the aged. At home, 12- to 14-year-old girls undoubtedly find that baby-sitting for neighbors gives a great fillip to self-esteem, so it is quite possible that girls, particularly, are eager for experience of service at a younger age. But the lack of it is likely to be more serious (even if unrecognized) at 14 than at 12 even when youngsters at that age are not conscious of this source of malaise.

In my work in American schools, wherever I have seen students able to contribute as adults to community work, to urban renewal, to hospitals, to youth counseling centers, in tutoring situations, in day care, in farmwork, I have observed a glow of well-being, a kind of relief as of a new-found equilibrium, which I have not seen elsewhere. In fact, the only schools I visited which seemed totally satisfactory to the students were two small schools—one a private rural boarding school, the other a public school for human services—which stressed, respectively, the requirement to work on a farm and homestead and the opportunity to undertake human services in the city. At their best, the art studio, industrial arts (when not improperly despised), and improvisational drama and movement have immense importance in this respect, as in so many others. So also has biology, if it properly explains the care of animals and plants. But for some young people in their middle teens at least, more direct societal contributions are necessary also.

I am not one to recommend drafting anyone for anything. But I certainly suggest that this country start providing opportunities for teenagers to spend a year or several months contributing to meeting human needs and combating the prevailing "public squalor" to which John Galbraith referred; and that this should not be an obstacle to their subsequent educational chances. Of course, a period of voluntary service of this kind does not mean that other aspects of learning are necessarily ignored—indeed, the interconnecting of theoretical and practical work can be extremely valuable—only that the balance between taking and being allowed to give should be restored.

A NEED TO NEED

Needing Other People. It is not merely for reasons of schematic satisfaction that I go on directly from a need to be needed to a need to need. One of the important things people can learn in adolescence is that none of us is expected to be perfect and all-sufficient in our working lives—or indeed, as people. Paradoxically, this applies particularly to the person of many talents; Edward Edinger puts the point very well when he says that such a person must "voluntarily accept being a real fragment instead of an unreal whole."[3] If in adolescence one is helped to enjoy the need to need others who are different from oneself and who complement one's weaknesses and strengths, the attraction of being a member of a group of peers should not have to represent a desire to submerge one's identity, as it so often does today.

In collaborative learning there is a true emphasis on diversity, a belief that it is satisfactory to need someone who is pleased for you to try out your ideas on him, or is more humorous, less serious than you, less down-to-earth and more imaginative, better with his hands or more inventive, has more experience of city or country—and who in turn enjoys being needed and has other needs which you can meet. In the younger phases of early adolescence the need to need may well find its expression in hero worship, which is of course invaluable for finding one's own identity. Properly nourished, this can grow into a satisfaction in being able to turn to friends and colleagues while sensing oneself as competent also to be comfortable on one's own.

Learning by Needing. In thinking of the need to be able to acknowledge one's need for others, I have come to see that this is closely allied to learning by needing.

Needing others is not a challenge to identity, but an imaginative extension of it. So is learning to extend oneself in such a way that one can discover a new lack and wish to overcome it. When I learn because I shall be punished or fired from a job if I do not learn, or be given a gold star or a promotion if I do, I remain dependent for my actions on the judgment of others. If I learn because my vision of myself has extended, I grow in self-respect and hence, indirectly, in my ability to offer equal respect to others. Learning by recognizing a need to learn, because otherwise one cannot solve a problem or complete a creative project which is an extension of oneself, is neither strictly intrinsic motivation nor extrinsic, as these terms are usually understood. It is a kind of personal motivation which is very important in adolescence. This viewpoint is the antithesis of the emphasis on so-called skills learning, which, so far from seeing learning as an extension of the self, reduces it to a choice of three evils: enforced drudgery, a way of pleasing adults, or a form of deferred gratification from which the young may learn to live always in the future, when the "skill" can be used.

The notion of learning by needing is an extension of a widespread concern that children should have an improved self-concept in learning. It is a way of linking self-concept with the actual learning process that is quite direct, since it involves both improving the sense of self by having the courage to face a need in one's self and also developing the competence and energy and means-to-end realism to deal with the need constructively. Learning that arises from an increasing recognition of a need to need is "creative learning."

A NEED TO MOVE INWARDS

A number of people who have been working towards an integrated day in the elementary school are now searching for an appropriate educational equivalent for sixth-graders and beyond. I would suggest three main changes of emphasis. There is a greater need to affect the outer environment, rather than simply to explore it. There is a need for a more conscious understanding of the relationship of the work of an individual or small group to that of a class or larger group as a whole: that is, a greater sense of community. And there is an increasing concern with understanding the behavior of self and others, which with encouragement can develop in time into an inquiry about the behavior of societies. The first two of these developments are dealt with later on in this chapter. The third is the least recognized, perhaps because it is the most secret.

As children grow into adolescents, the phase of total involvement in investigating materials and trying to understand the physical world of the here and now is gradually modified (especially if it has been adequately experienced) to allow for an increasing interest in understanding human behavior, including one's own. In other words, we would rightly expect the inquiry of pre-adolescent children to be concerned mainly with the material environment, and that of mid-adolescents to be focused on human problems: the one centered on the outer, the other on the inner world. I hope I do not skew the evidence by bringing in a preconception here, but it has seemed to me interesting that over the last few years in England and Ontario, and now in the American schools with which I have been connected, the kinds of Open Inquiry which have most engaged the interest of 11- to 16-year-olds have been concerned with people: these have included, for example, studies of myself (identity), of how human groups work, of the physical, psychological, and sociological aspects of growing up, of sight, sound, happiness, anger, jealousy, and boredom (one English school° invented the most boring country on earth as a result of a discussion of drugs), of "now" and the future, of roles and relationships, including sex roles, of our parents' or grandparents' times, of change in the local community, living in a technological society, images of man, man and the universe, "why man?" war, and case studies of moral problems. I have put these in a roughly developmental order from 6th through 10th grade, concern with social questions tending to come later than the immediate concern with self, growing up, the senses and emotions; but I would certainly not make heavy weather of this, since students should be able to interpret all this material in accordance with their personal stage of development. Furthermore, a great deal depends on the imaginative and symbolic depth and the breadth of scientific understanding with which an inquiry is tackled.

One Open Inquiry which I have not yet seen, although I have proposed it a number of times, is an in-depth study of adolescence by students in their teens. An inquiry into "growing up" in earlier grades will be sure to lead some boys and girls to inquire into variety in rates of growth and of development of sexual characteristics, a topic which is very important in allaying the extreme anxiety that ignorance can engender; for the rest, interest usually centers on birth and early childhood. A study of adolescence at a later stage would range more deeply into physiological, psychological, anthropological, mythological and economic aspects of this period of life. Some juniors and seniors, incidentally, might well want to correlate it with counseling younger adolescents. At the very least, a school library in a middle school or high school ought to have a plentiful supply of books on adolescence. It always strikes me as extraordinary

---

°Fairlop Secondary School, Ilford, Essex. This remarkable school, whose headmistress, Margaret Horne, was a member of the First Pilot Course at the Goldsmiths' Curriculum Laboratory, is the source of several innovations referred to in this book.

arrogance in adults that we feel entitled to know more about adolescents than we permit them to know about themselves; it is also very shortsighted. Since we do not provide ritualized procedures or even an agreed societal viewpoint on the passage from childhood to adult status, the least we can do is to offer access to the best information, scientific and imaginative, that we can provide. This is one of the rights of adolescents or young adults today.

I do not suggest that these human problems should be the only subject of study. Of course not. But if the interest in human behavior is not given the same attention as was the investigation of the material environment at an earlier age, one readily sees a mood of disillusionment or disaffection setting in: "What on earth is the good of all this to me?" they ask; and only the most docile, those least inclined to take psychic risks, will fail to share their discontent, whether overtly or secretly. It is a serious matter when the sense of inner connectedness with learning is weakened. Early and middle adolescence is an egocentric age. We should act as partners to that mood, not as adversaries.

A NEED TO AFFECT THE OUTER WORLD

As I go round schools, I find increasingly that my first suggestion is that children and their teachers should be able to alter the look of their classrooms and corridors, preferably in such a way as to convey in concrete terms some of the ideas on which they are working. At one stage of my study in 1971-72, I was overwhelmed by an accumulation of those corridors with built-in lockers—so bleak, so unchildlike, and speaking only of power and possession, and in some of the palatial new buildings I mutter to myself Tennyson's devastating comment on a grande dame: "icily regular, faultily faultless, splendidly null." These are no buildings for young people to spend their time in; they breed a sense of powerlessness, and unwittingly, no doubt, but significantly, they seem designed to institutionalize the human spirit.

Not long ago I had a very helpful conversation with a group of seventh-graders in a suburban school. They were the same ones I thought too distant and conceptual in their outlook to profit by a study of the future. Towards the end of their inquiry on education I asked them what study they might like to embark on next. A pause, then one small-looking boy said: "It's bad for us being in these rooms. Look, they're all the same shape. We ought to have round ones and all kinds of shapes, and we ought to be able to change them round. " Then another pause, and the next idea came from a girl, blushing and spluttering at an unexpected surge of feeling: "Human motives," she said, "that's what, why we do things." We went on from there to think of some of the human emotions they would like to understand better: fear, anger, jealousy, then on to animal behavior, and whether we could learn about ourselves from studying animals. These areas of inquiry were eagerly agreed on, and then the first boy reflected once more: "My father," he said, "well, we have a maid, you see, and he's never able to get to do anything in the house." He and I could see possibilities for an introductory study of affluence and poverty, their sources and their effects, but these did not yet interest the others. They wanted to change their school around and to study behavior, as did a parallel group talking with their teacher, who came up with a wish to set up their own museum and, once again, study human behavior. They were not yet ready to study political and economic questions, which they still saw as remote—more remote, I suspect, than the future would have seemed. Perhaps inner-city students, to whom inequity is anything but remote, might have shown more interest than these youngsters in studying affluence and poverty; but they share the concern to move inwards and a need to affect the outer environment which this group expressed.

While the study of human relationships becomes more significant, students' relationship to materials may become more manipulative, less responsive, in fact, both inner inquiry and outer effectiveness are different ways in which adolescents flex their muscles. It seems particularly important to help this age range to sustain "dialogue" with plants, animals, and inanimate nature. This is one reason why I become so concerned to find art teaching often reduced to "skills" teaching when the attitude to materials should be sensitive and exploratory, even reverent; and I have seen shocking wastefulness and fecklessness in the use of materials, which argues a poor relationship with the cosmos among youngsters who are often eager to take up the cry of ecology. Young people need to respect material, but this does not lessen the importance of using physical material effectively and with panache to create an environment which reflects their meaning and purposes. In this respect I have one warning about photography, valuable as photography is in other ways. I have several times noticed that when I have proposed collaborative efforts to alter the use and look of a classroom, corridor, or open space, teachers have gone off on a tangent: "We thought we might do a photography unit," they have said. It is a tangent, but not a *non sequitur*. Photography can be used as a substitute for effectiveness: instead of changing reality, you change its image. Photography is an important art form today, and its side effects include a growing confidence in the validity of personal choices and the uniqueness of individual vision as well as a sensitivity to what exists that isn't bounded by conventional distinctions between beautiful and ugly. But photography does not fully meet the problem of powerlessness. Perhaps these teachers' hesitations were due to a half-conscious desire to protect their students from failure. Teachers often express this fear to me, and I appreciate it, but I am less disposed to be protective. If human beings commit themselves to any worthwhile plan of action they always risk failure. (That is one reason why programmed learning that does not allow for failure is a hidden form of control, and dangerous as a main diet.) Plans to change the environment sometimes have to be undertaken with determination but also in a spirit of inquiry and means-end realism: How should we set about this with the most likelihood of success, what shall we learn if this plan fails, and so on.

In a society dominated by media and technology, acquisition of technological know-how is an important way of learning to affect the environment. It isn't surprising that many young people are fascinated by technically interesting art forms such as film, video, electronic sound systems and multimedia productions, and by technical studies leading to inventions or creative problem-solving with materials (which I see all too rarely in school science programs). All these are ways in which cognitive mastery can be achieved of a kind quite different from the verbal, analytical style on which schools are so narrowly focused, a kind associated in brain research with the right side of the brain. The same needs may be met by games and puzzles, which are fascinating to many younger and middle adolescents. We are apt to concentrate on their value in preparing in concrete form for fully abstract "formal operations"; but many games are also ways of domesticating adult reality and reproducing it in play form, a useful modern addition to the curriculum, though certainly no substitute for making actual changes in the environment of classroom, school or neighborhood.

Riddles, games, and puzzles, like modelmaking, are rehearsals for tackling reality which are very engaging; they are very valuable for younger and mid-adolescents, and they should not be thought of as appropriate only to younger children. On the contrary, they have additional value in that they create opportunities for practicing formal operations in miniature.

I have concentrated here on altering the physical environment because this need is so little recognized. It must be obvious that when young people are much concerned with roles and relationships and with testing the ground of the adult arena they want to try their hand also at decision-making. Most high school juniors and seniors I know today cannot really be bothered with running a school (any more than most of their English counterparts want to be prefects); that phase of life has filtered down to the middle-school age groups. But they may want to be consulted, even if they don't want to carry a school. As to ninth- and tenth-graders, one of the course members at the Goldsmiths' Curriculum Laboratory undertook a survey of some attitudes of 14-year-olds in England, which I often recall. To the question "Do you have arguments with your parents about the time you come home at night?" some 90 per cent replied, "Yes." To another question, "When you have children of your own, will you have them come back at the same time as you or earlier or later?" 90 per cent replied, "The same time." Consultation, not institutional responsibility, is their demand in school also.

Some alternative schools, in an eagerness not to be authoritarian, have failed to recognize that older students are not seriously interested in public responsibility (except perhaps in the exciting earliest phases of setting up the school). In fact, the second UNESCO conference on alternative schools, held at the Woodstock Center in Illinois in 1972, was devoted to decision-making, which confirms that it is a central concern of these new schools. In my view they would be much more profitably concerned with examining curricula, where there rarely seems to have been great inventiveness. It is far less important to most young people of high school age to partake in community meetings on a school's constitution as a way of affecting their environment than to begin to feel they can act from their own initiative in their learning and that if they do so their environment will respond, and thereby to be reassured that they are connected with reality. In this connection I have met choices in mini-courses, but few opportunities to engage independently in inquiries.

Another urgent need which has not often been met is to relate action in the community to interdisciplinary studies in school, so that learning arises from action and the action is focused and refined by learning. This is a major new problem and opportunity in curriculum building.

A NEED FOR INTENSITY

Our adolescents seem to need to experience intensity. I have come to realize this not only through observation and discussion of adolescents' satisfaction in having intense experience but also through conversations with older people who have arrived at some manageable sense of themselves and who look back at the experiences which seemed to shape them.

For some, the need for intensity is due to a need for an external reality to match the vehemence of their internal experience (particularly in the 13-to-16 phase of this age range), since as they move into their mid-teens many find themselves governed by their moods and feelings in a way which they have not experienced in previous years. For others, a reason for needing intensity seems to be that their inner sense of themselves is so little differentiated that they become literally apathetic—unable to undergo experience—unless they have some outer actuality to help them shape themselves. These two kinds of behaviors I have observed in numbers of youngsters in the last two years. For a third condition, I am grateful to the comment of Douvan and Adelson:[4] "In the normative response to adolescence, however, we more commonly find an avoidance of inner and outer conflict, premature identity consolidation, ego and ideological constriction, and a general unwillingness to take psychic risks." Our education should provide help for this condition also; one way at least would be to allow the young to have the chance to take psychic risks, and thereby expand the possibilities of self in a supportive atmosphere.

Probably the main "psychic risks" which can usefully be taken in school are these: to risk failure at a project on which one has set one's heart; to risk personal expression of powerful feelings in a number of media; for boys, to try out roles they may see as effeminate, such as working in dance improvisation, sewing or cooking; for girls, to become involved enough in their inventions or designs to stop pretending to be more sophisticated and less intelligent than they are; for all to commit themselves (and this is more alarming than it may sound) to paying full attention in a "dialogue" with a person, an object, or a piece of music; to risk one's arm for an ideal, or to make a fool of oneself for the same purpose.

In whatever ways adolescents choose (or find it necessary) to manage the psychophysical problems attendant on growing up, they need to experience what to them, subjectively, is danger; otherwise they do not get the full value of the adolescent phase of our lifetime search for maturity. Violence, heavy drinking, drug abuse, fast driving, all tell us this regularly; the search for conformist submersion in a peer group or early foreclosure in personal development does likewise and is no less serious, though these may induce less alarm in adults. Apart from boys' sports for potential stars, the only intense experience deliberately provided by traditional schooling (and that only for those who will play the game) lies in the teacher-pleasing stakes: "Please grade me, for otherwise I don't know what's important," as one seventh-grader put it. It is a measure of my concern on this score that I have even at moments begun to think there is merit in the early specialization we impose on college-bound youngsters in England. Some at least gain a heightened sense of self as they develop some mastery in a special field. Also, to have a good frame of knowledge enables them to move freely with difficult material that claims their interest, and this in turn can create an involvement in learning I have seen more often in sixth forms in England than in the equivalent junior and senior grades in the United States, where the curriculum is more diffuse.

The truthful experiencing of hopes dashed and hopes sustained, of the pain and joy of trying to create a movement or an object or a sound-series which truly brings the inner world out into the external, is an aspect of the arts which is particularly important in mid-adolescence. So it is disastrous that classes in the arts are so often undervalued in school programs, and the work in those classes is frequently no more than tricks and techniques which neither challenge nor give rest. Since adolescence is so private a phase (despite the peer-group chatter), the arts also have special merit through their ambiguity. This ambiguity is retained even if some of the intensity comes from communal creations. The making of a shared sculpture, or a powerful as opposed to a statutory school mural, or a dramatic improvisation, or a play or an opera, these are all activities on a scale which requires the energies of a gang of youngsters. I have rarely seen opportunities for the young to initiate and create together what they could not achieve alone. (The prevailing individualism may not lead them to propose such ventures.) Yet the intensity of shared creation is one of the great experiences of youth, and is also highly satisfactory later on, as diverse community art projects and amateur theater groups make very clear.

Nor need intensity always be associated with *making*. Intensity of listening or looking, sensitivity exercises, experience of quiet, these have their place also. So do rugged physical experiences such as those provided in outward-bound programs, exploring trips, camping with minimum equipment and food, visiting strangers in an unknown city, taking up a social cause and pushing it through. The sad thing is that school goes on and on—and on and on.

A NEED FOR ROUTINE

In speaking of a need for intensity, I am not suggesting a need for excitement. On the contrary, the need always to be "tripping" or enjoying a "group high," or at younger ages a restless, fidgety, selfish search for more and more different things to do in a day—these are part of a prevailing malaise, and it is certainly not for teachers to throw their bonnets over such gristless windmills. Indeed, one of the greatest snares of elementary "open classrooms" in this country is that teachers may give way to a demand for constant stimulation, so that children become passive (despite their activity), dependent on showy materials or on passing whims which arise in their minds without conscious volition. And one of the first impressions I had both in schools and among friends in the prosperous Northeast was of what I called the glutted child, for whom I immediately proposed a quietly ordered day and a minimum of materials so that he would have a chance to make do and improvise. In time, the glutted child becomes the despairing adolescent whom nothing satisfies because there has been no experience of intense satisfaction, no simple love, no "dialogue."

Many teachers who are "exciting" in this way come a cropper because they do not recognize that routine gives security and privacy, two essentials for adolescents. Indeed, it would be interesting to carry out a longitudinal study to discover whether in open situations there is a greater appreciation of routine among 13-, 14-, and 15-year-olds than occurs three or four years earlier. I emphasize this point less than some others I have observed because there is already so much routine in most schools. But this has been routine created for administrative convenience. I am more concerned with routine as an aspect of ritual; with routine as having aesthetic value, since it creates a beauty of order in time and space; with routine as releasing energies which can too easily be squandered on keeping one's head above water if one is an adolescent who is at the mercy of inner and outer disorder; and if possible, of routine as bearing a relationship to the rhythms of the seasons.

Drill in learning is a traditional form of routine. In general, I have found that teachers engaged in "open education" in elementary schools as well as those in free or alternative schools for adolescents, are more nervous of drill than they should be. I can quite see why: they are reacting against drill for drill's sake, drill imposed on children who have no sense of being partners in their learning programs. But drill is an aspect of all learning, beginning with learning to grasp and release objects, to crawl, to walk, to speak. When learners want to learn they want to practice, and this need to work with steadiness and a kind of willed determination shouldn't be ignored just because we have come to associate drill with meaningless rote teaching and inflexible procedures in teacher-centered classrooms.

As with many of the needs I have referred to, some people need routine because they find it easy to handle and some because they find it difficult. The same is true with another complementary need, that for flexibility; all young people (some more urgently than others) need to learn to understand their own rhythms of learning and withdrawal in work, in play, and in social life, rhythms partly physical in origin, but certainly aspects of the creative process in most people.

A NEED FOR MYTH AND LEGEND

Closely related to the need for intensity is the need for fantasy and myth. I am not at present sufficiently clear in my own mind about the importance of myth to argue the case in full in this book. I will simply say that I notice a lack of mythology and mythical reference, and I have also noticed how deeply involved young people are if they have access to imaginative as opposed to merely analytical studies of myth. I suspect that most young people in the United States have fewer resources of fairy stories, myths, and local lore— even of old wives' tales—than are available to the young of other cultures, including other industrialized societies. If this is so, it would be a natural result of two historical circumstances: the cutting off of the mythic roots of the American continent through the assault on Indian tribal cultures and the devaluation of the mythic roots of those who immigrated to this continent with more hope in the future than care for the past.

The profound sense among Afro-Americans and Mexican-Americans of the need to restore a continuity with their past and with the people in whom that past lives on is a wise intuition which other ethnic groups could emulate. In fact, with the wealth of human wisdom embodied in the European, Asian, African, and Latin American traditions housed in America, this country need not remain starved for the imaginative human understanding handed down by bards, dramatists, myth-makers, and creators of rituals of the past. There is, moreover, a special need to recoup the losses and assuage the guilt created by the suppression of indigenous myth.

As adolescents move more deeply into a concern with the nature of man and the place of man in the universe, they need to be able to draw on man's most profound symbolic insights as well as on the hypotheses of the behavioral sciences. These young people, probably for the first time in man's history, are part of a culture which does not provide them with symbolic clues to the hidden meanings of human life. For this reason, a major research study of the renewal of myth in relation to lifelong education would be very valuable indeed.

Without benefit of such research I can only make some intuitive guesses about the place myth might take in schooling. I wouldn't want to lay down any fixed progression: myths of the seasons, for instance, retain their significance throughout life. But in general I suppose that for younger children the important thing will be to help them feel themselves members of an ordered cosmos which they share with other creatures and with inanimate nature rather than a privileged species with a franchise to exploit. Later on, somewhere about 11 or 12, children would begin to grasp the scale of space and of past and future time. I would see this as prime time for studying creation myths. In their teens, mythology has important messages for people who are becoming aware of the uniqueness of their personal journey, of their separateness and of the inevitability of death. Stories like those of Odysseus, for instance, or such Western and Eastern tales as are collected in *The King and the Corpse*,[5] are found today to have inner personal meanings of which their first hearers probably weren't conscious.

Clearly myth must be treated as a living source of wisdom, not as a corpus of information to be dissected and then tidied away in a coffin at the end of a semester. These are stories made to be told or portrayed, and whenever possible they should be read aloud by the teacher or student who reads with the greatest sensitivity and style— or wit, for often our forebears were much less heavy-handed than we are in dealing with matters of creation, life, love and death. Beyond this, myths can at times be played out in ritual performances, and some groups may be inspired to create their own myths, myths of the future, like science fiction, as well as eternal truths. Music and dance and choral speech obviously enrich work of this kind, and if it can be done in a myth center (see page 66) all the better.

Here is another opportunity for older students to work with younger children, becoming skilled story-tellers or readers and actors of tales which the younger ones can act, illustrate and enhance in their turn. Sometimes we have to find ways of helping adolescents to admit to serious thoughts without feeling self-conscious. This kind of approach can do just that, for their action is done for others and has become public property, not personal disclosure. (In much the same way, adolescents use posters to present idealistic thoughts that they wouldn't wish to express more directly.) I imagine that in a school which had throughout fostered the imaginative personal life this embarrassment would be less acute; but fear of profound truths is a sickness of our society as a whole and we can't expect adolescents to be free of it.

A NEED FOR FACT

Oddly enough, people whose imaginative life goes unnourished are often weak on fact also. I have been worried by a lack of respect for detail and complexity which seems to me to prepare young people to become members of Orwell's Admass. That I have been made anxious by this disrespect for detail surprises me because in England I have been used to attacking a pusillanimous concern with minutiae and a failure to understand the necessary relationship of fact to the context which gives it meaning. But here are some kinds of behavior which I have noticed during this year. First, a lot of teachers seem so thankful that students are "having a good discussion"—i.e., actually utter—that they fail to probe. Many times I have wanted to say, "Stop, what is the nature of your evidence? Who will go and get some facts for us so that we can study this argument properly another time?" Or even, "How do you see a connection between this proposition and another that you made some time ago?" As we help students to develop "formal operations," we have to help them also to become more sober in the face of reality. This should be a habit of mind not in advanced students only, but throughout the student's education.

Second, in language arts many teachers seem to think that the way a student feels about a book or passage is more important than an examination of what the author was trying to convey. The emphasis on a child's independent judgment is good, but the separation of opinion from evidence or of feeling from understanding is not. I know that some people believe that comprehension exercises placed at the end of the chapter solve this problem. In my experience the children's response to these is desultory and docile; the argument appears to lose reality for them as they proceed through the questions. They look upon them as yet another test. One good reason is that they are not experiencing the need for fact or careful argument in their own thinking, and therefore do not appreciate its significance in the thinking of others. Another, of course, is that their aesthetic judgment is often correct: even today literature is often subjected to mechanistic, non-literary analysis. The test questions ask only for pre-set answers and do not stimulate a complementary creative response. They do not lead to "dialogue" with the writer and are likely to quash children's personal imagery.

These two trends are forms of anti-intellectualism, a vice of which schools are often accused in this country. But a third trend stems directly from intervention of an inappropriate intellectual ambition. I refer to the whole dogma of "teaching to concepts," which has led teachers to hurry along into generalities. This is a very grave failing because it supplants personally perceived meaning with publicly shared belief (in the sense of publicly shared construction of reality, publicly shared assumptions which go unexamined). If young people are to grow up to be autonomous, to have competence in decision-making, to imagine themselves in other people's shoes (especially when those shoes are pinching)—in fact, to have the many virtues we claim for mature members of advanced societies—they need to be safeguarded at this age from being bamboozled by their own rapidly increasing capacity to manipulate abstractions. As Jerome Bruner points out, the value of conceptual thinking is that "the organism reduces the complexity of its environment." The true problem is that teaching to concepts often results in denying the student's own complex experience, which includes relationships with other concepts and other experiences, personally significant factual relationships that cannot be shared; secondly, it often replaces this experiential fullness with an empty verbalism.

This misguided policy in the schools is compounded by the fact that there is very little opportunity outside them to develop the power of imagining. In fact, this is an example of a countervailing need caused by a change in our cultural circumstances. Sylvia Ashton-Warner has recently made rather similar observations about imagery in younger children in this country.[6] Originally there existed the oral tradition, in which one learned through listening to storytellers, bards, and preachers; much later came the printed word, and then radio. All these permit a stream of images to come into the mind. Much of the power of the great mythmakers and the simplest storytellers has been to encourage our sense of actuality by helping us to create our own figures in our own scenery. It is similarly important in dealing with more discursive or factual material to envisage the content, whether it is, say, historical narrative, biological detail, numerical and spatial relationships, or relationships between ideas. If everything comes to us in television, film, cartoon, or direct physical encounter, this vital capacity to imagine is not strengthened by practice and cannot easily be called on by an act of will. Ideas become simple, vague, and unreal, and facts lose their keen significance.

Recently I have come to suspect that some difficulties in reading may be accounted for by a failure to use visual or other imagery. I am referring to the many adolescents (as well as younger children) who comprehend the face value of words but don't form them into a meaningful combination. I have suggested to teachers that for quite a number of children it would be profitable to suggest they try to make a mental picture of what they are reading or imagine a noise, a smell, a blow, or a touch as they read. Teachers of creative writing have confirmed to me that writing improves in a quite spectacular way when children are encouraged to let imagery come into their mind as they write a story. Imagery need not be visual, of course. In line with this, I was talking recently with some teachers about visual literacy, and was misconstrued as speaking of visceral literacy—a splendid notion. For that matter, we need neurological and muscular literacy, too. Until we literally incorporate thoughts so that they become part of our physical being we don't fully comprehend their meaning and we can't act on them; and until we can move imaginatively into the world we perceive with our senses we can't truly associate ourselves with it and it is likely to seem external, mechanical and quite possibly hostile.

The answer to the problem of empty conceptualization lies not in a return to the dry fact-collecting of the past, but in an extension of the experiential learning that is the basis of open education at the elementary level. Not all learning can be fully experiential; some of it has to be taken on trust. But such trust should be skeptical and skilled, not submissive or woolly.

In the later stages of grades 6 through 10, it is all too easy for young people to reify abstractions. Aspects of American education encourage this tendency, such as the emphasis on right and wrong answers and checking verbal correctness in multiple-type tests. I know many 18- to 24-year-olds who can argue a theory very competently but have no imaginative entry into the statistics or conceptual frameworks they so readily quote. So it is very important that at this younger age inquiries be as specific and concrete as possible,

while the ideas that youngsters develop about ways in which concrete evidence is interconnected become increasingly sophisticated
as they move into formal operations. An essential characteristic of all
the inquiries I have found successful in American and English
schools is that while the ideas were complex and abstract the expression was complex and concrete. This is of fundamental importance
for younger and mid-adolescents, and much more thought should
be given to it as an aspect of lifelong education.

A NEED FOR PHYSICAL ACTIVITY

All young people across this age range have to learn to coordinate
and come to terms with a changing body. Yet I understand that in
some areas the provisions for physical education and sports, even including swimming, are minimal or are being reduced for reasons of
economy; and in some schools I have visited the only people who
seem to have adequate opportunities for physical activity are the
promising athletes; and among these, only the boys.

One of the things I have found most distressing in the upper
reaches of schools is the way adolescents have to sit and work all day
long. An age of maximum physical restlessness is met with maximum
rigidity, with no legitimate opportunity for bodily contact or expression of aggression—no break to have fun and burn off energies or
calm anxieties, no chance to get out of doors; instead, a rushed lunch
hour and a requirement to sit passive in class for hours at a time. I
cannot imagine a more penal form of servitude for the young.

A good recreation program, including access to lifelong sports,
plenty of opportunity for dance and sports, and for preadolescents
and some teenagers simple cubbish tumbling, and the assumption
that one can move around a classroom, along a corridor—these are
minimum decencies for young people in these middle years. The
provision ought, of course, to be extended to include exploration of
cities or countryside.

This all seems to me so obvious, especially for youngsters with the
restless energy so noticeable in this country, that I am embarrassed
to have to point it out.

Furthermore, I have seen too few schools which have extended
their concept of physical education beyond the conventional expectations of years ago. For instance, improvisational movement is one
of the most direct and valuable forms of human expression, involving both awareness of feeling and discipline of the body, and it

is exceptionally important to maintain and develop this relationship of feeling and imagination to physical movement throughout childhood and into adolescence, when it can be a potent form of self-discovery and emotional integration. Yet it is seldom provided in. American schools even for girls, and for boys (as in England) practically never. For boys, it seems, the aesthetic experience of the flow of movement has to be channeled into aggressive competition. Again, hatha yoga, which is increasingly widespread for adults as a form of physical and spiritual discipline, is rarely to be found in schools, and the interest of many young people in the oriental martial arts of self-defense is also rarely acknowledged, although where classes in karate or kung fu have been provided they satisfy a number of needs of young adults. They lead to physical mastery of a high order, they provide a strictly ritualized mode of expression of basic emotions and they make available the moral and spiritual control that non-violent self-defense demands. The cinema has been exploiting their potential violence; schools would do well to counter with an experience of their value in defense and inner control.

A NEED FOR STILLNESS

When all goes well, young people in their middle teens are committed to a search for personal meaning. Many of them are sensitive to what Abraham Maslow described as "peak experiences,"[7] which are sometimes experienced as religious, sometimes associated with the aesthetic or the sexual, but are always recognizably spiritual in character. This is no new phenomenon, but today it seems often to be related to another dimension, one that has no precedent: namely, the awareness among today's youth of the fragility of mankind's hold on life and our displacement from the cosmos. Thus many adolescents, being open to cosmic revelations and having been born into a species capable of genocide, find little to revere in adults who seem both hardened and foolhardy in their attitude to life. A first requirement of a good education is that those of us who have this vision too should share with them a grave but joyous response to the world.

This is an important step, but for two reasons I do not think it is enough. First, as the young grow older, they too will find it easy to forget the vision; ecstatic experiences are all too easily pushed aside from the memory as simply an outcome of adolescent sexuality. Secondly, we are beginning today to understand something of the physical and mental conditions that enable human beings to move into spiritual contact with their inner selves and thereby to reach out into cosmic consciousness. Orthodox Greek spirituality called this *hesychasm*, a search for stillness or calm. I shall use the word stillness also, as a polarity to physical activity, because we know that it is associated with lowered brain rhythms and muscular relaxation. Adolescence is a period for forming habits that are based on an extended image of the self; and forming a habit for this kind of centering, which is inner "dialogue" at its most profound, can give access to lasting wisdom of a kind that cannot be written off as adolescent emotionalism. Rather it involves a discipline which is anything but emotional, if emotional means involving energies that are out of control.

I am sure that stillness, in this sense, is an important educational need of adolescents. I am not sure at present in what ways this need is best met. There are significant movements for bringing into schools various styles of meditation, through Yoga classes, Transcendental Meditation, Mind Control, the guided fantasy of Psychosynthesis, and music therapy leading to "altered states of consciousness." I respect all of these, but I think we should also be looking to more traditional ways that lie within the usual competence of teachers, so that when such special activities are not available or for some reason are not acceptable in the school the need for peace can still be respected. Here, it seems to me, is an aspect of creative and expressive experience that is too little noticed. It is a function, for instance, of writing poetry in relation to music deeply heard; of the sensitivity exercises preparatory to dance and improvisational drama, and of quiet rhythmical movement in its own right; of peaceful "dialogue" with made objects or with nature; of bird-watching or of gently tending animals; of the rhythms of throwing on the wheel. To do these things well requires one to move into the deeper relaxation of one's body rhythms. Schools abound with opportunities if the significance of such experience is understood.

It is important that we reveal to adolescents in their search for true relaxation that there are alternatives to drugs and to dulling the senses into insensibility by activity, or even sound, taken to an extreme. And if teachers give themselves these same chances, instead of being busy teaching all the time, they too can become wiser and more lastingly at peace.

A NEED FOR SEPARATENESS AND
A NEED FOR BELONGING

I have chosen these simple and perhaps rather naive words, "separateness" and "belonging," to describe an important polarity because I do not want to be pressed into the technical language of psychology, sociology, or political science and thereby perhaps seem to be making a false antithesis between the individual and society or to be identifying without explanation with any one theory of developmental psychology.

In relation to both these needs, innovative schools have sometimes overreacted to the failings of traditional education. Traditional schools tend to fail youth because young people's true need to be understood as diverse is distorted: instead of being acknowledged as different they are urged to be competitive (and then, ironically, they are asked within this competitive framework to respect and support one another). In more innovative situations those who don't want to fall into the trap of selfish individualism sometimes underestimate the need for independent work. In my own case, I am conscious that although I have always stressed the importance of diversity, my thrust has been toward the value of individual diversity in common enterprises. It is true that as a rule the most satisfactory basis for grouping seems to be a pair of best friends (or two pairs of best friends working together).[8] But in every group of young people there are always some "happy isolates" who like to work on their own or to move from group to group according to the way their study is developing. Occasionally to undertake a chosen piece of work on one's own can be a great joy, and a significant aid to mastery for teenagers who usually like to work collaboratively. It is important not to react so strongly against the prevailing egotism that one ignores the value of separateness.

One example of the benefit of being allowed to go one's own way within a collaborative environment—of being a happy isolate—occurred with a boy in a study described in the next chapter in which 8th graders were convinced that we would all be living in caves in due course and focused on deciding on and representing the basic requirements for life in the cave. This one boy was preoccupied with hard drugs and asked if he might bring in facsimiles to include in the supplies being collected for the new era of cave life. The teacher checked with the Consortium member (an expert on drug education), and together they agreed that since the other students were not greatly impressed with his notion this could do no harm. Over the weeks that followed it was noticed that the boy removed these facsimiles of harmful substances and unobtrusively replaced them with others of life-giving drugs.

Sometimes a need for privacy can be met by much simpler physical means: students need to be able to withdraw at times to quiet places or alcoves where they can be still without having to pretend to be listening to cassettes or studying in individualized programs, subterfuges I often see them engage in when they can't stand the strenuous atmosphere of the workaday classroom.

By "belonging" I mean belonging *with*, not belonging *to*. Strong feelings for belonging to an institution are part of the childhood of mankind. These were natural, perhaps inevitable, at a time when family, school, religious organization, national subculture, or nation could still claim access to final truths. Today, as men look more deeply into themselves and towards each other in their personal growth, it is not surprising to find that young people seem to outgrow loyalty to institutions much earlier than their parents did. Belonging to a school seems to have little significance to teenagers today, except occasionally when there is an undesirable social or intellectual elitism involved. But young people do need very badly to feel that they belong with their peers and with significant adults.

With all the public attention given to peer culture, it should not be necessary to point out youngsters' need for companionship. Yet the way in which most junior and senior high schools and some middle schools are organized might have been deliberately designed to destroy the social fabric of adolescents' lives. I refer particularly to two systems of major importance in the schools: one is individualized instruction as usually understood, the other is any of the commonplace systems in schools such as non-grading, use of computer programming, and ordinary arrangements for electives. Most students with whom I have talked in high schools move about the school along totally separate routes. If they happen to meet someone in two different classes or get into the same elective for a period with their best friend, that is their good fortune. To the schools it does not seem to be important at all. The whole concept of getting to know people in some depth through working with them on common enterprises seems completely foreign to the school, and thereby to the students. If "peer socialization" takes the form of withdrawing from the rest of society or attacking it, the last thing we should do is to be surprised.

The need for companionship and the need to affect the outer environment are mutually supportive. If a group of students are seriously working together in *making* some study or some physical change in their environment which they cannot manage on their own, both needs are satisfied. This is one of the most important aspects of Open Inquiry. A sixth-grade teacher told me recently (as many others have) that it had proved difficult in her suburban school to get youngsters to collaborate, that they were self-centered and sometimes quite violently selfish. Parents were ambitious for their children, and her attempts to encourage a different attitude were not heeded. But when small groups had an opportunity in turn to make a film together, they immediately worked collaboratively, sharing the equipment and planning their shots effectively , because this was something they could not fully carry out and enjoy without agreement and compromise. Another teacher described how, when eighth-graders created and produced an opera, they suddenly began to understand that characteristics which usually annoyed them could be assets: the finicky perfectionist or the artistic dreamer were needed in such creative work, and the miser was good at handling the money. An interesting development in an English school which has taken a leading part in the innovations I was connected with in England capitalizes on the need for the young to work separately and together. Individuals or groups make a proposal to do a piece of work which particularly interests them in connection with an Open Inquiry, and the larger body of students then agrees to contract with them to do this work on their behalf. "Management checks" to establish whether the work is going on effectively are the task of the teachers, but the original agreement is a communal one, a good example of creative use of the need to belong with one's peers.

"Belonging with" includes belonging with grown-ups. We are dealing here with an age group of students who, on Lawrence Kohlberg's scale of moral development, are likely at best to be at a conventional rather than a flexible perceptual stage of moral understanding. In Piaget's terms, many are not likely as yet to be highly skilled at handling the relationship of ideas. If there were no other reasons but these, I would be alarmed at any notion that youngsters can bring themselves up if left to their own inflexible devices. But beyond this I would accept the argument made by Derek Miller,[9] now of the University of Michigan, and others that in societies which set much store in the development of consciously maintained identity, adolescents need other adults (over and above their parents) whom they can trust, respect, and confront, and that this is true of youngsters in any nuclear family, however admirable the parents may be. In this view, the loss of the extended family creates a serious gap in the identification process of adolescents. Since we are not yet accomplished at creating families by affinity and since young people are finding it increasingly difficult to find employment in their teens, the school or learning center is the most likely source of significant adults. Not all of them are necessarily teachers, of course: there are other community members, secretaries, teaching aides, building superintendents, gardeners, bus drivers, counselors, and, for the youngest students, more mature seniors to look to. One of the merits of working on service or community projects or on community electives is that one's catalogue of accessible adults is greatly extended.

If this view is correct, it is worrying that a number of teachers seem to feel it a duty to be professionally cool, clinical, and if possible infallible. It is also one of the most serious failings of many programs of individualized study that the teacher moves to the sidelines and becomes a writer and checker of ditto sheets, rather than someone working alongside the youngster. If coolness is an authentic personal disposition, well and good; but for many it is an assumed role.

I do not want to repeat much that my colleagues and I have so often written about the need for personal interaction and for collaborative learning of teachers with students, but I must say that it is honest personal interaction which I find most seriously lacking in many schools. And neither the free school movement nor the traditional schools seem to have this interaction as central to their purposes. On the other hand, I can also say that in some schools this situation is rapidly changing as more and more adults begin to work more seriously on their own lives. In fact, some teachers' growing sense that adult life is a search and a continuing creative task is perhaps the most encouraging instance—and the most important—of the impact of changing adult mores on a relatively static educational system.

3. Observation Points

I WANT NOW TO OUTLINE some of my own experiences in working in American schools. My proposal to the Ford Foundation was that I should not merely study existing developments in the education of 11- to 16-year-olds but should actively intervene in some schools to encourage them to move towards a more "open" program. (As I explain in a subseqent chapter, I am rather hesitant today to use the term "open education," since it is so often misunderstood. I prefer to describe these programs as aspects of a properly diversified education.)

The first steps in planning my year's study and travel were taken in the previous academic year, when I was teaching at Boston University. I arranged in the spring of 1971 to set up working commitments with a number of educators in different parts of the country who had already invited my help or whom I had met while lecturing in American universities. This was the nucleus of the group of eleven educators that subsequently formed itself into the Middle Years Consortium, which I describe in greater detail in Chapter 5.

When making my plans, I realized, of course, that in planning regular visits to six centers (in Massachusetts, California, Oregon, Pennsylvania, Wisconsin, and New York) and some contact with a program for younger children in Chicago, I was denying myself the opportunity to work in depth in any one place. But I wanted to see in a very general way (though hopefully not in a superficial one) whether there were any commonalities—whether their students were blacks, Ivy Leaguers, Spanish-speaking, or from blue-collar families—that like-minded educators across the country could recognize.

During the autumn of 1971, I spent some days in each of the seven localities referred to. The group of eleven educators met on Long Island in early November, with the help of a small grant from the State University of New York at Stony Brook. The meeting lasted five days. Those attending decided that continuing collaboration was of the utmost importance and made some detailed plans towards this.

I expected to continue visits on these same lines for the following months. But owing to the illness of some and changes of appointments among key teachers with whom I had intended to work in three areas (Walpole, Mass.; Portland, Ore.; and Milwaukee and Racine, Wis.), I found it not economical in time to continue to visit these places regularly. So the main schools which I visited and had reports on throughout the year were in three areas: two middle schools on Long Island, New York (one blue-collar to middle-middle-class and all white, another similar but including a good proportion of socially and intellectually advantaged); three junior high schools in San Bernadino Unified School District, California (one 60 percent black, 40 percent Chicano; one "racially balanced" with black students voluntarily bused joining children of mainly blue-collar families; one 50-50 black/white, middle/upper-middle class); and one school in Philadelphia whose student body was mainly black, with some Puerto Ricans.

In 1972-3 I have worked with groups of teachers in several middle or intermediate schools, three high schools, some classes for children with learning disabilities, and more sporadically in a few elementary schools—all in New York State and New York City. The comments that follow are based on work in both years, 1971-2 and 1972-3.°

I started 1971-2 with three sets of general questions in mind:

1. Would the kinds of programs which we had developed at the

° I have come to the conclusion, reluctantly, that I can't acknowledge individual teachers by name because although in some schools it was quite clear with whom I was working or whom I visited, in others there was no very clear demarcation. So I have to express my gratitude in a generalized way to the principals and faculties of the following schools: Shandin Hills Junior High School and Arrowview Junior High School, San Bernardino, California; Shoreham/Wading River Middle School, Shoreham, New York; I.S. 44, New York City; Robert E. Bell Middle School, Chappaqua, New York; Briarcliff Manor Middle School, New York; also the School for Human Services, Philadelphia; Timberhill School, Cazadero, California; and Manual

Goldsmiths' College Curriculum Laboratory for English pre-adolescents and middle adolescents be appropriate for youngsters in the United States? It seemed likely that they would, since a series of American visiting professors had shared in our cogitations and since we had tried to distinguish the fundamental values for which we stood from the modes of operation, which would vary from one school or region to another. In the same vein of questioning, was it possible in a plural society such as the United States to suppose that any one kind of program would advance the learning and personal development of young people from very diverse regional and ethnic groups?

2. What new insights might I gain about the educational needs of adolescents from this opportunity to study them in a culture that was in some respects alien to me?

3. What new developments would I find in American schools that would add to my own understanding of adolescent education, and could I evaluate these in such a way as might help to improve the lives of young people in this country?

Experience had taught me that a newcomer can sometimes identify strengths and weaknesses more easily than someone to whom they are so familiar as to seem obvious or immutable.

In working with schools in England I had found that no curriculum change was of value unless there were good personal relationships between teachers and students. An innovative school must have some of the qualities of a family or at least a community based on mutual respect; otherwise, changing our learning expectations is simply tinkering with externals. When a school (or a coherent group of teachers within one of the larger American schools) has this necessary human outlook, two proposals for change seem to be the best starting points and fortunately they are mutually supportive. The first is Interdisciplinary Enquiry, which in this

High School, Denver, Colorado. Some of these schools I worked with in the course of my Ford Foundation study, others subsequently as a consultant, and the last three I only visited and did not work with. There are of course many other schools which it has been very helpful to work with or visit, but these have programs that are specifically referred to in this and other chapters. Quite a number of the programs have been written up much more fully by the teachers themselves in articles published in *The Good Guy's Gazette*, an informal journal circulated by the Middle Years Consortium.

country I have come to call Open Inquiry, partly because concern for disciplines is less well-established here, partly because the acronym IDE (using the English spelling "enquiries") had a useful association with ideas, idealism, and ideology and I don't particularly like its American substitute, IDI. The second starting point is the shared positive appraisal of students by the teacher group. Accordingly, for the last 18 months, I have been concentrating on these aspects of curriculum. As I have indicated in the previous chapter, I see them as necessary although not sufficient elements in an improved education for adolescents and an invaluable beginning, since together they help teachers to become both more adventurous in the kinds of learning they emphasize and the kind of subject matter they acknowledge and also more observant of the diverse interests and learning styles of their students.

OPEN INQUIRY

The main features here are (1) that students have the opportunity to study in areas of investigation that they recognize as significant to themselves; (2) that this is open-ended inquiry, not so-called "discovery" guided by teachers towards a foreknown end, although this may have a place in other parts of a curriculum if teachers find it motivates students and helps to challenge them towards new understanding; (3) that teachers work together, contributing their viewpoints as specialists; (4) that representatives of the creative and expressive arts, including shop and home economics, contribute as members of the interdisciplinary teams. I see this as fundamental for historical as well as theoretical reasons. In my experience in England (and now in the United States), whenever these teachers have played a central part in an Open Inquiry it has had a far better chance of involving students' interest and also of leading to substantive learning than when "academic" teachers have tried their hand alone; (5) that although shared or contiguous space is not absolutely necessary, substantial blocks of shared time are—thus Open Inquiry, at least after the first tentative steps have been taken, makes demands on the macrocosmic planning of a school and cannot be undertaken privately in a self-contained classroom as is possible with moves towards "open education" in an elementary school; (6) that teachers are not disturbed if students know more, or learn to know more than they do themselves on a chosen aspect of a study —in a plural and "information-rich society" this is inevitable, whether the students' knowledge is the social realism of city dwellers, the more distantly acquired factual knowledge of some suburban children, or simply the outcome of an enthusiastic search in the process of the inquiry; (7) that in addition to some common work, small groups of students (or individuals) are encouraged to take up different aspects of an inquiry, preferably aspects which they identify for themselves; and (8) that as they become more confident, teachers encourage "open access" whereby groups or individuals move to the specialist whose help they need in different phases of their chosen search.

Even in rather limited or primitive forms, in the schools in which I have been a regular visitor or consultant, Open Inquiries seem to give students and teachers times of unprecedented satisfaction, energy, and mutual understanding. One very simple but most productive program was a course in geology given by an art teacher and a science teacher who had collaborated previously in an art and biology program. The last time I visited this project, it was in an early stage in which pairs of students chose a geological period which they illustrated with great care and growing expertise, using various three-dimensional materials. Subsequently, according to a report in the first issue of the Middle Years Consortium *Good Guys' Gazette*, "some students wanted to know more about earthquakes and volcanoes," since the school is near a major fault. "They made models, engineered models of volcanic activity, studying why it takes place, and of earthquakes of different types, learning why they move as they do. When they started they made a museum for themselves only, but as it emerged they recognized that it might be interesting to others." The total class became involved in setting up the museum in an unused room, inviting guests and teaching each other about all exhibits in order to guide their visitors. Here, then, is a very good example of ways in which students' own local or personal interests can expand a teacher's integrated project into a lively inquiry.

In another, more privileged school, one in a rich area, teachers discovered the joy that seventh-graders with a plethora of material possessions can find in making simple equipment for themselves, in this case a darkroom and pinhole cameras which they needed for an environmental study. Other teachers showed an impressive respect for the adolescents' need for physical experience to stimulate and satisfy imagination, ranging from one beginning group of teachers working on Indian cultures (who encouraged far more creative work —making teepees and bows and arrows, learning and planning tribal rituals—than they had previously dared) to a "visit to Africa" organized by a remarkable teacher. After a careful preparatory period in which they studied what the journey would be like and what they might expect to find on arrival, the children were allowed to stay overnight in school in replication of the flight, testing their expectations against fuller experience. (Reality testing of this kind is an important aspect of field studies and visits of all kinds.)

After similar experiences, some teachers began to move quite comfortably into more sensitive areas relating to personal identity or to the serious anxieties of many young people about the present and future of the human species. One group of seventh-grade girls, who were completely out of tune with school, worked in a home for the aged for some weeks of concentrated service; the experience of helping led to poetry writing, painting and photography, to very serious discussions of old age and death, and also to a quite intensive search for evidence about the economic situation of old people.

Two other schools discovered a concern for the future, from which it emerged that many seemingly cheerful, casual youngsters conceive our prospects as nasty, brutish, and above all short. They worked out their expectations of the annihilation of their town, or of cave-dwelling, through physical simulation of the ideas which concerned them in their imaginative life, but also through quite specific factual inquiry. In one it was assumed by seventh-graders that one could not imagine a future more than 15 years ahead; the last I heard of the plan was that much ingenuity was exercised in thinking what evidence archaeologists of the future would want about local life in 1972, and this was to be collected, placed in a capsule, and buried on the school grounds. In the other study, undertaken by eighth-graders, the assumption was that people would spend at least some period in the future in caves if they were to survive, and the ingenuity lay in making the classroom simulate a cave, in studying minimum food and air requirements and examining the varied view of individuals as to what else was essential to life. All of this naturally involved problems of leadership roles and personal relationships.

This last study was significant in two other ways: first, it hinted that the archetypal symbols such as caves identified by Seonaid Robertson[1] as being especially significant for younger children have drawing power for adolescents also. Secondly, it came spontaneously out of physical *making*, which is often more satisfactory than carefully planned thematic studies. In this case the art teacher had for some time had a notion that he would like it to be difficult to get into the studio, so students volunteered to make the entrance into a tunnel. Then they thought of making the room into a cave. Then they said, "Well, we shall all be living in caves soon enough. How would we manage?" It was then that other teachers in science and social studies were drawn into their inquiry. This progress, from making to inquiry, is what characterized to some degree the study of old age and the science-art study of earth sciences. It was a phenomenon very familiar to me in England.

One major anxiety was allayed by our work. It is simply not true that there are certain classes of children—suburban or inner-city, or black or white or brown—who are unsuited to work of this kind; that is to say, the question posed earlier in this chapter—about whether any one kind of program could advance the learning and personal development of young people from very diverse backgrounds—can be answered positively also. I often meet teachers who speak of the English schoolchild as if his or her wings were sprouting from each shoulder. American children are painted as having short attention spans and febrile energy, English as docile and content. I wish teachers who say such things could have seen some of the English classes I have seen. I would agree that there are some greater difficulties for American adolescents than for English, but I can also say from my past two years of work in American schools that greater freedom does not mean chaos, so long as teachers seek out ways of establishing the dignity and self-esteem of every child. This requires sociological understanding of the very different problems of, for instance, the affluent but neglected student, or of the poor and defeated. It also requires personal insight into individual variations, as between the intra- and the extrapunitive, between those who find escape in activity and those who withdraw, between the dependent and the rebellious, and so on. Provided teachers do not opt either for authoritarianism or for laissez-faire (two very common temptations), inventiveness and involvement lead to good order and self-discipline.

Among the teachers I have worked with, there has been a clear recognition that some students need a much firmer framework than others. An excellent development in one school is that the teachers are going to take on the scheduling of students themselves, trying to match students with teachers according to the degree of control or flexibility they seem to need. There is also a general move towards preparing students gradually to take more responsibility for their own learning, moving them from very firm contracting to a freer self-discipline as they seem ready. (My guess would be that toleration of flexibility will be found to vary from time to time within many individuals according to other aspects of their lives, but I respect the intention and the effort to create an adaptive system.) A differentiated treatment can seem unfair if youngsters cannot fully perceive the nature of equity. But where a teacher "levels" with a student and says, "I think, don't you, that you really need to have a firm agreement which you can keep, so that you and I can have confidence in each other," or words to that effect, the student does come to recognize that he and his teacher are both on the same side, even though as a discombobulated teenager he is sure to forget it from time to time; and the same of course goes for girls.

Partly because the changes we were looking for could not be trapped in any test that we knew to exist in the fall of 1971, partly also because we certainly would not wish the work to be deliberately assessed by narrow instruments such as standardized tests, we did not include pre-testing or post-testing in this my 1971-72 study. Process evaluation would have been most valuable, but would have been a major research project at each site. What we can point to is the confident assurance of good teachers that youngsters working in the ways I have described began to learn more competently and with greater involvement than before. On the basis of these results, these teachers want to continue working along these lines. Regarding the so-called basic skills (though if there are skills more basic than inquiry, making, and dialogue, I would like to know of them), the teachers are confident of a noticeable general improvement. A windfall of evidence from one school fell into our laps: those who had been working on the combined social studies, science and art program on the future showed an average of three years' "growth" during the academic year in the Iowa tests, against a figure of 10 to 20 months for the rest of the school.

APPRAISING STUDENTS

The other main thrust of my inquiry was to help teachers to become more perceptive and systematic in their observations of students and to see if they might develop more fully the notions of shared appraisal of relative strengths which my colleagues and I had developed at the Goldsmiths' Curriculum Laboratory. At the moment, in most junior high schools and high schools I have visited, the student disappears down the crevices between subject areas in a way very familiar to me from English secondary schools; and the middle school faculties, although usually organized on a team basis at least for "academic subjects," do not seem to have used this arrangement very widely for what should be its primary purpose—better understanding of each child. I cannot see how one can hope to assess an individual's needs and provide an appropriate program without such shared analysis.

In *Young Lives At Stake*, I suggested a steady process of appraisal throughout a school year, with reports to parents staggered instead of all the work arriving in one swoop twice or three times a year. I proposed that the basis of these reports should be appraisal sheets in which a large portion was common to all the teachers mainly concerned with any one student; and I suggested that for the time being, until we can get used to looking out always for students' strengths instead of beating our breasts about their failings, the main process should be one of putting a checkmark against a child's name if he or she has evinced a relative strength. Thus a group of teachers may decide to look out for such behaviors as the following: works well on his/her own; works well in a group; has many ideas; is interested in putting ideas into practice; is accurate; works without a tight contract; carries out a contract conscientiously; responds to others' needs, etc.; or any other values that they may choose to concentrate on over a period of time. In comparing checkmarks, which can be done quite easily if the planning is systematic and not upset by mass reporting periods, collaborative groups of teachers develop much greater insight into the students, and also into themselves, for they discover how their perceptions of individual youngsters reflect their own priorities and characteristics.

I believe that most or all of the teachers in the schools with which I worked would say that they are now more attuned to their students; in fact, some reported this in an answer to a Consortium questionnaire. However, my view is that this area still presents the greatest weakness with which we have to contend. I have in particular observed that teachers working with analysis via objectives and with pre-test, post-test systems have a pretty clear idea what mark a student has arrived at in an imposed program, but they may have a good deal less human insight than the traditional class teacher. They show less recognition of the student as a whole, even of that part of his wholeness which emerges in their discipline, and they have even less access to his wholeness as a person operating with his own temperamental disposition and his own imaginative intellectual, manual, or other strengths. (See "Individualized Learning," Chapter 4.)

Another difficulty is that it takes time for specialist teachers to think beyond their specialism to the school program and beyond that to the reason for the program and its appropriateness as a whole to any individual student. To get into the habit of seeing the student's day as a whole and to plan with each in the hope that it will have meaning for him or her as a whole (even though not all of it is necessarily particularly interesting to each) involves some change in the teacher's selective attention—a new focusing of the visual field —which presents greater difficulties, it seems, than becoming more open and flexible in ways of working with students may do.

Anyone—preservice student, in-service teacher, administrator, consultant—who makes the opportunity to follow a student or a small group through a day or more in a traditional school comes away with a salutary image of incoherence, monotony, and an extraordinary arbitrariness in the varying mores that individual teachers require. In more innovative schools we should be doing better not only in these respects but in our understanding of what is appropriate for the immensely varied individuals whom we teach. One of the great advantages of the system of shared appraisal that I have summarized is that it aids such understanding. As a tiny instance of this, I recall an appraisal meeting of a team last year. The science teacher complained that one boy came up with many ideas for inquiry but didn't bother to carry them out; he didn't understand why this was. "But he's an ideas man," exclaimed the mathematician. On the basis of this kind of regular exchange, it becomes possible to foresee a program worked out for and with such a boy, agreeing to let him be, perhaps, or to encourage him rather firmly to choose an idea and work on it, or to suggest that he might care to work with someone who would enjoy realizing his ideas. In such small ways a student's day can begin to take shape in teachers' minds because the student's personality has begun to assume a shape, being seen through the eyes of several different colleagues. I do not suggest that this is enough either. I am convinced that it is necessary for schools to develop a system of advisories, so that each student knows that one teacher particularly will enter into a dialogue with her (him) about her (his) program. This advisory system is the essential lynch-pin whether the school is divided into teams, as so many middle schools are, or is still using a purely departmental plan; in either case, maintaining an advisory group is a task for all teachers, librarians, and counselors, including of course those who teach the arts or practical subjects. The advisor is the person to whom all information about members of an advisory group is channeled and who is called on to explain and if necessary defend his or her clients; and the advisor is the link between teachers and principal or counselor.

Finally, I notice that the new techniques of evaluation being developed in various places to evaluate innovative high schools have moved away from concentrating on the student's product in spelling, composition, answers to multiple-choice questions, and content tests of various kinds to include process evaluation. This is a very useful development, but it is programmatic rather than personal. Since Americans are so deeply committed to evaluation, I hope that new ways will be found here of evaluating open-ended adolescent education in its many aspects, and that these will include further guidance on personal observations of children. My proposals, even when more fully articulated as they were in *Young Lives At Stake*, are only a primitive beginning. They need fleshing out if they are to be of full practical help to teachers.

TEACHERS' ATTITUDES AND COMPETENCE

As answers to the questions I posed at the start of my study began to emerge, I also became aware of an underlying additional question about the competence and interest of American teachers. As I shall be repeating in this and the next several chapters, I have been favorably impressed on this score, but generous support in the classroom, in collaborative study groups, and in experiential workshops, together with an effective network of communication, is required to make changes substantial and widespread. These are essential not only to enhance the competence and confidence of teachers, but also to counter a rigid hatred of change in some communities which threatens all innovation.

Many teachers feel marked anxiety as they begin to work more flexibly and to interact more freely with students. Thus they are vulnerable not only to external pressures but to internal doubts and hesitations. This is hardly surprising in view of the changed relationships and learning expectations involved, but the experience often comes as a surprise, so it is a situation of considerable tension for many teachers. On the one hand, they feel that if they do not change their ways they are failing their students and themselves. As one said to me, "My personal values are changing, so my work with the kids must change, mustn't it?" On the other hand, when they do change they are haunted by increasing anxieties: Are they letting the children down? Is any real learning going on? Sometimes the cause of this anxiety is that those same inner changes, although compelling, are not yet firmly based enough to sustain the change in ways of working with children that their very urgency inspires. Sometimes learning expectations are little changed: teachers want to develop more creative and exploratory work but are not prepared to relinquish the familiar landmarks of a fixed curriculum. Sometimes there is an underlying fear of failure—and many are well aware that if an innovation fails it is the teacher's fault, whereas if a conventional program does not produce acceptable results the fault is ascribed to the child. Often teachers feel guilty, perhaps because they are enjoying themselves, or because they are breaking away from long habits of relative dependency and obedience. Nor can they rely as they could in the past on those comfortable fat textbooks. Sometimes one finds a hint of a fear of success, since success leads to increasing demands on oneself for further inventiveness. Teachers who are spunky enough to engage in these innovations need affectionate support.

The kinds of problems teachers meet will naturally depend on personal temperament. Jennifer Andreae, an experienced English consultant at the elementary school level, makes a helpful distinction between the "plungers" and the "gradualists."[2] Many American elementary teachers, surging forward on the excitement of an idea, are plungers; but I have not met this often at the adolescent level, except in free schools or an occasional alternative program within a larger school. In fact a much more common situation is to find that a team has spent two or three weeks in a summer workshop planning, and over-planning, exactly what steps it will take in setting up an inquiry. Come the semester and in come the children: if it is sensitive the team will retreat in confusion from a plan which it can see leaves no place for children's collaboration; if it is innovative in imagination only and not in fact, it will juggernaut its way through. Sometimes one will find a plunger on the same team with gradualists; this leads to painful controversy but it is an invaluable experience if the team survives the tensions.

Whatever one's temperament, the most advantageous attitude is to enter innovation in a spirit of inquiry. One is involved in the necessary strain of a creative process, but one can also be a little bit distanced from it and can afford to be kind to oneself. The best example of this attitude that I know is a newly formed team of teachers whom I have been able to visit more often than most, some eight times over five months. They told me they had started by over-planning and had retreated. Next, they decided to consolidate and move into correlated studies in an inquiry on Indians: plenty of books, quite a lot of angles of study, but the classes moved from teacher to teacher in the usual 40-minute stretches. Next, with the help of a media specialist and the art departments, they conducted a much more active and inventive study of media, still with the same class periods, but with one excellent modification: one full morning each week there were mini-electives within the inquiry, so that a new step was taken toward open access of children to the teachers they needed, and soon this was extended to two-fifths of the time scheduled. Then came some withdrawal to intradisciplinary work, so that each teacher could feel comfortable that his or her specialism was being kept in trim. During part of this time the English and social studies teachers collaborated in a splendidly free "writers' workshop," which consisted of two weeks of steady writing for two hours every day with plenty of stimulus materials: records, tapes, news items, pictures, story lines, titles, and (a great advance) the teachers, aides, and student teachers serving as "editors" at desks around a large room, waiting for clientele to come to them by choice and when ready. The whole room was decorated with slogans and phrases to encourage the writing. Subsequently two weeks were set aside for students' individual projects, another successful period.

The team's next plan was to propose a study of the future, with students staying in groups of 15 or so (all available assistants being welcomed to keep the numbers down) and ignoring changes of periods. I suggested that the team should have consultancy schedules, whereby students particularly interested in some scientific or political aspect of the future could sign up with the teacher strongest in this field. I thought this would be an easy move towards open access. "All morning?" I suggested. "No," they said, "an hour a day. That's all we're ready for. Next time we may be ready for open access or at least open consultancy appointments. Not yet."

This example is given in some detail because it illustrates a number of important principles. First, the team was pretty realistic. Other people might be able to work faster or differently, but they knew their limitations. Secondly, it represents some of the many stepping-stones from complete separation of powers, which really denies the value of collaboration, through correlation or integration and gradually towards that most desirable state where there is open access between students and their teachers. Thirdly, it shows how the roles teachers can handle become far more flexible; in the process, they discover that they can stand less on their dignity with children without losing proper authority. Fourth, it demonstrates that inquiries can vary in length and in the number of teachers who take part in them, so that specialist teachers do not suppose they have to collaborate in this way at all times: there is a continuing place for demarcated studies. Finally, these teachers succeeded in part because they had the creative support of an outstanding assistant principal, who himself had the backing of an innovative school district.

There are strong personal conflicts between members of this team which may cause it to break up, but the progress of their work was significant. We should expect regrouping to be quite commonplace, particularly in these early stages when changes in learning expectations and teaching styles can create great anxieties. Painful as it is, that is really part of the inquiry, the discovery by each teacher of his or her strengths and weaknesses, likes and dislikes, and limits of commitment. For this reason, among others, it seems clear to me that some schools at least should try to introduce changes in a less abrupt, more friendly and collective fashion than I have usually met with in this country, so that volunteers are welcomed into collaboration without any threat being posed to the more separatist or traditional teachers.

Innovation, at present, does almost certainly require the deliberate support of a "teacher liberator," whether the principal, an outside consultant, or a teacher with some acknowledged responsibility for curriculum development. In the schools I visited in 1971-1973, this role was played sometimes by the Consortium member, sometimes by the principal, and sometimes by me. I don't think one should think in terms of changing school administrators or teachers; that seems impertinent. But I do think of liberating them—from unexamined assumptions, from anxieties about process, and as far as possible from nervousness about ignorant criticism. Thus the "liberator" is a partner to the individual's own inner wishes, not an external change agent.

My work as a consultant has made me understand more fully than before what Socrates meant about the educator as midwife. One may, of course, bring in ideas of one's own, but they are useful only if similar values are springing up among the people one works with. Ideas have to be lived in the hearts, minds, and viscera of the people who are going to put them into practice; otherwise the process will be obedient, not creative, and the same will go for the part the students are allowed to play. It is much harder to carry out an idea than to suggest it, so people in the field need time with someone like-minded, time to voice their hopes and anxieties and to begin to think in some detail round practical possibilities. Again, an outside visitor can be useful simply by reaffirming within the school building those humane values which teachers and administrators know they stand for in their personal lives, but somehow lose touch with inside the school walls, with its reminders of powerlessness or mechanization.

Innovative principals, in particular, often badly need someone from outside to talk to, a person who can look with another pair of eyes at the people likely to be involved in change, and who is competent to discuss scheduling and buildings. For teachers it is the change in learning expectations for children which takes the most time: they need time to talk over disappointments and fears. But for a principal who is offering supportive leadership, the main need is often to have someone around who will spend time and care in giving him or her that same kind of creative support.

4. Some Developments in American Education

NOW TO TURN TO SOME other proposals for changes in education which I have found most widely discussed, and have seen in operation in American schools.

OPEN EDUCATION AND OPEN SPACE EDUCATION

I have found an extraordinary amount of confusion between these two terms. In some parts of the United States the phrase "open education" denotes excellent programs such as Lillian Weber's Open Corridor in New York City or the Follow Through programs supervised by Bank Street College of Education, the Educational Development Center, or the Chicago Institute of Juvenile Research. But in others it seems to connote one of two things: either chaos or recent open space buildings. It seems urgent to me that the difference between open space education and open education be made clear, for it is possible to work in a diversified and responsive way with children in any old building; and open spaces unwisely used create opportunities for educational practices that are totally antithetical to the values for which proponents of open education stand.

In view of the many existing misunderstandings and also the peculiar anxiety that is always associated with adolescent education, members of the Middle Years Consortium agreed to speak of open education only when spoken to in those terms, and in other situations to speak of flexible, differentiated, experiential, or open-ended education, though of course being well aware that these words too can be used for mindless activities.

"Open education" is doomed to failure if it means "being locked

63

in an open situation," as James B. Macdonald and Esther Zarat have put it. This is particularly so in adolescence, when there is a great need for security and order as well as for fun and freedom of movement. If open education is to be used with justification as a "hurrah" term, it must come to be associated with openness in many well-established senses. It should mean mutual trust between persons; it should mean the collaborative learning of teachers and students; it should mean candor, so that students are not processed according to a hidden agenda but are able to understand the meaning of their education and to make shared decisions about it; it should mean as seldom as possible closing a door to a student's effectiveness by doing for him what he can do for himself or what another student can do for him; it should mean to the greatest possible extent open access among students and teachers and the breaking down of formal scheduling barriers; it means a flexible curriculum in which children's and teachers' diversity is respected; it means that no one is imprisoned by a role; it means using the environment as an open resource; it means open doors to parents and community aides and others in the community; it means that sharing is not cheating; it means open-ended studies that go beyond what teacher or child have envisaged; it means that although teachers vary greatly in the degree of delegation they can handle, even the more directive types are always on the lookout for keys to unlock the creative energies of individuals and groups. It does not mean an open conduit polluted by the disorder of the streets; nor does it mean that every question is so open a question that it is somehow demeaning to come to a decision.

Open space education is a matter of buildings, and therefore for adolescents mostly a matter of middle schools, since these usually seem to be housed in the newest buildings. There is a widespread move to organize these new schools on a team/house basis, for which open spaces are felt to be appropriate. I find it hard to give a balanced estimate of the educational value of the schools-without-internal-walls which I have found in many prosperous areas. Open planning is, of course, an intelligent attempt to cut costs and to avoid obsolescence by making buildings internally flexible. The problem lies not so much in the buildings as in the attitude that goes with them. At worst, they are the crassest form of human engineering, an attempt to force people to work in a certain style. It happens to be a style I approve of, but I do not approve of strong-arm methods even in a good cause; and of course, teachers who are not willing, not able, or not ready to move away from the formal class lesson recognize this as a strong-arm move, so that like other people under threat they regress, become more rigid and more uncommunicative, and have more headaches and other anxiety symptoms.

If open space buildings are intended, as the rhetoric proclaims, to provide for flexibility, then the wherewithal for flexibility must be provided. The wherewithal is of two kinds: one psychological, one physical. Psychologically there are a number of requirements: it is essential to prepare teachers for working collaboratively and with unfamiliar techniques and also to support their early efforts. This requires workshops and also a kind of nonthreatening intervention in planning and carrying through initial programs. It is no less important to recognize that for some teachers, and not all of them old, working in open spaces is not now and perhaps may never be the situation in which they can work best with youngsters. It should be possible for such people to be free to work in other ways. If physically they need to work in more differentiated areas, they should be able to spend at least some time in seminar rooms or even in standard classrooms. (It is interesting that one of the controversies about new buildings for English middle schools (ages 9-13), which are mostly not of the totally open plan in use in the United States, is whether the withdrawing-rooms, as one might call them, are best when built of seminar or of standard classroom size.)

Again, in terms of physical flexibility, it is amusing but also deeply distressing to note how limited people's vision of physical openness usually is. So many of the schools I have seen or know about allow open teaming between the so-called academic subjects; but the arts, the crafts (or manual arts), music, home economics, and physical education, including dance, all tend to be tucked away in another open space on another floor or within an adjoining complex, so that openness between ideas and their imaginative expression, or between practical and theoretical studies, is very hard to come by.

Another modification urgently needed is this: to make open spaces human. It should be a rule that some of what a school district saves on walls should be made available to the school over the years in the form of materials that teachers and children can use together to transform their environment so that it meets their changing needs. They should be able to build darkrooms and make wigwams or small geodesic domes (or temples, if they must do Egypt). I would like to see not only math centers but myth centers, parts of the space in which some magic can be created by lighting or decor. There should also always be a choice of cubbyholes or lairs, indoor tree houses or human-scale maze boxes, places for students (and teachers) to withdraw to when they need planning time, brooding time, or just a good snooze. I learned only last year about the progress of one middle school where five years previously I had met my first grand modern resource center; it was like a Roman temple. I protested that children need cubbyholes. The principal thought this made sense and invited the children to make the center fit their needs. They rapidly made it quirky, personal, habitable—a good home for learning.

I stress this point because it goes against one of the current pieties —or fads. Many teachers feel ashamed of not being able to forget that they are territorial animals and also that withdrawal to recenter oneself is an important part of being human. Teachers, no less than other people, need to be able to exercise some mastery over their environment, so that it is not impersonal but reflects something of the individual's personality and interests. It has greatly interested me that one of the most significant things about the better English primary schools or about secondary schools working in Inter-disciplinary Enquiry is that clusters of children move to the room or space of the teacher whose specialist help they need, but they also do much of their ordinary getting-on work in the room or space of the teacher most compatible with them. Why should it surprise us that teachers' and students' needs run along the same continuum, some needing peace and quiet—"I will 'ave 'ush," as the Yorkshire saying goes—and others enjoying mess, laughter, and excitement?

In sum, I suggest that open spaces are very appropriate to the kind of education I have been writing about provided, first, that neither children nor teachers spend the whole day in something like the main hall at Grand Central Station (but fuller than the station is today), since they need escape hatches; second, that access to the arts and other practical subjects be open; third, that the environment be flexible enough to meet the changing needs of the occupants. At present, most open space schools seem to add to a contagious sense of powerlessness.

TEAM TEACHING

I have not met with much of the type of team teaching that was promoted some years ago by J. Lloyd Trump[2] and his associates, although doubtless it is in operation. Perhaps I may therefore simply quote an earlier comment from *Young Lives at Stake,* in which I said that team teaching "institutionalizes the choice of the lesser evil," giving tutors the chance to know their students better through group discussion but denying close contact with teachers in the fields of the teachers' greatest interest.

The newer meaning of team teaching is an almost standard arrangement in the middle schools I have seen or read about. Students are divided into pods, grade divisions, or houses, usually numbering about 100 or so (according to the local staff-student ratio), and their "academic subjects" are taught by a team consisting of a math, a science, a language arts, and a social studies teacher. This is a very reasonable use of open space and a natural development from, or modified return to, the procedures of the old K-8 schools. It is one viable model for a middle school, ensuring that a child is not parceled out among specialist teachers who never meet each other and see him only occasionally. From my biased point of view, my contacts with schools (and I include visits in other years) have been somewhat disappointing. Very often, students move by stations to the four teachers in turn, and there is very little collaboration except for an occasional project (although in some districts extraordinarily generous planning time is allowed). On the whole, I have found most teachers still hampered by their specialist qualifications rather than seeing these as some of a number of personal strengths they can contribute to a partly shared program. These teachers are in an ideal situation to develop Open Inquiry for part of the program. They are also well placed for shared appraisal of students, the other fundamental asset of teaming I have emphasized in speaking of "focus groups,"[3] namely, that teachers can work together to look at each child individually. This understanding of teaching I have rarely met, although it is developing in some Middle Years Consortium sites.

I have said that the teachers' situation is almost perfect, but in speaking of open space education I have already suggested a major flaw which applies to the scheduling of most middle schools. This is that the teams are confined to "academic" teachers; the others—art, drama/dance (if any), music, physical education, home economics, and manual arts, or shop—are treated as a separate constituency. This is disastrous. The gap between art and life (see "The Child's Growth Through Art," Part II, Chapter 1), which is the most serious weakness of much schooling at this age, is made almost unbridgeable, especially when as so often happens the academic and the practical teams box-and-cox so that shared planning time becomes impossible. I have talked with some teachers and princpals during these past two years, and they are beginning to develop new means of collaborating. In one case, it involves adding an additional "roving" art teacher; in another, giving students open access to the studio as they have to the resource center or library (each teacher having a slightly larger group of children than he otherwise would, but knowing they can go freely to workshop or studio); in yet another, having a great deal of material for *making* in the "academic" spaces and drawing on the advice of the art or shop teacher. Again, in some places the problem is solved by the "practical" or art teacher becoming the facilitator of interdisciplinary projects, so that they ooze art, regardless of schedules. One hopeful sign is that some teachers are becoming aware of the importance of physical expression and interpretation of ideas, as I have already described.

Akin in some sense to the separation of academic from art teams is the hard-edged separation often found between academic teams. In Open Inquiry it should be possible for individual youngsters, or groups, to have occasional access to the best advice on specific problems that a school can offer. I have been happy to find in some schools a very good organization of teams, whereby each teacher is a member of a grade (or sometimes, admirably, an ungraded) house team but is also a member of a specialist team, so that there is good collaboration across disciplines and within them. I have not yet found the more sophisticated notion which a group of head teachers in England proposed at the Goldsmiths' Curriculum Laboratory: that an individual should not only represent a field of studies within a team but should also be the specialist in, say, history *or* geography *or* anthropology, or in biology *or* physics *or* chemistry, for the school as a whole, available to help other teachers and at least screened students in his special field. The only instances I have met of this differentiation in the United States applied to the acknowledged specialisms of members of a unified arts team.

As Leslie Smith pointed out in his study of timetabling,[4] there is no intrinsic difficulty about teams of teachers making agreements of this kind among themselves. The problem is mainly one of changing our visual image of the individual teacher's work and the curriculum as a whole.

The most serious disadvantage of teaming in middle schools is one of which I became aware only in the later months of this survey while working in schools where teams of four (or occasionally two) "academic" teachers were established for some time. This is the tendency of teams to settle down into a complacent mediocrity; the members become so comfortable among themselves that they are unresponsive to the needs of students and to the changing mood of educational thinking. There are four of them in a team; they are four-square, and each fortress is impregnable. I have spent many hours with administrators trying to think of ways in which there could be more fluidity and challenge: for instance, could two members of a seventh-grade team move up to the eighth grade with the students, or might one or more teams want to consider some mixing of grade levels? None of them would budge, and since the administration had quite properly delegated as many of its organizational roles as possible, they could not be made to budge. In one school, the best we could do was to agree that the faculty would surely allow that the needs of someone who was unhappy and wanted to change teams must have priority over those who preferred to stay put—and that this, plus a couple of retirements, could create some movement.

I must admit to great disappointment, since I have for years been praising the creative capacities of small groups, and now I find them being uncreative and also, according to several art teachers and others, increasingly "cliquey and offhand."

As regards teams of four, I have also been wondering what fifth wheel we could introduce to disconcert people and add to the interest of their lives. Of course, the obvious candidates are the teachers in special areas (the art, media, shop, music, physical education, and home economics teachers), providing the basis of the interdisciplinary teams I had always envisaged. I have also come to think there is a good deal to be said for two-person teams. In my experience in the United States they tend to be more flexible and inventive than the teams of four. I think there are things to regret here: in English schools I have been glad to see students in their early teens have contact with specialists who have a real feel for their specialism. But the two-person team, by the breadth of what has to be taught, does provide its members with an intellectual challenge. Another plan I've heard suggested but haven't seen in action is for two teachers to stay with a group of youngsters, moving alongside them collaborating with different teachers of different specialisms, say, four to six moves in a year. This might be a good solution, if it did not in turn prove too inflexible.

The present situation may not sound very serious, but I believe the problem is an important one. It confirms that there is urgent need for research on the psychology of teacher teams, to study the kinds of people who team together most effectively, in terms of mutual support and inventiveness, the optimum life of a team, the advantages of teams of various sizes, ways in which teams can be helped to become more open to children's needs and colleagues' contributions, and the pros and cons of more informal ad hoc forms of cooperation.

If I were principal of a middle or junior high school that still had independent specialist teachers, I would hesitate a long time before proposing the standard organization into academic teams I have described. I find a good deal more verve and freedom in those schools where the principal simply tries to schedule in such a way that teachers who want to work together can do so, whatever their subject disciplines. It is the institutionalizing of teaming that creates such harmful rigidity. An arrangement of this kind based on personal wishes may well prove to be a better stepping-stone towards more self-scheduling and more flexible collaboration.

FOCUS ON SKILLS

Here I have to say that I decided early I would not offer detailed comment on the teaching of reading. To do so is not within my field of competence or of interest. I don't in the least underestimate the value of being able to read with enjoyment and discrimination, nor the concern of parents right across the major socioeconomic groups. I merely feel that the emphasis on reading in America has now reached the point of a neurosis, a neurosis which leads to rigid, defensive behavior. The result is damaging to innovative programs, since proposals are largely judged by the degree of attention to reading they promise; and thereby it is damaging to reading, since it is through programs which involve reading and writing in a quite natural way that children learn to read with confidence and enjoyment—because they need to. It is in this context that remedial help is best given. (See pages 13 and 25.)

The problem is that reading is cut off from writing, writing from speech, and all three from experience. Moreover, the value of children's personal experience is thrown into question, especially if they come from a minority culture, and the school is so busy teaching reading and writing that it has no time to provide rich new experiences about which children could talk, write, read, paint, dance or act. So the vicious circle draws tighter.

I must admit that I have a good deal of anxiety about the whole concept of skills. First, I suggest that to group reading and writing with mathematics is to accept without examination antique notions of the 3 R's. Today we should realize that mathematics is in no way on a par with reading and writing. It comprises one of the great human language systems and is also an essential lens through which man perceives the universe; and mathematics is the supreme example of the beauty of the immutable. Reading and writing, on the other hand, are merely useful handmaidens to verbal communication, unless they are done with style and concern.

In many classrooms it seems that handwriting is no longer seen as having the character of an art nor the composition as being an outward expression of a whole person; and I see too little acknowledgment that written reporting or argument is a means to becoming the "exact man" whom Francis Bacon proclaimed. As for reading, which should lead to a dialogue with minds far distant in time and space, it has been reduced to the status of an intransitive verb.

My second difficulty affects every area of the curriculum, for I have become deeply suspicious of the whole concept of skills as it is now presented. In the process of industrialization it became economically convenient to break down the processes of production into parts, or "skills", then people could be trained in these skills, and their different activities, when combined, could replace the complex individual work of the craftsman. This may be excellent for the assembly line, at least economically speaking; but to divide learning into skills which are taught independently of need and with no sense of the nature of the material (material such as mathematical and verbal symbols, clay, paint, wood, etc.) is appropriate to the circus, not to the school. The time for drill is when a person's courage is up, his enthusiasm running high, and when he is able to envisage himself as being skilled in some area that he minds about. The ambition then is qualitative. A person in that state of mind wants to do something well, to be skilled, not merely to possess a skill.

These principles apply, as I have suggested, to reading. I have already reported a general satisfaction among teachers with the way youngsters used books in early attempts at Open Inquiry. I am certainly not surprised. There is an unmistakable air of satisfaction and competence that young people get when they begin to view themselves as specialists at work on an inquiry or a creative project. This greater self-confidence is also likely to be reflected in standardized test results, unless the test atmosphere is grossly diminishing to a student's ego.

The confusion between having a skill and being skilled affects the teaching of the arts very seriously, for to work well with clay or wood or in photography or dance or music is to move as deeply as one is able into the outer material and also to draw as deeply as possible from the inner sources which give meaning and shape to experiences. In doing something in the arts as well as you are able, you honor the material with which you work and you respect yourself in the process. To want to *have* a skill, as a possession, is much more frivolous; much of the work I have seen in the studios is in this sense frivolous, involving techniques—a new one each week—rather than an exploration of material and a search for an authentic personal relationship with it. It is frivolous because it trivializes an opportunity for an intense and healing experience of "dialogue."

INDIVIDUALIZED LEARNING

There are two main ways of breaking away from the traditional class lesson. One is to develop a highly diversified program which allows for individual development within a collaborative social framework. The other is to set children apart from each other, working on carefully systematized assignments. In the one case the teacher moves from being a lecturer and interrogator to being a facilitator, advisor, consultant, encourager, extender of ideas, confidant, sponsor, "gadfly," and "midwife." In the other the teacher becomes a provider of assignments, a manager of a classroom, and a marker of grades.

The trouble with the term "individualized learning" is that it is used to describe both these polarities and various intermediate possibilities. Great confusion results in teachers' minds. It is necessary to find a distinguishing term. Therefore I propose to use *diversified learning* to describe "open" or collaborative education, and not to attempt to reclaim "individualized" for what I conceive as better purposes.

The merit of individualized programming is that it enables teachers to estimate much more precisely than they could in class lessons exactly where children are on a continuum of factual knowledge. If you assume that there is one best learning route, then it is clearly humane and efficient for children to be able to take it at their own pace. A truer merit, when teachers have really put their minds to this operation, is that they develop a good collection of diagnostic and resource materials, analyzing the particular weaknesses that hold a child back, and pointing his nose to a file where he will find additional help. (Of course, some published programs have built-in mechanisms for this purpose, but on the whole these seem to be materials very tightly related to the specific program rather than something available for revision or coping with individual blind spots.) In my view, there is a place for diagnosis leading to coaching and remedial help of this kind: it is one aspect of any needs-based curriculum. There is also a value in getting off in a corner and studying independently, especially for some children; others with whom I have talked about individualized programs tell me they find it almost impossible to learn without human contact with a teacher or fellow-students. Needless to say, it is the mark of the overwhelming superiority of diversified programs that this kind of difference can be recognized and allowed for.

Most individualized programs that I have observed are little more than self-pacing. When they play a major role in the school, they are entirely foreign to the spirit of diversified education. They deny opportunities for risk-taking. They permit no decisionmaking or offer it on a trivial level. They narrow the focus by separating the wholeness of human experience into a series of disparate programs. In the early stages of individualizing of this kind, the relief of being able to exchange pleasantries with one's fellows instead of being silenced in a class lesson, together with some feeling that it is more grown-up to be allowed to work on one's own, outweigh the boredom of impersonal learning. It is easy, it is restful, it is safe. But in schools where working to objectives, pretesting, doing an assignment, post-testing, pre-testing, doing an assignment, post-testing, and so on are the ways students spend their day as they move (often along separate ways) from one class to another, I note a growing boredom and disillusionment. The teachers are quite excited about their creations, having worked on an independent task toward a competent conclusion; not so their students.

Earlier I pointed out how important it is to reflect on prevailing tendencies and to act to countervail them when they are inimical to the development of young people as substantial persons and responsive social beings. Individualization of this kind confirms more than it countervails a trend of our times towards shallow and impersonal relationships which lead to being self-regarding because it is difficult to recognize other people as being as fully real as oneself. I'm not surprised, therefore, to learn from some of the "non-academic" teachers in schools dominated by highly individualized programs that students are increasingly unwilling to sing together, to make murals or mobiles or whatever together, or even to work together in a kitchen. Each, I have been told, wants to "do his own thing." Divided we are easy to defeat, easy to control, easy to soothe with placebos.

Individualized learning is used also to describe various kinds of non-graded scheduling. In these cases my comments in a previous chapter apply, both those on youngsters' needs for companions and in some instances those on their need for interaction with adults.

The advantages of *diversified learning* are very different. Such an education includes the possibility of individualized programming when a student has work to catch up on, or likes to spend part of his or her time in the safety of a predigested program, or wants to work quickly and effectively through some material for which he (she) has a recognized need. But it also provides opportunities for human contact, for individual and group decisionmaking, for working alongside a teacher and fellow-students in order to expand the significance of some simple question, for contributing one's strength toward a common goal, and for re-creating wholes through interdisciplinary study.

When the term "individualized learning" is used, as I have occasionally found, to describe a very careful, personal advisory system in which each student daily or at least regularly discusses his (her) plans with an advisor—who, incidentally, may think that he (she) is best suited by firm contracting or free inquiry and will make agreements on this differentiated basis—then the term points to an essential characteristic of a diversified program, one that quite often is not recognized by new teams of teachers working together in open-ended programs for the first time. This is an excellent and important development.

In general, I would say that teachers I have observed working on fully individualized programs in the usual sense are serious, well-intentioned people. They want to satisfy themselves and please the parents and the school board by being able to identify individual "progress"; but they have failed to understand the inner significance of their action, which is to dehumanize learning, to reduce autonomy, to deny experiential learning, and to ignore individual differences except in regard to speed and aptitude in their special field. I am glad to note that when a "teacher liberator" comes on the scene many of these teachers confess to anxieties on precisely those lines. Then all their planning and analyzing becomes a valuable resource, to which they can turn to help some individuals at some moments of their development; and they are free to return to working with children.

FLEXIBLE ELECTIVES

Short-term electives, or "mini-electives," have a great attraction for adolescents and offer satisfaction to teachers. They are an element of curriculum which English teachers have not developed to nearly the same extent as have Americans. They meet the restlessness, the immediate curiosity, and the desire to get a hold on the world without always having to go into things too deeply, that characterize many young people in the middle grades. They furnish an opportunity for teachers to fascinate students with the things they themselves find fascinating; in some cases this can lead youngsters on to work more deeply in a field they would not otherwise have thought of entering. Mini-electives can be a separate part of the program from Open Inquiry, but they can also accommodate special interests which arise in inquiry.

In one middle school where the program of mini-electives is particularly inventive and is a lynch-pin of the curriculum, each child regularly takes part in two mini-electives lasting some six weeks each. I was impressed to find there that the concept of "need" had been very sagaciously applied. For instance, in deciding who might go to a small but much-desired course on filmmaking given by a filmmaker in residence, one student was given priority because she was highly intelligent, almost excessively verbal, and more mature than her sixth-grade class; another was picked because he was Hispanic, had some language difficulties, and had found it hard to settle down to the seventh grade of this new school.

Such a system of electives seems to me an admirable development. The only serious criticisms I have heard were at high school level. Thus, although some of the most prestigious colleges are loosening up their formal requirements for obviously talented students from innovative schools, the same freedom is not permitted to many upwardly mobile students who have a weaker educational background and who are aiming toward the large state universities which have computerized entry requirements. Sometimes the charms of a lighthearted approach to curriculum can blind inexperienced students from inexperienced families to the relatively rigid requirements they will have to satisfy. There has to be a means-end realism about these students' life chances. This may be regrettable, but it is reality.

Another difficulty I have noticed is that while a combination of "basic skills" and "mini-electives" is neither coherent enough nor imaginative enough as a total diet, it is one to which some schools seem to be attracted. The weakness here lies not in the electives but in the concept of unrelated basic skills, and thereby in the lack of opportunity for varied collaborative inquiries in which young people can follow their bent and still create a collective program on a scale worthy of their energies. This is particularly important at present, when students come late to diversified education. In a few years' time, when some will have this experience right through K-12, there may well be a good case for having one year at about age 13 which would be conceived mainly in short-term electives, based on students' needs and interests and teachers' personal choices.

COMMUNITY ELECTIVES

Increasingly, innovative schools are looking outside the school faculty for community members who can add to the variety of offerings made to adolescents. One of the most important aspects of this move is its benefit to the community: numbers of people find themselves enjoying teaching an occasional class, and they become more fully aware of youngsters' needs and of reasons for educational innovation. Many become aware of themselves in new and helpful ways. Some begin to realize that good teaching is hard and skillful work. And, in general, one can see the beginning of a new development in human societies in which members of a community begin to renew themselves through their shared concern with the young. In one small pilot study it became evident that the community volunteers teaching students in various parts of a suburb and city enjoyed the experience much more than the students did: the students agreed that "it was okay—but it was still school." This seems a very appropriate outcome, inasmuch as most community electives tend to provide students with a form of consumerism as opposed to a good deal of creative thinking by the volunteers.

I approach the question of community electives with two preconceptions. The first is that it is quite extraordinary to keep active young people within any one building for the greater part of their waking youth. The second is that it doesn't make very much difference whether you go to your classes by high street or corridor: what really matters is why you go and what happens when you get there. I do not want to sound blase about this. The schools-without-walls programs, which are the most embracing and most noticed instances of community electives, are clearly an adventurous new development and an invaluable demonstration of the importance of using all community resources in the service of the young; the original idea has had a promising liberating effect in school systems across the country, a successful high-impact strategy. It is rather that I wish they were not viewed as a breakthrough *de novo* to a new institutional creation, but as a natural part of the redefinition of our social institutions as a whole—and as a natural development of open-ended education. Administratively, schools-without-walls take to the limits the idea of open-ended education; to the limits, that is, of a conventional view of education, which expects schooling for all young people up to 18 and also expects education up to 18 to be separate from the continuing education of adults. But the curriculum is rarely innovative.

I prefer to look forward, on the one hand, to a much greater development of environmental studies from Headstart on and of service programs for all young people who want to contribute to their communities. How better, how else, can they acquire an adequate sense of themselves or the community? On the other hand, I like to look also to the development of interage learning. We should be envisaging schools without age walls from at least 14 years old onward —and possibly younger.

AFFECTIVE/CONFLUENT/HUMANISTIC EDUCATION

When I first began my study, I shied away from these kinds of developments, particularly when they were associated with the term "affective" education. It seemed to me that damage was done by making affective education into a program rather than a dimension of all that goes on in learning. This move appeared to put a seal of approval on the division of affective from cognitive against which I have battled for a long time. I felt that if people were involved in collaborative learning, with the cognitive-affective-conative aspects which that difficult process requires, if you had an education in which open exploration of personal concerns was accepted, if the arts were seen as essential media for expressing and notating experience and for deepening and exploring one's understanding of the material universe, one's understanding of the psychology of self and others and their mutual relationships, and one's understanding of the spiritual dimensions of the whole, and if one had plenty of opportunity for physical activity, fun, laughter, and pain, then one would be doing pretty well, without ever mentioning a separate entity called affective education. Today, two years later, I still feel that programming "affective" sessions for certain times, to be undertaken by certain people, may be a retrogressive move. On the other hand, I am beginning to understand better the way in which changes take place in American life, where the habit seems to be to polarize, to label, to build an image and promote a new specialty, and then to hope it will become integrated into a new whole. So I feel my antipathy may have been premature. I respect very much some of the work being done under this rubric, and I only regret that I have not found special attention being paid to the crying needs of the pre-high school adolescent. The admirable DRICE Program (Development and Research in Confluent Education), led by Dr. George Brown of the University of California at Santa Barbara, for instance, did not operate directly in a middle or junior high school. In any case, I hope that a more integrated or organic approach may be found to be enriching and drawing on the inner world of experience. Otherwise, there is a danger of emotional gimmicks and of trivializing amateur encounter groups very different from the humane notions of the sponsors of affective, confluent, and humanistic education.

PARTICIPATORY OR SERVICE EDUCATION

When I first began to sense the overwhelming influence of consumerism on education in America, I thought I would have to spend much of my study year in developing ideas about how young people could participate more fully in American society during their school years. So it was with great relief that I learned about the work of the National Commission on Resources for Youth (NCRY). Activities in human services were familiar to me in the United Kingdom, but I sense a more intense relief in the United States at being allowed to be useful. It might be due to longer schooling or to some more profound difference of weaknesses and strengths in the two cultures. Certainly the relief I speak of was there, ranging from the delightfully-revealing comments of a *Foxfire* journalist ("*Foxfire* gives you something to do while you're in school"), through the interested detachment of a tenth-grade Philadelphian working in a mental hospital ("It's observing more than helping; I learn about human nature"), to the ecstatic discovery of a Californian working in an excellent school-hospital collaborative program, about her feelings watching operations in the hospital where she works and studies ("I have learned how precious life is").

As I look back at two schools to which I referred earlier, the service-oriented high school and the rural boarding school, both of which seemed really satisfactory places to grow up in—and also to occasional opportunities in other schools for intimate relationships with one or two teachers and fellow-students—I have come to realize that in a sense curriculum is only a poor substitute for the life of an informed and creative family.

The two main developments sponsored by NCRY, its Youth Tutoring Youth (YTY) and parenting programs, both meet the most profound needs of adolescents. YTY is particularly interesting since it deals with reading, the great bugbear, in a constructive way; it exploits the well-known dictum that we never really understand anything until we teach it, as well as encourages self-esteem through cross-age helping.

I hope that one day we shall begin to be able to take the next step, whereby we find nothing odd in having teenagers explain to adults what they are learning or engaging in inquiries which especially interest their community. Of course, adults will first have to get over an outmoded shame at ignorance and learn that it is inevitable in a world of changing problems and proliferating information and knowledge. We have spoken a good deal of collaborative learning of teachers with students; we should begin to think of lifelong learning as a collaborative process also. In fact, few of the present problems of students and teachers will be solved except in a context where lifelong growth through education is fully accepted.

CAREER EDUCATION

In the early months of my study for the Ford Foundation, I was shocked because it seemed that this country was involved in a veneration of the theoretical over the practical, whereas I am convinced that men and women need to sense themselves as competent in the physical world. I suspected also (and later had good evidence) that members of minority groups were being badly counseled by being made to go into vocational-industrial arts programs which were generally despised; in this way, potentially good courses were being despised because they were being used for socially divisive purposes. I also noticed a number of affluent suburban young people acknowledging their need for human physical competence by going into subsistence farming, simple general contracting, and so on. American youngsters seem to me remarkably handy and inventive, but this strength was not being respected in many high schools.

About halfway through my study I began to realize that the pendulum is now swinging in the opposite direction. When I read an official draft program from Washington suggesting the entire school program needed restructuring, with the focus on career development, and when I reminded myself of the nature of man, who does not live by bread alone, it occurred to me that the bewildered dinosaur scans again, as he has so often in every country. I can only profoundly regret that just when the search for identity, the broadening of interests, the development of inquiry, the experience of creative art and practical making are most needed and most likely to be rewarded in an effective leisured and working life, our incipient new understanding of what general education might stand for should be thrust aside in favor of so limiting a viewpoint. General education has not been tried and found wanting; but as G.K. Chesterton said of Christianity, it has been found difficult and never tried at all.

My own position can be summed up in terms of three English study groups: the Crowther Report (1959), the Newsom Report (1964), and the Schools Council Committee Working Paper on the Transition from School to Work (1973). Crowther argued the case for a good prevocational education, stressing the need for a broad enough base and a sufficiently sophisticated "numeracy" and "literacy" to ensure that people had enough flexibility to meet the challenge in later life of radically changing patterns of employment. Newsom urged that young school leavers should not have packaged courses in which their studies were consistently related to their vocational choices: they should have choice based on their personal interests (a choice which could, of course, include orientation towards a career). The Schools Council Committee agreed to a statement to which I contributed as a member, making a stand for an education that was both liberal and prevocational.[5] This would provide a broadly based, personally interesting education leading by its liberal character to increased self-knowledge and a general social competence. It would also respect young people's proven interest in careers by ensuring ample opportunity in its prevocational aspect to study the world of work through open inquiry, together with a wider range of practical courses which might be vocationally useful. The aim of these would be to give young people confidence in themselves as practical people competent in the modern world, not to narrow their focus too early to a specific career field. We believed that this growth in practical competence was important for college-bound as well as for job-bound students.

As I see it, employment is an essential part of most lives and a rewarding aspect of some. Therefore, any education that is appropriate to adolescents will include the following:

1. Discovery about and reflection on the world of employment as one aspect of self-knowledge and one aspect of knowledge of modern societies. There should be a general background of interest in human work from the earliest stages of education, as the new Career Education plans recommend; there should also be specific opportunity for Open Inquiry not later than eighth grade. This study should be as experience-based as possible; but employers' concerns being what they are, the experience for these younger students will often have to be vicarious, through film, role-playing, some visiting —and the reporting back of young workers, an important and neglected aspect of youth helping youth.

This type of inquiry can be supported by *making*, and be devoted to the planning, producing, and marketing of some salable objects. Such programs have already proved their worth in a number of high schools, and for ninth-graders in junior high schools. The inquiry should be seen as no less important, but no more important, than the studies of other aspects of human life today. When Socrates talked of education being about the proper way to live, he did not mean it would be about the proper job to have.

2. Learning an adult "survival skill" of one's choice. These today are more than the three R's: they include auto repair, hairdressing, cooking-catering, elementary electronics, house construction and decorating, and carpentry—all valuable skills also to those who may not take them up for life. The aim would be that every youngster, like every aspiring actress who learns to type, should be able to say: "I am likely to be able to earn my living through this preparation, and I may choose to do so, but I am not bound to by the fact that I learned it in my teens."

This attitude is important for three reasons: It reduces anxiety about jobs, which is, alas, well justified among many minority students; yet it does not create a rigid mental set or a feeling of inferiority through some miscounseling. Second, it creates in all students the sense of human competence I have described. Finally, if the options include a range from tasks involving elegant manual dexterity to tough physical challenge, it gives an invaluable counterpoise to other studies. This I have realized from meeting some students on an urban renewal program who were able to bear school only because their anger and anxiety could find an outlet in heavy physical labor—of their own choice.

3. For a minority of students, fully fledged vocational schools which give the option of basing most learning on vocational interests.

4. From age 14 onwards, the opportunity to earn money for part of the day, with recourse to school seminars on both the content and relationships of the work situation and to coordinating teachers. In that way practical problems about relationships at work can be ironed out and become a source of learning about human beings, oneself included, and about the working aspects of human' lives.

I have met some, of these arrangements in a number of different places across the country. I have not yet discovered a full program which acknowledges them all.

SUMMARY: Innovation and the "Forgotten Years"

If one looks at the vitality and the commitment of the groups who support the innovations to which I have referred, it may seem odd that the middle years are still generally considered the "forgotten years." Indeed, there is a vivid interest in some quarters in the promotion of middle schools as an escape from the disappointment felt about junior high schools. But there seems to be less evidence of a vigorous concern with the life experience of young adolescents in the society.

At times it seems as if adolescence were seen as a social problem rather than a vital period of growth and of establishment of the personality, a period which a society should provide for with affection, good sense, and patience. This is not true of the earliest years, on which much attention has been focused—and rightly so, of course, since these years should be enjoyable in themselves. If they go badly, they can create patterns of behavior which it is difficult to counteract. Yet anyone who has worked imaginatively with teenagers can think of young people whose faith in life has been restored by an adult's faith in them; and most of us know that even after a good start, adolescents are still vulnerable to serious damage by a hostile school unless family support is extremely strong and understanding. Further, there is evidence that at fourth-grade level children get "turned off" school. It is at this age that the more formal methods obtaining higher up in the schools begin to affect the lives of younger children. Thus, unless adolescents are rescued also, the effects of improving the fate of children in kindergarten to third grade may be short-lived.

Ralph Inge once wrote, "The Dark Ages knew that they were dark." I have the feeling that early and middle adolescence are the dark ages of American education. Certainly there is a pervasive sense of uncertainty and sometimes gloom, except in some middle schools. Most people seem to think it a difficult age to teach—which it is. Yet there is no widespread feeling that it is prestigious to take on this challenging task. On the contrary, whereas high school teachers seem to have some sense of themselves as professional specialists in their disciplines, having clear connections with higher-education colleagues, and elementary teachers find satisfaction in the human and endearing aspects of their teaching, only a few of the many middle-grade teachers I have met express the self-esteem that this centrally important work deserves.

As I try to identify sources of my discomfort, I realize that one of these is the dogma of the four-year high school diploma. The corridors seem endless because the time spent moving along them lasts so many years, except for "high fliers." Even though a school may attempt to become more collegiate than any I have seen, a kind of gray virtue settles on high schools which seems to me to mask an underlying discomfort about the appropriateness of having young adults of 17 and 18 in school, especially if they are not developing that sense of themselves as competent junior specialists I referred to earlier. Even the freest and most responsive of the alternative high schools rarely seem to provide the sense of being in the mainstream of life that one finds in a good community college or (and this is significant for my argument) in a good technical or day college in

England, where students can go at 16 and find themselves alongside older people. (I understand that nearly a third of the 'A' levels [17/ 18-year-old exams] are now prepared for in technical and day colleges.) My mind keeps flashing back to a discussion between an excellent English headmistress, a group of her equivalent of ninth- and tenth-graders, and me. "I'm really worried," she said to them, "that so many people want to stay on into the sixth form [an equivalent of the junior and senior years]. They ought not to be lingering around here. They ought either to be out at work or at a local college, or preferably both!" It is from the starting point of an alien's discomfort on this point that I have been thinking about the pros and cons of all-age schools, middle schools, junior high schools, and three- and four-year high schools.

If one examines middle schools, one can see that they could be very viable places for the young to be based at. I don't suggest (despite the publicity attending them) that many have shown the imaginative flair one might have hoped for. Even the key fact of physical restlessness seems to have been little acknowledged, nor has the sense of fun, the extreme talent for boredom, the demand for hard gratifying work leading towards practical, visible results. Nevertheless, there seem to be enough people in a middle school who are at the top end of childhood, with its sense that life is manageable and that communal life is fun as well as being a serious business, to enable these schools to provide a context of security, enjoyment, and appropriate challenge, even for those who are already more moody and more solitary than most.

The weakness is that the middle school does not solve the problem of the ninth-graders as they move on into the four-year high school. In the high schools I have visited or among the high school personnel with whom I have talked, there seem to be two main attitudes to this age group. One is (and this I have met even in schools providing exceptionally interesting and inventive alternatives for juniors and seniors) that ninth and tenth grades are the grades for "basics," after which more interesting times may come—an old story. The other, less common and found only in the few alternative high schools catering for ninth-graders, is that they have really not noticed any difference between the freshman and the older students. The second is, of course, far the better position to take, and many of the most urgent difficulties of this age group are dealt with simply by being treated like an older person and also by not being too visible. But I suspect—and in fact have heard from some youngsters in this situation—that they are more confused and disrupted by the casual, get-on-with-your-own-life and don't-let-me-interfere attitudes of the usual alternative school than they like to admit. The fact is that they *are* at a different state of development from older students: for many the physical changes are still confusing if not actually physically disturbing; few have yet come to terms with their developing sexuality; and they are likely to be subject to unexpected moods, to be less accomplished at maneuvering abstract ideas, and to be more punitive and guilt-ridden in their moral notions than many of them will be a couple of years later.

I cannot see that the junior high schools are well situated to meet ninth-graders' needs. The old rituals of graduation and of responsibility of older for younger students, in an institutional sense, are moth-riddled. The only way, I would have thought, to revive these schools would be to acknowledge the ninth grade as something quite special, with serious and important work to do outside the school. This acknowledgment of the 14-year-old as a part-time adult with a capacity for socially significant action, a sophisticated view of life, possibilities of creating newer ways of living and thinking other than his parents knew, enables him or her to admit also to being a part-time child, who needs security and help with moods, who is in close touch with powerful unconscious symbolism, who comes up against problems in the peer and adult world that are hurtful and hard to deal with.

For the modern ninth- and tenth-grader it is just possible, with good human relationships and a truthful curriculum in and outside school, to make school as school tolerable. But at that age this is not really enough. I have already made suggestions about further studies that might be undertaken. I think these apply particularly to the older members of the age range I have been looking at. These young people above all should be working in community projects, traveling, testing themselves for endurance, earning enough money to give them some independence, having their imaginative life encouraged and their educational needs more fully understood. It seems that they are the most consistently failed by the schools.

5. Some Steps Toward Change

THE MAIN PROBLEM IN CHANGING EDUCATION in the direction of openness or diversification is that this is not a model which can be imposed or copied. It is a way of life, a way of perceiving children and oneself, a risk deliberately taken. In the long run it is a source of profound personal satisfaction, but for many teachers the reward is not immediate; it comes only as they develop a new personal style. The problem created by a desire for models is evident enough in this country at the elementary level, where the American respect for English experience has created instances of blind obedience to supposed dictates. There are increasing numbers of successful open classrooms, but these have come not from imitation of a model but from good support systems of advisories and workshops, which have led to quite remarkable adaptations of inner feelings as well as outward acts. This impulse will continue to accelerate and spread, given courage and good luck, whereas attempts to copy a model have soon failed, as witness some teachers who have leaped into "open education" and retreated rapidly and others who continue with ill-considered programs, thereby bringing into disrepute a whole movement towards renewal in education.

In the middle grades also, many teachers and administrators are searching for models, but this search is ill-fated since there are no models available. In some aspects—for instance, in liberalizing the teaching of English or in the new movement to change in which my colleagues and I participated and which characterized also the work of some middle schools and some Schools Council projects—there is help from England; or the Swedish experience may be relevant to career education; and so on. But to all intents and purposes American educators are as much involved in the creation of a new and barely tried approach to the education of adolescents as anyone else on the globe. In some respects, because of the more advanced economy, they are meeting the future earlier than any other nation. They are not quite on their own, but nearly.

Many aspects of American life are totally antithetic to diversified education; but there are also traditions and dispositions that are very favorable. Some disadvantages for the new kinds of education include perhaps a tendency for intellectual systemization and preplanning without reference to what actually happens; an immense capacity for paperwork; an urge for conformity and for shared endorsement of private experience; and among the public an extraordinary narrowing of focus, a desire to control education without taking the pains to understand it. The advantages for new education in the United States seem to me to be a ferment of social inventiveness, which has led to the invention of free schools, community schools, and mini-schools; respect for record-keeping and research; the increasing desire of many people to strengthen their inner lives; and a prevailing concern for persons, a profound wish that all should be well for individuals. Also many older educators remember, and some influential independent schools still bear witness to, the innovations of the progressive movement. Having experienced both the strengths and failings of the movement and also having absorbed the thinking of the last two decades, they are in a sound position to make further moves. English primary schools continued to develop on these lines, but the English secondary schools were barely touched except for some secondary modern schools immediately after World War II. So American educators and teachers are working in more familiar territory than their English counterparts at the secondary level.

Changing schools requires an attitude which is not so widespread as it ought to be: a faith in teachers. It is no longer acceptable for administrators and university teachers and curriculum developers to behave towards teachers with any sense of superiority. The whole notion of "teacher-free" materials was a disastrous form of contempt. Teachers have an immensely difficult task which few of their detractors would like to undertake. If you seek to use them to create a millennium on the cheap, you will rightly fail. They need and deserve precisely the kind of trust and support they are urged to offer to students in open-ended education. Hence there has to be a complete break from the scientific management tradition in American education, which is always based on a linear industrial model, whether one of full integration of production through delivery or of a wholesale/retail variety. The program envisaged must be at base one of mutuality and exchange. The task is to help people who share such values as I have outlined to get together wherever they are and exchange help at the grass-roots level. A strong support system is desirable also, in terms of advisories, teachers' centers, and workshops for teachers and interested parents and community members; in terms of theoretical research; and in terms of exchange of information and even friendship across the country.

One of the major problems in a single school—and, indeed within a school district—is whether change should proceed by polarization or by more collective procedures. Here the cultural difference between our two countries is so great that my opinion may not count for much. I appreciate the notion of a pluralistic society in which parents can choose among a whole range of educational options. I appreciate also that an administrator may feel that providing such options as if they were of equal value may be the only way he can expect to survive, or to get some changes made. What I fear is that mini-schools within or separate from a main school may act chiefly as a safety valve, ensuring that the children of "liberal" parents get open-ended education whereas there is no incentive for the schools even to consider change for those left behind in the main school.

I also have to admit to being shocked at the way that American education is so often treated as a product, something about which the consumer (always the parent, not the child) makes decisions without engaging in serious inquiry that might qualify him to contribute to the decisions of professional teachers. The result in my experience is that youngsters with liberal parents who could well survive and profit from some fairly tough confrontation with a traditional teacher tend to meet only their own kind, and too often a kind of softness results which makes it more difficult than ever for them to find their personal "shape." Some perceptive youngsters are aware of this lack in their diet and deeply regret it. On the other hand, children of authoritarian parents have to go on through conventional programs, with their powers of empathy, their autonomy, and their creative imagination untended. Administratively this system may be convenient, and it is easy to dress it up as democracy. It runs entirely counter to the needs of children in an effort to comply with the demands of parents.

A further disadvantage of such arrangements is that faculties are polarized also, instead of learning from one another. Since I believe that shared appraisal of youngsters, undertaken by teachers with very diverse viewpoints, is a central task of teachers in the adolescent grades, I have to urge the case for small-scale experiments, in which teachers engaged in innovation do not cut themselves off from the rest of the school. And I suggest that this gradualist approach will give the best results in the long run. A school with a polarized faculty is not the best place for youngsters, especially since paranoia sets in so easily when people harden into opposing camps.

If one works in the gradualist style, one works as a teacher does in open-ended education: one encourages volunteers rather than drafting corvees; notes and supports small moves toward inventiveness or collaboration; ensures that all planning work of an innovative team is done openly or is well recorded for others to know of. As I have already mentioned, I was particularly pleased to find that in two schools where an art teacher acted as facilitator things moved very smoothly, with the interest of faculty gently extending beyond an initial handful of colleagues. This has confirmed my view that not much good is done by simply repeating that the arts should be central to the curriculum: put people in a position to take risks and ensure that there are artists among them, and the very character of the arts and of those who represent them in a school will ensure that their standing in the school is transformed. I have also found this true of media and shop specialists, and in some cases music and home economics teachers. It would be true of teachers of improvisational movement and drama if they weren't so appallingly scarce in American schools.

As a first step towards bringing people together who feel a need to change, I have found it helpful to distinguish four categories of teachers: (1) the early innovators, some outstanding, others ineffectual teachers who hope that a change of style will rescue them; (2) the second-line innovators, people who do not move very quickly since they are successful in traditional styles but who, when they do come into an innovative program, can be a great strength for it; (3) the good or at least adequate traditional teachers who remain well satisfied and have every right to continue in the style that best suits them; (4) the incompetent and/or disaffected.

As I have said earlier, I am confident that there are enough competent people in groups (1) and (2) to make significant improvements in adolescent education, but they need help with communication to ensure that they do not alienate the third group and are not destroyed by external pressures or by the animosity of the fourth.

The strongest members of group (1) are, of course, already liberated and competent in their work with youngsters; all they need is a collaborative setting in which to work in a way that is necessary for their own peace of mind. Many of them are extremely vulnerable in the cold climate of the conventional school, and too many of the more talented drop out or are pushed out of teaching. But when they can take their place in a group and gain the friendship and support they need, they are able to support the more shaky determination for change of colleagues who are less imaginative and less committed but who are at heart uncomfortable with their present style. I am glad to say that in two cases where teachers began, with my support, to work as a creative group of six or seven people, they have recognized the value of a vulnerable colleague of this kind, and I learned later that they had sworn to resign as a body if he (or she) were not retained in the school.

In the second group I would distinguish two different kinds of persons. Some are excellent teachers, who have a lot to lose by changing a style of proven value. They need to be convinced that change will be beneficial. In England we found that mature teachers of this kind were often in no hurry to change, but could become very interested in the innovative work of others if their advice and help were needed or if they could occasionally free themselves of other commitments to act as consultants to groups of students in Open Inquiry or to come in and give a talk that summarized current developments in a field into which youngsters were moving. Quite often, after an initial year on the sidelines these teachers would help to create a new innovative group, and in many cases were extremely effective at the second phase.

These admirable teachers need to be distinguished from another kind of second-line innovator: those who haven't been thinking very much lately, who have drifted into conventional ways of working, perhaps under pressures from parents and community which they haven't cared to withstand. I am not too despairing about this group, but they need patient support. In first working with them, one is often met by a barrage about individualized learning (in the narrow sense I have described earlier), and a welter of behavioral objectives which are not necessarily appropriate for many of the children but are given equal weight, as if quantity could substitute for qualitative judgment. But if one stays with such teachers for a while and has some feeling for the pressures under which they work, then some at least come with great relief to shed the busywork and to plan thoughtfully towards some more liberal programs.

This second group profits from the liberating experience of workshops where professional concern for youngsters and work on their own personal growth are fused; for usually, in getting out of touch with students, they have also moved into a state of general indifference towards their own lives, or they have failed to make a connection between the changes in their own values at home and their professional behavior, so that they experience a discontinuity which is quite tiring but which they do not fully understand. Teachers' centers and advisory services are extremely helpful also, and it is to be hoped that these will be developed in many more areas than at present.

The greatest unmet need I have noticed is provision of conferences for principals which would give them time to move deeply into problems of relationships and curricula in their schools. In some cases other experienced teachers might join with them; in others, these teachers could be regular or visiting faculty, who describe new developments in their specialist and interdisciplinary work. These should be prestigious conferences in comfortable surroundings and should take place in term-time. My long experience of policymaking conferences of this kind at the Goldsmiths' Curriculum Laboratory strengthens my conviction that they are an important missing link in the American in-service provision. There we had about twenty people for ten weeks, but only from 10 A.M. to 4 P.M. daily, to allow for travel. I would think a residential conference of three weeks would suffice to permit principals already wanting to make a move to arrive at decisions and a personal commitment towards them. Such decisions, in which administrators and teachers invest their self-esteem, lead to action, as the research on Goldsmiths' work made very clear. Conferences of this kind might not be particularly cheap, but they would be extremely economical in terms of cost effectiveness.

When it comes to problems of communication with parents who are opposed to more open-ended education, there are very serious difficulties, which in my view have not been sufficiently recognized. More attention seems to have been paid to the rigid and harsh behaviors of many schools than to the outside pressures which can easily crush attempts to change.

Owing to my decision to work in relatively favorable situations, I have found many instances where teachers (and administrators) are hamstrung by requirements that are out of line with adolescents' or younger children's needs. If one believes that improvements come from working with relative strengths, the searchlight might for a while usefully be turned away from the well-recorded difficulties of those in a community who try to liberalize a school and onto community pressures against liberal educators.

Some misunderstandings can readily be ironed out. Young children often, for instance, enjoy new programs so much that they dash home and say, "I did no work today." They need to learn to analyze their own work in such a way as to see that they have been doing such and such an amount of reading or writing or mathematics. A pity to divide their view of the world, maybe, but better than that their voluble innocence destroy a valuable program. My own belief is also that an emphasis on a child's relative strengths, a clear statement of the program planned for him in order to capitalize on them, and evidence that teachers have engaged in serious shared appraisal should allay the anxieties of parents, especially if descriptive reports can be used instead of unexplained gradings. In this generation it is certainly necessary for the innovative to evince practical wisdom. One can appreciate that in a time of economic doubt and some serious disillusionment about the whole state of being in the country it is natural for members of the public to focus discontent on school costs and to reject the kind of personal openness which characterizes the innovative teacher. Nevertheless, the fact is that unless serious research is engaged in, leading to good systems being set up for exchanging information and advice about ways of involving parents and allaying their anxieties, the movement for renewal may be crushed first in one place, then in another, before it has had any chance of showing its strength or even being recognized as a significant phenomenon.

Ample research in a number of fields is a necessary element in a program of change. Since this has not been a research document but a book of reflections and observations, I hope it will stimulate ideas for new research on adolescent education which others will wish to undertake. In the field of communication with parents and other community people, for instance, information on the characteristics, sociological and psychological, of those who are vehemently opposed to liberalizing education would be invaluable, since it would help administrators and teachers to meet criticism with understanding and perhaps to avert the downfall of their hopes. Thus, one kind of study that might differentiate the part played by parents in an upwardly mobile suburban area as opposed to that played by the general community could indicate some possible approaches. (And an inquiry into the influence of realtors on school board policy might be very fruitful.)

As to the organization of middle and junior high schools, I have already suggested a case for research on the pros and cons of teaming. Furthermore, there has been little, if any, work done on the after-effects of workshops as against the more expensive but far more systematic support of advisories or on the ways in which these two services can best be related. We have very little knowledge about what support teachers feel they need, and how useful they find the help offered to them.

A further need is for a much closer partnership with anthropologists, sociologists, and psychologists in the understanding of adolescence because most schooling has been divisive and competitive. So far, very little research has been possible on the behavior of young people in collaborative situations other than gangs. Open-ended education offers important new opportunities for collaboration among teachers and behavioral scientists and adolescents. I would also like very strongly to propose the setting up of an interdisciplinary group to examine educational needs in adolescence and to concern itself also in very practical ways with the question of how best to bring awareness of these needs to young people, to teachers, and most especially to parents. At least part of the group's work should be undertaken with adolescents engaged in an Open Inquiry on adolescence.

For some time I have had in mind two pieces of research on curriculum which are immediately relevant to what I have observed in schools. I have already mentioned a study of the impact of mythology. Valuable as it would be in itself, I would hope very much that it could be undertaken as part of a more wide-reaching study of the spiritual aspects of the education of adolescents. I do not, of course, have in mind any kind of breach of the fully secular tradition of American public schools; that would obviously be out of the question. But the fact is that the separation of church and state has led to a failure to acknowledge that the great majority of human beings— and I believe the great majority of Americans—view themseves as having some unique relationship to the cosmos, one which might be summarized as a spiritual relationship; so far as this is ignored, the image of man that is given to youth is distorted historically and does not give them properly balanced evidence on which to arrive at their own personal values. This is a serious problem that needs investigation.

My second piece of research would be valuable in connection with Open Inquiry. There is an urgent need for a curriculum project which would identify some main areas of interest of adolescents today on which inquiries could be based. It would indicate some of the directions in which Open Inquiries have developed, or might be likely to move, and would suggest access routes to resource materials and the special contribution of new media and data-storing technology. A study of this kind would not predetermine any new inquiry, but it would give teachers some indication of the kinds of concerns that emerge overtly or covertly among adolescents and the kinds of connections they may be likely to make. It could provide some kind of scope sheets which would be helpful to them in making their tentative preparations and, in some cases, suggest new lines of study if a group of students ran out of ideas. To take a simple example, the observations I undertook in my Ford Foundation study revealed there was a significant interest in the future. Few teachers I talked with expected this; and the students' expectations of the future might well disconcert teachers who had not encountered them. In fact, on several occasions lately I have taken areas of investigation such as the future, which I know have proved significant to young people and have asked how they would expect an Open Inquiry to go; in general, the expectations have been less directly human than the actual situations I could describe. A "connection bank" based on experiences in school would not only help to ensure that inquiry programs involve substantive learning; it might also deepen our understanding of the wisdom and seriousness of adolescents.

I have suggested that an adequate support system would involve in-service commitments through workshops and advisories and residential conferences, together with research projects concerning the participants in the educational process and also the curriculum. Beyond this, there is a need for teachers (and students if they are interested) to feel that they belong with others of their kind across the country. In this last respect, the example of the Middle Years Consortium seems significant.

The members of the Middle Years Consortium who first met in Stony Brook in November 1971 were: Robert Bassett, Assistant Superintendent of Schools in Walpole, Mass.; Al Dobbins of the Whitaker Middle School in Portland, Ore.; Donis Dondis of the School of Public Communication, Boston University; Marie T. Genest of the San Bernardino (Calif.) City Schools; Dennis Littky, Principal of Shoreham/Wading River Middle School, N.Y.; James Macdonald of the School of Education, University of North Carolina at Greensboro; Thomas Minter, Superintendent of Schools, District 7, Philadelphia, Pa.; Mary Ann Penny, Consultant on Intermediate Education to the Ontario Board of Education, Willowdale, Ontario; Daniel Scheinfeld, Director of the Follow Through Program, Institute for Juvenile Research, Chicago, Ill.; Florence Scroggie, Consultant to the North York Board of Education, Toronto, Canada; and myself.

As a group, we come from widely scattered places across the United States and Canada and include educators holding quite different kinds of appointments within schools, school systems, and universities. But although our jobs and our geographical bases are so different, we are united by a close proximity of our ideas and attitudes.

In the British Isles, with its comparatively small population and manageable distances, people who have similar ideas find each other with relative ease. Although I am not overwhelmed by the much larger population of North America nor by the even greater multiplicity of cultural traditions, the land does seem to be too big. Large-scale business enterprises producing a uniformity of products can span it efficiently, but it is difficult for like-minded people who are not in a position to flock together in large conferences to have any family feeling or sense of proximity with natural friends and allies who are separated from them by vast distances. The result seems to be that much valuable energy is dissipated, and people feel themselves cut off and isolated, although the total number of colleagues across the country who agree with them may be quite large. In England it was possible to think of ripple effects going in many directions because there is a discernible pond, a felt unity that comes partly from geographical proximity, partly from historical tradition. North America can never become a pond, but here one can think in terms of networks of small friendship groups that span the continent. The Middle Years Consortium is a venture of this kind.

One important feature of the Consortium is that it narrows its focus to a manageable field by concentrating on an age group, and this differentiates it from many excellent people who believe they can work an all-inclusive reformation from K through 12. In fact, some parameters are necessary, and such people usually work within a limited locality or within a single subject field. In either case, they can profit by the advice and collaboration of a group which is concerned with every aspect of a certain phase of educational growth. This kind of expertise is familiar in early education but rare in the later years, where subject specialisms cause professional divisions.

One main interest of MYC at present is to develop an informal exchange of reports and suggestions among its members and the teachers with whom they work. The first issue of this exchange, *The Good Guys' Gazette*, was circulated among cooperating teachers in the summer of 1973. It is an informal journal, and readers are asked to duplicate it and circulate it as freely as possible. There is no doubt that inventive teachers want to work out their own programs; nevertheless, they are thankful for stimulating ideas and for narrative descriptions of programs carried out by people with whom they are connected, even at a distance.

Another main thrust of the group is to develop support systems in the areas of those members who are especially concerned with in-service. This in turn leads to the identification of teachers who are more than competent to run workshops for other teachers, to further the grass-roots exchange to which I have referred. This is a component which is very seriously lacking in programs of change at present. It is nearly always to university teachers, a small number of well-known consultants, or English visitors that school systems look for leadership in open-ended education. MYC's alternative is to discover strong people at the local level who can work together, though still making sure that they obtain refreshment themselves. Some local people just work as members of focus groups in their schools; others should be working in workshops also; and yet others should be seeking appointment in due course as "teacher liberators," members of school faculties who are able to concentrate on curriculum when this is not a main interest or field of competence of the principal.

Those of us who have been working towards creating small local networks of like-minded teachers find that there is a hunger for meeting, talking, and exchanging ideas. Many are willing to contribute articles to the *Good Guys' Gazette*, which should be a unifying factor as well as being useful practically, and the sense that there are other identifiable teachers across the continent working along similar lines and willing to share their experiences gives a feeling of "belonging with" which may well lead to further developments.

Altogether, I have been interested to notice that, both in its own nature and in its hopes for teachers, the Middle Years Consortium meets the requirements noted by Elizabeth Simpson in her recent study of educational change.[1] "In the long run," she points out, "new ideas, attitudes, and ways of behaving cannot be presented, enacted, or imposed by others, whether groups or individuals, students or teachers. Acceptance and open-mindedness must be 'meanings perceived as related to the self.' " She calls for six characteristic requirements: partnership in decision-making; the satisfaction of belonging to a group which provides mutual support; attachment to forward-looking reference groups which are responsive to teachers' proposals; a communication network for teachers and students to avoid the sense of being isolated; a recognition that change in curriculum is in a relation of mutual entailment with change in the school's social system; "propaganda" and reinforcement from reference groups and also "the confirmation of some valued part of our identity."

For myself, I find membership in MYC very encouraging. I like the fact that it is an informal friendship group which is not regional nor even national in its preoccupations, yet is extremely close-knit. I am sure there is a place for new ways of communicating between educators which are not hierarchical and do not suggest that wisdom comes from one source alone and that the contribution of teachers is to be seen at best as useful feedback. I hope that other people will create networks for mutual help and for strengthening the collective fabric of education.

References, Part 1

Chapter 1.

1. Ivar Berg, *Education and Jobs: The Great Training Robbery*, Beacon, 1971.
2. Sherwood Washburn and Ruth Moore, *Ape Into Man: A Study of Human Evolution*, Little Brown, 1973.
3. Mario Fantini and Gerald Weinstein, *Disadvantaged: Challenge to Education*, Harper & Row, 1968.
4. B. Inhelder and J. Piaget, *The Growth of Logical Thinking from Childhood to Adolescence*, Basic Books, 1958.
5. L. Kohlberg, "Stage and Sequence: The Cognitive-Developmental Approach to Socialization," in David A. Goslin, ed., *Handbook of Socialization Theory and Research*, Rand McNally, 1969.

Chapter 2.

1. A.H. Maslow, *Motivation and Personality*, Harper & Row, 1954.
2. Claudia Naranjo, *The One Quest*, Viking Press, 1972.
3. Edward Edinger, *Ego and Archetype: Individuation and the Religious Function of the Psyche*, Putnam, 1972, p. 14.
4. Elizabeth Douvan and J. Adelson, *Adolescent Experience*, John Wiley, 1966, p. 89.
5. Heinrich Zimmer, *The King and the Corpse: Tales of the Soul's Conquest of Evil*, Joseph Campbell, ed., Princeton University Press, 1971.
6. Sylvia Ashton-Warner, *Spearpoint: Teacher in America*, Knopf, 1972.
7. A.H. Maslow, *Religions, Values and Peak Experiences*, Ohio State University Press, 1964.
8. John Allen, "Pairing and Grouping," *Ideas*, no. 21, December 1971.
9. Derek Miller, *The Age Between: Adolescents in a Distracted Society*, Cornmarket and Hutchinson, 1969.

Chapter 3.

1. Seonaid M. Robertson, *Rosegarden and Labyrinth*, Routledge and Kegan Paul, 1963.
2. Jennifer Andreae, "Stages in Implementation," in *Open Education Reexamined*, Donald and Lilian Myers, eds., D.C. Heath, 1973.

Chapter 4

1. James B. Macdonald and Esther Zarat, "Study in Openness in Classroom Interaction," University of Milwaukee, Milwaukee, Wis. (mimeographed).

2. J. Lloyd Trump and Dorsey Baynham, *Focus on Change: Guide to Better Schools,* Rand Corporation, 1961.

3. Charity James, *Young Lives at Stake,* Agathon Press, 1972, pp. 45, 234-37.

4. Leslie Smith, "Timetabling for Flexibility," *Ideas,* no. 20, October 1971.

5. "Careers Education in the 1970's," Schools Council Working Paper 40, Evans/Methuen Educational, 1971.

Chapter 5.

1. Elizabeth Simpson, *Democracy's Stepchildren,* Jossey-Bass, 1972.

Part II
Porpoises and Rainbows

I HAVE ALWAYS LIKED and admired porpoises. In fact, I identify so closely with them that when I read recently of two porpoises saving a girl's life in the Indian Ocean I thought, "Well, good for us!" I respect their secret intelligence, their comradeship, their E.S.P., their playfulness—and I am also conscious of looking rather more like one than I could wish. On a transatlantic voyage there is a good chance that one will see a school of porpoises and also a double rainbow. So I use these images to describe a very enjoyable period of my life, roughly between 1967 and 1970, when I began to engage in many kinds of work beyond the special focus of the Lab's concern with the education of younger adolescents. This involved a lot of travel and wide contacts with people of diverse special interests. I visited Africa as a British representative on a small British-American team of advisors on social studies in African primary schools. For a while I joined the International Committee of the I.E.A. (International Evaluation of Achievement), Civic Education section, and established its English committee. I became particularly involved in questions of museum education and served on the English Committee of the International Council on Museums (Committee for Educational and Cultural Action) and chaired its subcommittee on museums and schools. In this period, too, I came to the United States and did some lecturing and consultancy in Ontario, which has a great and well-deserved reputation in England for its educational system. I was also a member of the Schools Council of England and Wales' Committee on the Transition from School to Work and became chairman (until I left for the States) of its Research Project in Art and Craft Education, for ages 9-13. It was a time of great interest and expansion.

I have put together here, with a few minor alterations, three speeches related to some of these projects: "The Child's Growth Through Art," given to the International Society for Education through Art in August 1970; "The Real and the Unreal," a speech to the Ontario Institute for Studies in Education conference on teacher education, in April 1970; and a paper given in Leningrad on museum education in May 1968.

I have also included three articles. The first is "Sharing," from the 1971 Museums' Annual. The second, "A Shared Search for Values," is a brief study of moral education published in *Learning and Living* in September 1967. The section concludes with a slightly expanded version of an article called "Nesting," which I contributed to *Ideas*, the journal of the Goldsmiths' College Curriculum Laboratory (no. 21). This article isn't particularly connected with the flurry of activity of this period, but I wanted it placed here rather than in Part III with my other articles from *Ideas* because I relate it to another kind of personal growth, a move in the search to be able to write in a less professional, more personal style than I had hitherto dared. I think it is very important for some educators (not all) that the intimate connection between the professional *vita* and the personal life should be openly admitted. "Nesting" was a first step in that direction.

6. The Child's Growth Through Art

By the time the International Society for Education through Art (INSEA) held its biennial conference at Coventry in England, in August 1970, I had come to know a good many English art educators —partly because of my convictions about the central importance of the arts in education, partly because I had become chairman of the Schools Council for England and Wales' curriculum research project on art and craft education (ages 9-13), which was carried out at Goldsmiths' College. Nervous about accepting an invitation to speak there, since I am a convinced but personally inexperienced advocate of the visual arts, I was assured it was because I was a "generalist" that I had been invited. It seemed that there were not many who were seen as friendly to the arts.

At the time I was also booked to take part in a UNESCO conference in Dubrovnik, so someone would have to read my INSEA paper for me. When the UNESCO engagement fell through, I found myself with a ready-written paper on my hands, a rare event for me since I like to have the feel of an audience while I speak. I read the paper in the train and did not like it too well, not so well as I do now. So in speaking it I tried to underline more clearly what the central question in my mind had been and why I had underlined the particularity of art and hence its relation to sense perception. I had recently published Young Lives at Stake, *in which I proposed that the three central processes of the curriculum should be Enquiry, Making and Dialogue. So now my question was this: if all the rest of the school curriculum were as it should be, what then would be the special function of the arts? (At present, their function is clear: to keep as many children as possible sane in school by giving them ex-*

103

perience of what all education should be like.) I don't regret my insistence on particularity as against the dangerous abstraction and empty generalizations of much so-called academic learning. But if I had had more papers to give I would probably have spent equal time on other glimpses of the importance of the arts to young people, in deepening and clarifying experience, for instance, in involving a disciplined behavior, in creating an outer form to match an inner vision and helping self-discovery through this process of exteriorization. Today I would be more concerned with the focusing of the whole person, body, soul, and spirit in the creative process.

In 1970, when I gave this speech, I wasn't aware of the significance for education of the recent studies of the left and right hemispheres of the brain, the one concerned with verbal, analytical responses, the other with visual and aural patterning and problem-solving. Within that framework, the INSEA paper and many other parts of this book can be read as urgent pleas to schools to foster the right hemisphere as well as the left, and Open Inquiry or IDE/M, which emphasize flexible choices between a variety of symbolic systems in developing and expressing meaning—such as visual models of ideas, improvisational movement, math and language—provides constant opportunity for ready alternation between left and right.

My own admiration for the arts is such that I find it impossible to understand how any teacher can dare to feel superior to the art teacher. So it has come as no surprise, but a great pleasure, to find that in the United States and Canada arts, crafts and media teachers are marvelous facilitators and leaders of innovation in collaborative work with other teachers, just as I have found them to be in England. Alas, the non-artist's view of the matter has met with acceptance by some artists in schools. At the earlier SEA workshop which I described in the paper, all the other members of our coiling course were art teachers. "But you are an intellectual," they said. "You'll find us boring. You won't want to talk to us." We talked seriously and lightheartedly as we worked, for the better part of ten days. On the last day I said, "Can you honestly say that in the last ten days I have said anything in any way more intelligent than anyone else here?" They had to admit that I hadn't.

AT SCHOOL I WAS BAD AT ART. Ironically, it is into a visual memory that all my experiences of failure, boredom, and teachers' disapproval are concentrated. I picture the art studio, a room remote from the rest of the school, a grey room with a north light—and no one who was not bad at art at school can imagine the moral chill that a north light can convey, especially in a cool climate. In a corner stands a bust of Dante, waiting to be drawn. I doubt if I then knew that Dante had written, "Abandon all hope ye who enter here." But abandon hope I did, once a week for years. That is my memory of art at school.

Forty years on, a second venture. I was visiting Seonaid Robertson, and being Seonaid Robertson she was naturally doing something to improve her house or garden. There was some soft cement there, into which I put my fingers, and knew I must try potting. She found me a place at an SEA conference. There I learned for the first time what it might have been to work with physical materials. The discovery of the strength and determination of this other was a revelation. In fact, the meeting with clay as partner and adversary was so overwhelming that I had to escape quite often into words. So my memory of the SEA at Chichester is a double image, reading Sophocles in a sunlit garden, and an ever-open studio. I could alternate between these as I pleased—as I needed, as each demanded.

I begin with my own experience because I believe strongly in the importance of communicating through the particular, and I fear the assumption that man is most noble when his statements are most general. I begin here because I also imagine that I alone among us am unable to speak about my subject, "The Child's Growth Through Art," from experience. I did not grow through art but, lacking it, lurched belatedly into a diminished maturity. Nor do I want to emulate the impertinence of the evaluator who believes that from outside a situation he can ever truly say what happened: understanding a process is more than being able to point at points in a supposed continuum. I remember once meeting a 13-year-old boy in an Approved School (a school for children who have been in trouble). He told me to look out for an abstract sculpture he had done. "How shall I recognize it?" "I call it 'The Strangulated Birth.' " "Will there be a man there one day?" "Yes, I think so. . . . If only, if only my family and everyone didn't mind so much about money." This sensitive, damaged boy might a few years on be able to tell you how his art contributed to his growth. I could not. I could only say that something very important was happening, which might not have happened if there had not been an outstanding art teacher in the school.

The phrase which haunts me as I write this paper is Rauschenberg's declaration that he operates in the gap between art and life. I don't know what he meant by it, but to me it expresses, although only by implication, the malaise of our lives. Alienation might be summed up as the existence of that gap. For reasons which I hope will emerge from the rest of this paper, even though it will not be possible today to spell them out, I believe that we have reached a stage in the development of human societies when the gap will surely destroy us if it is not healed, if we do not learn to come and go freely with the environment, if we silence our hidden selves to the extent where we need to demand that others control our public behavior, if we deny ourselves the human task of living hazardously, and if instead of delighting in authentic experience we allow ourselves to be cozzened into accepting the decaffeinated, the refined, the homogenized substitute. (Even the use of the word image as a euphemism for salesmen's falsehoods shows how direct the challenge is.)

In a heavily controlled society, be it tyrannical, bureaucratic, or just staid, art has to be deprived of its capacity to disturb. Whether the artist is simply professionalized or is accorded a titillating reverence as a shaman figure, by dividing him off from the rest of us as someone unusual and basically different from his fellows, we damage him and we damage ourselves. (I speak as a non-artist.) We suffer because our alien preconception blinds us to his perceptions; he suffers because we create a way of life in which he cannot be understood.

Schools are pale imitations of adult life, so since there is a gap between art and life today and since teachers mostly see themselves (despite Dewey) as preparing the young for life in the adult world, schools have traditionally been places where children's artisthood has been carefully destroyed through their general education, except, that is, for a few whose hands and eyes serve their purposes so well that they can hope to have the special status of Artists.

The challenge for art educators is to break with this tradition. I doubt if anyone else can do so much to heal the gap between art and life. And it can be done only by helping ordinary lives, in school and out, to be more like art. The task of the art educator is to liberate, foster, and maintain behaviors which to other people may seem to be art, but which to him are just living. And it is not only the children, it is his colleagues as well who need this kind of healing, the more so the less they recognize their need.

I hope this doesn't sound like empty rhetoric because I mean it quite literally. Perhaps I may be allowed to explain my general position. In writing elsewhere[1] about the rationale of the curriculum, I have argued that the essential characteristic of a good curriculum is to embody certain kinds of behaviors, and that this is more important than its specific content. It is not so much the program, more the way of life, which matters. There are three fundamental behaviors which I am concerned with. The first is *inquiry*, and this includes exploration, experiment, and the search for explanation. The second behavior is *making*, and this includes not only invention *de novo* (for the child) but also realizing, executing, applying, even maintaining, not just doing what you are told. The requirement of making is that the child contributes from his own sources. Finally there is *dialogue*, by which I mean not communication, which arises naturally in its proper context of inquiry and making, but openness to experience, whether experience is of material, of an object, a creature, a person (oneself included), or of a process. Dialogue concerned with awareness, not with use, and is therefore essentially opposed to the use-morality and use-aesthetic which too easily predominate in school as elsewhere.

These three behaviors are to me the polar opposites of apathy, passivity, and oblivion. I call them living behaviors. They are the way the small child behaves (with plenty of tantrums if he is prevented), but are so easily destroyed that very often they have to be consciously encouraged even with five- and six-year-olds in our schools.

If I speak to you, as art educators, about these activities, I hope you will think them a passable description of art in school. But I state them as requirements of the total curriculum. A good science teacher, a good social scientist, a good counselor, a good school principal—in short, any teacher—should be engaged in them. The difficulty is that so many teachers are not. Take scientists, for instance. Most professional scientists work within what Thomas S. Kuhn[2] has called "normal science." This is genuinely exploratory and inventive, but it is work within strict foreknown limitations. Thus, their students who become professors of the teachers who will teach in our less adequate schools may well be twice removed from great innovative science, teachers thrice, children four times. I remember once hearing a very distinguished scientist describing to a mixed group of teachers from colleges of education what it was like to be at the forefront of science, the rhythm of withdrawal and engagement, the hunches, the happy accidents, the feeling for appropriateness, the occasional marvelous moments of a perceptual "Aha." He was roundly attacked by the science lecturers in his audience, who one by one described science as the orderly collection and examination of "facts." ("Facts" has quotation marks around it because I cannot bear to appear to accept it without them.) Among artists the gap is not so great. If it had been a great artist or designer talking to art teachers about his work, even though the difference in quality of their work might perhaps have been very great, his listeners would have been at home with his way of thinking, would have had some personal knowledge of what he was talking about.

In describing the total curriculum in terms which might be descriptive of art, please do not think that I am trying to reduce art to being the same as everything else; on the contrary I find reductionism of all kinds abhorrent. My argument is only that in a school the artist has a double function: he represents certain values, skills, and concerns which are specific to the arts, but he stands also as a reminder of what all learning might be and school learning too rarely is.

What about the artist's specific function? You will have many important ideas, born of your experience and your expertise, of what the art teacher stands for specifically as an artist as against this general commitment to living behaviors. Possibly as a generalist in curriculum I may have rather different perceptions; and if that is so, either argument will be comfortable all around or the dissonance may be useful.

To me the artist in the school (specialist artist or primary teacher with an artist's bent) is first and foremost guardian of the senses.

This seems far more significant for education than any tradition which links aesthetic, by some kind of morganatic marriage, to "beauty." To be a guardian of the senses sounds safe enough, but it is to walk straight into vipers' nests of traditional antipathies that are based on errors so sinuous, so mutually entangled, that it is hard to tell head from tail or "t' other from which." I suspect that they are all interrrelated by the dubious mediation of an "undistributed middle": a fallacy which briefly says, "Here are a lot of behaviors which are different from the objective exercise of reason, and therefore they are all the same"—and all bad.

The first vipers' colony is the long tradition in Western and Eastern cultures which prefers the universal to the actual, or the ideal to the incarnate. Enshrined in Platonism, Gnosticism, and Neoplatonism, it later marched alarmingly well alongside a kind of science which aimed to discover totally impersonal objective knowledge. Relativity should have set this ally reeling, and in due course the blow will be acknowledged, but it will take time. Our leading artists, as the distinguished biologist C. H. Waddington has pointed out[3], rapidly understand the profound significance of such scientific discoveries; we cannot expect everybody to be quite so quick off the mark. In the meantime this error is represented throughout education by a lingering superiority ascribed to the pure as against applied studies, an attitude reflected in the honor accorded to fine art as against craft or industrial arts. It is, of course, strongly supported by any elite social system in which the privileged do not handle actual material: it is natural then for the aesthetic to be divorced from its simple pristine meaning of the perceptual and the perceived, and to refer to the beautiful; hence, to be concerned with objects of high culture, and so withdrawn from the multitudes.

My second vipers' nest nestles in another gap, the supposed gap between thinking and feeling. T. S. Eliot attributed this "dissociation of the sensibility" to the seventeenth century. Again, it went well with the development of mechanistic science, and over the ensuing centuries the antithesis played its part on the broad cultural level in the alternation of classicism and romanticism.

In too many of our traditional schools, feeling is simply written off. Of others, the best that we can say is that they display a promising schizophrenia, in that they separate feeling from thinking and

Art can be expressive of a childs feeling

associate the one with the arts and the other with real work; hence they see the arts as simply therapeutic, but they do at least accord it a fair stint of time on the timetable. But there are schools, also, where a true synthesis is being attempted, and where children are permitted to integrate feeling and thinking in their perceptions of the world. In my experience this happens only when a teacher of one of the arts, or again a primary teacher whose perception has not been destroyed, is right in the middle of the children's learning and is not limited to a two-hour stint in the weekly timetable.

Take, for instance, a couple of 10-year-olds who had been completely involved with others in observing and testing the actions of a spider which had appeared in the classroom—good scientific work. Then they disappeared. Half an hour or more later they emerged from under a table. They had been painting powerful pictures expressing the force of the experience and their ambivalence towards it. Without this the episode would not for them have been complete. Take again, a boy of 12, more technical in his approach to art, who in a project on "Images of Man" needed to express his image in the form of a picture or three-dimensional work, got stuck, found a book on Arp which helped him to see how he might go about it, finished that piece of work and, having evolved a technique which he enjoyed, decided to use it to convey an image of profound significance, his perception of death. Take, finally, a group of 13-year-old girls, engaged in a study of early childhood, who moved back from observation in a day nursery and a study of child development to the matter of conception and birth. They celebrated their learning by including in their material not only simple sociological data and precise biological statements and sketches, but a series of marvelously welcoming collages done in the needlework room, depicting the entry of sperm into the womb and the development of the fetus. Incidentally, that embroidery teacher told me the other day that she did not think her science colleagues would ever see science again in the old terms, since they had worked together in an interdisciplinary team. Certainly these girls achieved a totality of comprehension which we all might envy.

My third error is again a gap, again with vipers. I see the artist, being the guardian of the senses, as also therefore guardian of the particular against the general, the percept against the concept.

[handwritten marginalia]: Their environment as a good idea as the picture — Long portray: what student wants to portray it not what the teacher says

"Conceptualizing," said Marshall McLuhan[4] "is just games people play." We don't have to go so far as that; we don't have to succumb to that either/or dichotomy to affirm that perception is undervalued in our schools. Children are forced to pay too much attention to the general, too little to the particular, and this despite Piaget's warning that until somewhere in their early teens they need to work most of the time in concrete terms, to be able to refer back constantly to the concrete instance. C. Wright Mills[5] has attacked the kind of "Grand Theory" in sociology which is dominated by the interrelationships of abstract terms, with very little care for the actual, perceived situation. To many children much school learning is similarly devoid of content. We laugh at medieval schoolmen for arguing about angels on a pinpoint, but have we enough sympathy for schoolchildren who are moved too early into abstractions just as remote from what they see and understand?

The false gap between perceiving and thinking distorts children's education in two ways. First, it means that they do not move freely from the general to the particular and back again, and so lose an important aid to thinking. They learn all the time to communicate through verbal and mathematical symbols, but they are deprived of the iconic, and equally of the enactive modes of representation. The graphics element in many classrooms is limited to sketches of objects, such as musical instruments and scientific equipment, and to etiolated crayon illustrations of familiar historical narratives, with (in England) a couple of models of Norman castles thrown in. This is not enough. Few children learn to use the sketch or three-dimensional model as an aid to clarifying their ideas, seeing relationships between data, and predicting the way in which a study may develop by visualizing its implications. An architectural teacher I know requires his students to formulate images of a process which are so specific that he can be sure that they have fully grasped it conceptually, a kind of graphic algebra which we might well commend to schools. Once again, you can recognize a school where artists are all over the place by the freedom with which children make their problem-solving processes visible and work them out in concrete form.

The second distortion is that they learn not to trust and refine their perceptions. It always pleases me that in the Book of Genesis we are told that God, having made the world, "saw that it was good," and it amuses me that some English translations diminish the splendor of this carnival (as W. H. Auden describes this moment in an artist's work) by substituting "knew" for "saw." Doubtless God could have unpacked His vision, and given Himself long and tiresome inventories of the reasons of His success, as He saw it. But this is not always appropriate. Much of our life is lived rapidly at the level of what Michael Polanyi calls "subception,"[6] where we know more than we can say. To come to be confident in the probable rightness of one's perceptions of a situation, to learn to worry at them at the perceptual level until they are more coherent and inclusive, to be aware all the same that one's perceptions are properly and inevitably personal, and to allow for the fact and for the relativity of others' perceptions also, these are important lessons to which I suspect that the art teacher may greatly contribute, just by working with children as an artist in the context of their academic studies.

The polar opposite of this view, namely, the common undervaluing of perception arising from a belief that true knowledge is knowledge of general statements, is not merely damaging to thought processes. It is part of a dangerous mistrust of experience and of perceptual judgment. It matches, for instance, the kind of morality which falls back on general moral rules, when in the actual arena of moral conflict it is more important to appreciate how situations arise out of the unique interrelationships of unique persons. In the era of personal relationships towards which we are moving, ethics are giving way to aesthetics—that is to say, to the perception of moral actualities—and it is better so.

Another evil also stemming from overrating the abstract is more strictly relevant to the arts in education. If you are always concerned with conceptual understanding, ultimately you deny a child's right to privacy, because ultimately you deny the propriety of ambiguity, in which he shelters his secret understanding: the teacher expects to be able to understand everything he says and does. As I write the highly conceptual stuff that I am attempting here, even if it is embroidered with the occasional viper, I am deliberately foregoing privacy in order to avoid ambiguity. If I have managed to make myself clear, I have narrowly limited what you are expected to draw from my statements. But if I had written you a poem, or danced you a dance, you would not have drained my cup; there would always have been more, some of it hidden even from myself at this time. The ambiguity of art lies not only in the fact that it draws on configurations that are nonlinear, in that its order permits analogy, pun, and coincidence, all of which have no place in the overt order of rational discourse, where the particular is merely an instance of a general rule; it lies also in the greater potential of the particular. The significance of the general statement is by intention limited; science, where it is best displayed, is deliberately concerned with prediction concerning classes of objects in controlled situations. But the significance of the particular is inexhaustible, and therefore ambiguous, and therefore mercifully private, while being deeply evocative for those that have eyes to see or ears to hear.

Finally, may we return to Rauschenberg and the gap between art and life? I think it has significance for art education of another kind. I believe that life has ceased to be *living* because the non-artists among us have learned to play safe and to rely on the authority of others, on the simplified stereotype, on the reward of the tick of approval in our exercise books.

In contrast, artists are used to being at risk. Every time the artist uses a tool or sets a word in a poem, he engages in hypothesis in action and enjoys the possibility of error; and no one else can decide for him whether he was right or wrong. But academic teachers always have higher scholarly authority looking over their shoulders. Most have been taught critical thinking rather than the hazards of inquiry and making. When I think of my friends who are engaged in the arts, and remember how direct they are (though not always very good at words), how sensitive to actuality, how responsible to themselves for their decisions, or again when I think how much more interesting art students seem to me than many other students of supposedly higher "intelligence," I have to remind myself that it is unlikely that there is any correlation between handiness and this kind of adventurousness. It must be, if my observations of them are right, that their education has been less destructive than that of the majority of more academic students.

So I make two final pleas. Please care for those who are not particularly handy, who perhaps have no great gifts for poetry, for sounds, or for movement either. If you abandon them they have less

Calls for Artists to share in education and with youth make the school

of a chance of learning to live at risk, which in the long run is our best chance of continuing to exist at all. Please make your studios and workshops open houses for everyone in the school, however improbable as clients some may seem. There are ways in which they can become involved in your world: many artists, for instance, have ideas which others carry out, they invent but do not realize. And some young people love the life of the studio even if they are better at enjoying the process than at producing a product.

My second plea is that you do not withdraw totally into your studios and workshops. Come out and work alongside your colleagues for part of the school day, so that your values can illuminate the general curriculum. There are important moves all over the world toward the collaboration of teachers of different subjects. This is a great opportunity for artists to close the gap between art and life.

I don't believe these proposals for integrated or thematic or interdisciplinary work, as it is variously called, will much improve the adolescent's lot unless two things happen. The first need is for the work to be genuinely open inquiry and creative in character, with teachers and students taking risks in their learning. The second is for there to be a representative of at least one of the arts in each small interdisciplinary team of teachers. When this happens, the artists, in partnership with others who have the same sort of attitudes even though they represent other subjects, naturally come to take a lead because they are best able to cope with risk. By this simple means the artists among us, whatever their special field, can come to be at the center of the school's life instead of decorating its outhouses, and the school can come to be a society where art and life are not divorced.

In the schools where this is beginning to happen I am confident that children grow, though I still could not tell you precisely how it happens. That is the secret of each particular child.

References

1. Charity James, *Young Lives at Stake*, Agathon Press, 1972, p. 152.
2. Thomas S. Kuhn, *The Structure of Scientific Revolutions*, University of Chicago Press, 1970.
3. C.H. Waddington, *Behind Appearance: A Study of the Relations*

Between Painting and the Natural Sciences in This Century, MIT Press, 1970.

4. Marshall McLuhan, in a talk on the B.B.C.

5. C. Wright Mills, *The Sociological Imagination*, Oxford University Press, 1959.

6. Michael Polanyi, *Personal Knowledge: Towards a Post-Critical Philosophy*, University of Chicago Press, 1958.

7. Two on Museums

My connection with museum education arose from my coming to know Renée Marcousé, the remarkable Honorary Secretary of ICOM International Education Committee, who was until 1970 an Education Officer at the Victoria and Albert Museum in London. More than once, we had gone as a course from the Lab to work with her in a museum, and in the winter of 1967-68 she and I and Edwin Mason worked out a Pilot Study, testing out a way in which we might help children to work more perceptively and with greater enjoyment of objects.

Our purposes were twofold: to help young people, first, to develop a personal connection with objects and, secondly, to visit museum galleries with confidence and some sense of direction. The plan was a simple one, and was based on the notion that if youngsters are encouraged to make choices from among a limited number of objects, which they can at leisure look at, handle, and record (in sketches or words), they will be able to enter into true "dialogue" with the ones of their choice and will learn that their taste is a valid expression of themselves and that they are valid persons.

Classes of young people came on two visits with their teachers (who had already met and volunteered to go through the same process). In the first visit they did not go into the main museum but worked in a demonstration room with a selection of 36 very diverse objects. A simple questionnaire was so formulated as to require them to handle as well as to look very carefully. They were each to choose six objects for their personal collection, record them, look if they wished for information about them on a file of cards on a side wall; some then described their choices. In the second visit they were

116

guided to the specific galleries where they would find many more objects related to their special choice, the idea being that they would not be overwhelmed by the scale of the place if they knew what they were seeking and why, and could move in with some sense of being initiates.

Dr. Marcousé worked with 10-year-olds, 14-year-olds, and 17-year-olds from nine schools and recorded the detailed arrangements in an article published first in the (English) Museums' Journal in December 1967, and later, alongside my Leningrad speech, in Ideas 12/13 in February 1969. Her observations were extremely favorable, especially where the teachers made good use of the project on their return to the schools.

I mention this study because both she and I have found that it has value outside the field of museum education. I have used it in working with American teachers, both in a university graduate course and in a workshop; in each case we brought our own favorite object since access to handling museum objects is difficult here. We examined them carefully, being asked to decide on the six objects we would choose for our own collection and to record in any way we preferred the one object we liked best of all. I well remember the silence and absorption in my Boston University course as people pondered, and sketched or recorded in notes or in poetry. One man sat down and wrote six poems, to his wife, children, and best friends; he had never written a poem before and was overwhelmed. After a long silence we came together, and one by one displayed our choices and explained them. It is marvelous to learn how differently, and in some cases how richly, people observe the world.

One woman came over to a man who had given an extraordinarily sensitive appreciation of an object she had brought: "I can't give it to you," she said, "because I love it so much, but you have such a much better sense for it than I that I would like to lend it to you for three months." Months later I had a letter from a woman who had chosen one object only, a stone I had brought down from Maine. She described to me how that extremely spare choice had been her first recognition that she was in search of her basic self and her first step towards discovering herself through simpler and more direct relationships with people.

Renée Marcousé subsequently worked in the same way with

English children bringing in their most loved objects into a classroom (and discovered, among other things, that sophisticated 12-year-olds doing really well at school may have a continuing love for their teddy bears). This project, which was designed to lead to personal discovery through creative writing and other art forms, impressed her as being extremely significant in the search for identity at a younger age. [This study will be published in the forthcoming report of the Schools Council's Curriculum Project in Art and Craft Education (ages 9-13).]

I have referred to our shared study at some length because I think it has importance in education at all ages and is easily replicable. My speech in Leningrad and my subsequent article in the Museums' Annual (or Annuaire des Musées) are much more general. The ICOM conference in Leningrad and Moscow was agonizing in some ways, because we sat in the Hermitage for days with the greatest treasures in the world just along the corridor—and made public statements to each other. But it was a momentous occasion, the first ICOM conference on education and the first to be held in the U.S.S.R. It also was admirably planned in that we did not read our papers but spoke about them for 10 minutes. I found an immense response throughout this international group when I talked of the need to get away from lecturing children, and especially of the need to trust the creative involvement of smaller groups of children and adolescents.

In both pieces, especially the short article "Sharing," I was beginning to move towards a concept which I later thought about a great deal, that of "reschooling society." I believe that adults will only understand the culture if they combine consciously to teach it to the young and to each other. One easy aspect of this would be the kind of pepperpot distribution of experts throughout the community which is required to make an "outgoing education" truly effective in England, and in the States is most fully developed in so-called schools- or colleges-without-walls. The first place to start seems to be in the community's other public settings, such as museums and parks, which should not only move outside to give leadership and encouragement to schools, colleges, and neighborhood groups throughout a constituent area but also engage the energies of a far wider social group than the usual "friends" of a museum.

The Museums and the School Curriculum (1968)

IN CONTRIBUTING THIS PAPER to our ICOM symposium I must explain that unlike most of us here I am not a member of a museum staff or an expert in museum education. I am simply one of your clients. As Director of a Curriculum Laboratory I work with experienced teachers to effect curriculum reform in schools. Having been honoured by an invitation from Madame Antonova and the Committee to present a paper, I think the most useful thing I can do is to outline some of the changes in the curriculum and way of life of schools which I believe will influence the requests that they will make to you over the coming decades. And because education is neccessarily a partnership between all those who have something of importance to offer to young people, it is my hope that you will not wait for us in schools to change and improve our ways, but will actively sponsor and promote these changes. This would be only what we would expect from museums in view of the creative and imaginative part they have played in education in the past.

My message to you briefly is this: let us not spend our time giving more and more technically efficient answers to old questions. Let us reconsider our questions. This is the continuing challenge of living with rapid change. If one looks back over the years in which the educational policies of museums have developed one can recognize three assumptions that have dominated the educational scene. All are important, but all, I believe, need to be scrutinized and reinterpreted. They are (1) that in a modern society education is not a privilege of an elite but part of the normal provision made for all our members; for this there are three familiar reasons: that our level of education determines our individual human development, the quality of our communal life, and our national economic viability. To these I would add a fourth, that it may well determine whether our human species continues to survive and to emerge; and (2) that the function of education is to transmit a society's cultural heritage—and again we are beginning to recognize more fully the international flavor of this heritage; and (3) that children's learning is enhanced by direct personal experience.

In this context, the contribution of museums has properly been seen to be vitally important. We have wanted all our children to encounter excellence, and where better to look than to our treasure-houses?

But if we were fully successful in carrying out our present policies, the increasing use of museums by a rapidly increasing population would make the situation of museums intolerable.

Already there are signs of this. At worst, for instance, the inconsiderate (or ill-considered) demands from schools lead to the phenomenon of droves of children being shepherded around museums, being sat down on the floor and addressed by a museum lecturer who has to instruct them *en masse* in a didactic fashion which has long been abandoned in our better schools. Or it leads to the sight of children dashing round a museum clutching a questionnaire or assignment sheet prepared for them by teachers or museum staff. One must imagine that the life of many museum educators is a logistical nightmare, as they try to provide an experience of their rare treasures to an ever-increasing school population. And at the end of a long and trying day we have to look at these children and ask ourselves what they have experienced. Have they enjoyed delight in precious, beautiful, and interesting objects, or have they experienced going in a bus to a large building, being sat down on the floor and addressed by a stranger in unfamiliar and rather awe-inspiring surroundings—or (and perhaps this is rather better) have they enjoyed some of the fun of a treasure-hunt, but without knowing how to enjoy the treasure? (A teacher friend of mine once gave out a questionnaire which included the instruction to find and describe a certain picture. Faithfully one girl searched, and faithfully described: It is an *oblong* picture, she wrote; and she moved on. Experience of excellence?)

I have suggested that we may hope for a reinterpretation by schools of the educational assumptions that I listed, a reinterpretation that would greatly relieve the present difficulties and which I hope museums will encourage, for it will greatly benefit the young. If I may deal with them in a reverse order, the changes I would expect and hope for are these.

First of all, we are, I believe, becoming a good deal more sophisticated than we were in our understanding of the nature of "experience" in education. Many years ago, John Dewey made a valuable distinction between undifferentiated experiencing and "having *an* experience," which he saw as needing to be completed, confirmed and interpreted by the skill of a teacher. Having *an* experience does not just happen. We are beginning to see more clearly that it requires not only a teacher's skill, but a pupil's personal involvement and commitment. For this, the affective context, the feeling-tone of the occasion of learning, are vitally important: even the grasp through experience of something as impersonal as a mathematical concept will not occur unless these conditions are favorable; clearly in museums, where we should be concerned with the delighted appreciation of beautiful and interesting things, (or at the very least with the formation of a lasting attitude which recognizes their importance for other people), this affective factor is even more significant. To have an aesthetic experience, to become personally committed to it, and so deeply involved in it as to achieve a consciousness of self that is not self-conscious, this takes time, it takes support, it takes encouragement.

It is possible, of course that some individual children in a conducted tour will have *an* aesthetic experience in this sense, but if we are to ensure the maximal value of the occasion for individuals and also go beyond isolated personal experience to the rich shared experience of friends and colleagues in a group, with the growth of mutual respect and understanding that should ensue, we require a care in planning, a delicacy of touch, a personal welcome that will come only if we give priority of concern to it. We need to have at the forefront of our minds the concept of personal development and the enhanced dialogue with oneself and other selves that can arise from an encounter with objects.

Secondly, we need to reconsider the concept of education as passing on the cultural heritage. Too often, this has been interpreted as transmitting unexamined social norms and a body of factual information about the culture. But if we are clear-sighted we cannot fail to see that the cultural heritage which modern societies transmit is a heritage of change. "Man creates and recreates his culture," and in so doing must constantly question and reevaluate his environment, setting himself free to invent and design new possibilities. Ours is a culture based not on the acceptance of unquestioned truths, but one which prizes exploration and *making* above acquiescence and cultural docility. (It is in keeping with these changes, incidentally, that I suspect young people feel less awe than we did at the achievements of the past, but desire a greater empathy with the men who achieved them.) This is true of all countries in a technological era, regardless of their political complexions; it is a necessary concomitant of technological change. Unless we are to encourage a questing creative behavior only in a technocratic elite, condemning the majority to accept the fiats of that elite—and I am sure this is not the intention of any of the nations we represent—our schools must move more and more towards a problem-solving, exploratory and creative education.

In the context of this kind of thinking, we can see another way in which museums can contribute to the personal development of young people. This is by helping them with their investigations. It follows that we can expect to move more and more away from the didactic lecture and from common assignments towards the use of museums by small groups (or individuals) who are engaged in self-directed enquiry. They will probably continue to come in busloads if they come from a distance, but their use of the galleries will be more informed and more diversified. The role of the teacher in this kind of work is increasingly that of adviser and consultant, and he will look eagerly to the true expert in the museum to play the same role, but at a higher level. This change of role is in line with another development: the old didactic techniques, even the use of the assignment or questionnaire, arose out of a faith in the importance of factual knowledge. But as our world culture explodes into vast new areas of knowledge (one might borrow from astronomy and say that from now on the expanding universe of knowledge will be, paradoxically, our steady state) we are coming to believe increasingly in something we have talked about for generations and so rarely practiced, the importance of "learning how to learn." Gradually we are learning to practice what we have preached, and are concerned to help children to acquire effective habits of investigation, to use expert evidence, to evaluate opinions, to try imaginatively to see other points of view, to perceive relationships between facts. In all these processes, museum education has far more to offer than the mundane fact-collecting encouraged by some schools has often suggested in the past. "The merely well-informed man is the most useless bore on God's earth," said A. N. Whitehead.[1] The merely well-informed child is little better, and is ill prepared for modern life.

Finally, I hope that I did not seem tiresomely provocative in suggesting that the idea of education as a human right needed to be scrutinized. I meant, of course, only that we need to interpret it more subtly and sensitively than in the past. If we care about the personal development of young people (and by this I do not refer to competitive individualism but to personal growth within a collaborative framework) we come to see that human diversity is there to be valued and encouraged. We see also that much of our mass education has been an essay in injustice, for it has been too little differentiated. Equality does not consist in providing the same fare for different people, but in the equal provision of appropriate (that is to say, diversified) fare. There are two criteria for appropriateness: we have to recognize the diverse potential and special personal interests of the young, and we have to allow for and compensate cultural deprivation. Museums would put such a policy into practice in different ways, but one could well imagine that some might decide to give some degree of priority to two quite different groups of young people, those with exceptional aesthetic or scholarly interests and those who would not otherwise learn to feel at home in a museum, using it with confidence and discrimination, and so with enjoyment.

Developments in educational policy such as I have described will involve museums in increasingly complex tasks and many difficult decisions. You will require closer collaboration than ever before with sociologists, social psychologists, psychologists of perception, representatives of the mass media, experts on audio-visual aids (whom we can expect increasingly to find in schools and teachers' centers), educational theorists and practicing teachers. The National Committees of ICOM can set a pattern of this kind. But although the problems are complex, and will demand much more research and experiment than we have had, they bring with them their own intrinsic satisfactions. They will, they must, help to reduce the agonizing conflict between quantity and quality which exercises us today.

In this conflict we have to come out on the side of quality, recognizing that it is better for some children to enjoy a rich and leisurely dialogue with our greatest treasures than that a larger number should have an abrupt and superficial glance at them. The museum visit, as a singular event, ill-prepared for, hurried, and not subsequently exploited and confirmed in creative exploratory work, is an unforgiveable waste of our cultural treasures, and of your time. Let us not regret too deeply the passing of that phase of museum education. Far better collaboratively to ensure a better use of what museums can offer—and also to seek other encounters with excellence which a culture can provide, through children's theatre, for instance, or visits to places of natural beauty, or through the acute perception of a fossil, a rock, or a blade of grass.

SOME PRACTICAL PROPOSALS

It is not for me to propose educational actions for museums; but if my comments are not to seem purely theoretical I should add some examples of the kinds of developments which would be in line with the policies outlined in this paper. Some are, of course, already widely practiced. I do not claim that what follows is original, only that it gives examples appropriate to educational thinking today.

Preparation. (a) To set up or expand existing consultative and advisory services for teachers, so as to help them to make good use of museum resources. (The best way, of course, is to give them experience at their own level.)

(b) To develop courses in the pre-service education of teachers giving them experience of modern use of museums, encouraging choice and the recording of chosen objects.

(c) To create materials which would of themselves guide teachers and children, e.g., by providing what one might call "question-mark kits" containing objects, models and photographs which would arouse questions. The visit to the museum becomes the second phase of co-operation as children come to us with questions and problems ready formulated for study in the galleries and for consulting museum staff. (As ever, it will be necessary to guard against ill-considered fact-collecting.)

(c) To work in collaboration with TV and other mass media, which can usefully provide preparation, especially where CCTV is available, and where museums can work with a consortium of schools.

(e) To sponsor research into the use of audio-visual aids, in order to find out how far they aid and how far they impede experience of objects in their own right, whether they should be used as preliminary to or subsequent to a museum visit.

(f) Perhaps to develop museum outposts, where relatively commonplace objects, but ones which are too precious to be circulated to schools, could be housed on short-term exhibitions, preferably again in consultation with a consortium of schools.

Minorities. To develop in multi-racial societies collections giving witness to the culture of minorities. (I have in mind here particularly our need in Britain to show collections, not necessarily of great monetary value but of cultural importance, which bear witness to the cultures of our newcomers, Indians, Pakistanis, Africans and West Indians.)

Accommodation and Welcome. To seek ways of making museums attractive to the young. These are likely to be found to include: the provision of special accommodation where children and teenagers can behave naturally, i.e., make a noise; giving the opportunity (if it is conceivably possible within a museum's regulations, as fortunately it is in Britain) to handle genuine objects; if possible having space where they can enhance the visit by painting, writing, acting, in addition to the drawing which can be done in galleries. They are likely also to include the development of individualized guides, such as walkie-talkies, press-button explanation and films and concept-loops which explain how exhibits were made or used; development of concept-based punch-card or other systems that children could use in order to follow up an interest (preferably this might go beyond the walls of any one museum and might refer to objects in old churches or houses where these exist); intercom systems which would enable children (who had been given the code so as to avoid nuisances) to ask questions which were not answered in the ordinary data given to the public.

Consulting the Young. May I suggest that on this aspect of a museum's work much can be learned by discussion with young people themselves. A friend kindly made a tape recording of a discussion with fifteen-year-old boys of low academic potential from a deprived area who had experienced their first induction into a museum. In twenty minutes or so they produced the following (and more):

Special rooms for younger, middle-aged and older people (the last they thought would need more peace and quiet, expressing a sympathy typical of our often maligned younger generation); the first should have the chance of noise and activity and doing things with objects, and would enjoy a discotheque!

A change of image of the warder, whom they disliked as suspicious and ignorant.

The opportunity for young people to study to become what one might call middle-men, who without being extremely expert could help and advise people of roughly their own age.

Opportunities to handle some things in the galleries, under supervision.

More effective lighting and display such as are used to form commercial displays.

Alongside displays of, e.g., metal-work, to have displays of the tools with which they were made, and if possible films or at least transparencies showing how they were made.

Alongside costumes, to have films of fashion parades showing the costumes in use, and doing so in a kind of theatre decor, again using contemporary objects, which would show the environment and customs of the period.

The use of competitions.

Reference
1. A.N. Whitehead, *The Aims of Education*, Macmillan, 1929, p. 1.

Sharing (1971)

WHEN I RETURNED TO LONDON recently after a year abroad, a friend said to me, "We've done you well this year. You've got two beautiful new Elizabethan miniatures and a magnificent Italian primitive. Mind you go and see them." This is the most succinct statement I know of the traditional sense in which we share museums, that of shared ownership.

Public ownership, with its attendant notions of the accountability of officials and of public representation in decision-making, is a noble concept which remains fundamental to a just society. But there is a growing demand that the formal procedures of democratic control be supplemented by more informal, direct, lower-level kinds of partnership. I see this as one example of a general change that is affecting many of our social institutions. Take the family, for instance. Whether it was bound together by property ownership or by close kinship relationships of the extended family group, the family has been a fortress for its members, and at times a prison. Similarly the neighborhood, or maybe the clan or tribe, has been an enclave, seeking self-sufficiency, notoriously hostile to outsiders. Most obviously akin to the museum has been the school, also a publicly owned institution. It has been seen above all as a place which children are compelled to attend daily to be taught by people who have no other function in society. Until recently the school has not usually invited the community to share in the task of education; outside help has not been welcomed, and there has been little understanding of how children should move out freely beyond the school walls in order to pursue their studies.

In a landscape of hard-edged institutions such as these, it was natural to see the museum as the place where our shared treasures were to be guarded, interpreted, and shown to visitors; far more than as a creative center of cultural development for a community. Today the modern museum which chooses to play its part in the new moves towards greater interdependence throughout our social and cultural life can greatly increase its influence. The new ways of sharing museums are not strictly innovations since individual museums throughout the world have been extraordinarily inventive over the years. The change is rather one of emphasis. For instance, when one aim is to encourage informal study groups of children, adults, or both together as constellations of interest and support, the circulating exhibition gains a new importance, exhibitions being needed both as "starters" that may spark off new interests among them and also as "feeders" specially chosen to add depth to the ongoing work of such groups. The solar system can contain not only planets of this kind, but fixed stars as well, sub-museums set in schools or other public buildings, which can house objects that may be commonplace in the eyes of a great museum, but very nourishing to outlying communities. Exhibitions are all the better if they can be supplemented by speakers, or at least by evocative films or lively discussion materials. Again, as societies, schools, community centers begin to create and perhaps exchange their own collections, they should be able to look to the community's specialists for expert advice. Every community needs people with expert understanding of man's cultural history and of the natural world. It is only social sloth which makes us assume that all must be based on school or university and that to work in the museum service means necessarily to work inside a museum. A small group of people working from the museum could revolutionize the cultural life of a city or large country area.

Sharing does not consist only in receiving. Lay people have much to contribute to a shared museum. It is clear that many men and women greatly resent a social situation where they are dwindling into consumers; they have a profound need to feel themselves to be productive, and to be so. As the level of general education rises, museums can make better use of the non-professional, one who knows enough to facilitate the learning of others, and enough also to know when he must refer to an expert. It is good to learn that at least one museum invites young people from their middle teens onward to help in the museum, supplementing the indifferent warder with the eager participant, perhaps a specialist in the making.

In terms of training, the shared and sharing museum is so rich in possibilities and requires such flexibility of outlook that sharp differentiations of roles in the museum service seem inappropriate. There are some people, of course, whose vocation for detailed scholarship or for conservation is so clear and so completely satisfactory to them that they should not be disturbed. But for many it is both a relief and a spur to have a variety of roles at any one time and for others to be able to change roles from time to time can be a delight. I would hope particularly that people in their 40's or thereabouts would have the opportunity to change directions, since in these middle years aspects of the personality so often come to the fore which have previously been ignored and undervalued.

The task of training staff for the shared museum, whether one considers initial training or induction in middle life, seems to be to seek out and confirm people's relative strengths, giving them scope to realize the powers of which they are already aware. It is a good thing also to prod them a little so that they discover new potential in themselves. Thereby they are more ready to notice it in others; the capacity of human beings for continuing growth throughout life is one of the great revelations of a flexible community.

8. The Real and the Unreal

This is a lightly edited version of an extempore speech given at the Conference on Teacher Education, "A Search for New Relationships," held in Toronto by the Ontario Institute for Studies in Education in April 1970. A blurred tape, a clipped accent, and a torrential delivery combined to create some lacunae. But even if some of the passages sound somewhat disjointed, the general sense seems clear enough.

My connection with Ontario began in 1969, when I came to the States as a British representative to the Fourth International Curriculum Conference. Kenneth Prueter and Wilfred Wees from OISE were there, as was Kel Crossley from the Ontario Board of Education. We met with others in a crowded hotel bedroom to discuss whether I might have something to offer to Ontario education. As a result, I was invited over from England by the Board and OISE. I am happy that there are two Ontarians in the Middle Years Consortium and that from time to time I continue to work in Ontario, which has an education system from which we all have a lot to learn.

Towards the end of the talk I described a proposal for new relationships between pre-service teacher education and advice to schools which the Lab was developing. The plan did not come off. Instead I came to work in the United States. But I think it is an idea worth pursuing.

I BELIEVE THAT WHAT WE ARE DOING is mostly educating people for unreality. Unreality seems to me to include, among other things, the stereotypes of people. When you look at the stereotypes, you don't actually see the people. You have ideas about what they must be

130

like, and so you fit them into those ideas. In moral behavior, unreality seems to be to think that there are certain fixed rules by which we can organize our lives. Closer to reality is the recognition of "perceptual ethics"—the situation is always caused by the people, and it is by the acknowledgment of the people with whom one shares the situation that one's ethical decisons are made. Unreality seems to be a search for certainties in knowledge. And it is extraordinary to me that when we go on in this search for what is supposed to be the highest form of knowledge—physical knowledge as in natural science—we find uncertainty at the heart. The uncertainty of relativity, the uncertainty of indeterminateness. Yet we are still there hoping for some kind of certainty. To me, at the heart of reality there is uncertainty and at the heart of uncertainty there is reality.

I never really like talking about education without talking about people—and not stereotypes of people, but actual persons I have known. People are what education is all about. As I came down in the lift today to speak to you, I noted down that perhaps, just for today, just for this morning, education will be the affirmation of the value of persons in the delight and terror of shared uncertainties. You therefore cannot talk about education—that is, about people— without having a few people that among us we can somehow share. One such person is a poet. I happen to know the poet, and this is the poem: "My home is my heart and the journey is long, but I shall come there in peace." The poet was six and she didn't write it down —I remembered it and wrote it down. She just produced it with that wonderful mixture of intensity and casualness of a child, as if she were saying: "I've got lots more of those."

There are some people who are not aware what teacher education is for, and who are not equipped to share uncertainties with people, especially not with children. I choose some examples from one group of graduate students training for teaching, a group that I happened to work with before I moved over to working entirely in in-service planning with experienced teachers. I asked my group: "When did you last talk to a real, live, living child?" One of the group said: "It was last Christmas, eleven months ago, when I got very cross with a group of children because they had knocked over my dustbin. I didn't have sixpence to give them when they sang Christmas carols for me." This young man had had no opportunity of having any contact with children because of the extraordinary thing that has happened with the nuclear family—the generation gap. But he had thought that he would come into teaching.

Another student in the group—a very interesting musician—had taken some kind of general degree at one of the universities. I gave him a book about creativity and said: "Have a look at that—you might like it." A week later I asked: "How are you getting on with it?" He said: "I can't get into it at all." I said: "That's funny, it's all about you." "Oh!" he said, "Really?" The next day he had read it and understood it. He had seen that it had personal relevance to him because he was one of these creatively intelligent people the book talked about. He had learned that learning is something very difficult to do when the learning is irrelevant to you. Irrelevance in learning is a kind of disassociation.

Another student frightened me more than either of those two when he said: "At my department in the university, we soon learned what line the professors took and we took that line ourselves. What's the point of taking a line that the professors are not going to like?" It's frightening that such a thing is happening in our universities. In this group of teachers in training, there were two hundred students from different universities and many, many of those agreed. Unfortunately, the statement that scared me did not create as passionate an argument as it should have. They had already accepted unreality as inevitable.

One final example was a student, a girl this time, who came to me and said: "When a student asks you a question, you answer with another question. It's not fair. When a student asks a question and gets an answer, that is something." I said: "Indeed it is, but it's not something that we want." She was abashed and she was angry and she was frightened.

I remember a young teacher saying to a group of experienced teachers: "To me, the thing about teaching is that every day you have to go in there and examine what you've been doing and try to work a change." All of the others in the group of thirty teachers were angry, saying that that was absolutely unnecessary. They had settled for some kind of certainties.

I have just one other story which occurred with teachers in training. I asked them to write down the first three things that came into their heads when I said the word "teacher." When I came back into the room, all but two of those thirty students had written down something like "boring," "blackboard," "gray." One rather nice one had written "mortgage," which I thought was absolutely up all our streets. Although these were people keen to teach, when they came to the crux of it, the immediacy of it, this was how they saw it.

We know some of the positives that we are trying to implement, but I have been thinking in terms of unreality in order to give some of the negatives. One of these negatives arose when many of us met at Lake Mohonk for the Fourth International Curriculum Conference last autumn. One of my colleagues from Britain, a Welshman, had been off to a school in New York. This man is an expert on primary education and really knows primary children. He was talking to a six- or seven-year-old and asked him: "What's your family?" The small boy answered: "Well, I've got a mother and a dad, and my mother's younger than I am." Mel pressed him a bit— yes, and he had a sister and he was older than his sister; no, he was younger than his sister, but he was older than his mother.

You or I, not being experts in primary education, might think that we had misunderstood the boy. But Mel had probed sufficiently to know that this child simply did not understand the concept of younger and older. Mel followed the child into the classroom, and there on the board, written up for the lesson, was *Paleolithic man* and *Neolithic man*.

Here is the beginning of the education of a person into unreality. In education in unreality (as in history, for example), teachers have got some idea that history starts at the beginning of history, not that learning starts at the beginning of learning. And it goes on in the class lesson, with teachers talking to children in the back row who . . . well, you know the scene as well as I do. Nobody knows what is going on in the minds of those children in the back rows, with all the youngsters in the front rows putting their hands up. It is the guessing game—what is in teacher's mind. Puzzle: "Find out what's in teacher's mind, and tell her." She should know without being told!

Then think of the arrogant way we judge people. We send people out from school, not saying, "We have observed this person and we know this person in our estimation, but you must not be tied by us." We do not observe that this person is particularly notable for a fluency of ideas or, let us say, for liking to work on his own rather than being willing to join in with other people, or that he has certain kinds of manual dexterity which we think might be useful. We do not say that here is another person who is accurate, not very inventive, but accurate, trustworthy, loves to be useful, loves to be in with other people. We do not say that as far as we can tell, this is how he would be happiest to spend his life, but please let us put him in other situations so that he may turn out to surprise us yet. Instead of that, we say that we have somebody ready for examinations; we have someone with a 1 in physics or a 3 in geography—which tells nobody anything about anybody. The assessment is a totally depersonalized form of quantification and, in our country, very inaccurately organized and applied. Unreal appraisal that comes from unreal relationships in the classroom.

Another thing that we do in education is to separate feeling from thinking and denigrate feeling. We think that the arts have something to do with feeling and, therefore, they are something quite separate. We do not engage in the arts as a form of deepening our experience as well as expressing that experience. Again, we teach science not as real science but as dogma. I contrast it with Paul Park's work in an area that I think is absolutely fundamental—this experiential kind of science where the child is invited to formulate questions and work through them himself.

Basically we exclude life from the classroom. Life, the themes of life that matter to children—these are not the concern of the people who have come into our teacher training colleges, whether graduates or nongraduates. There is a tendency for the graduates to be rather worse, rather more damaged, than the ones who come straight into teacher education at eighteen. This is my experience and has been my experience in my college for many years. Of course, this is not true of everybody, but on the whole graduates show less ability to involve themselves, less happiness in free and fresh inquiry. This may not be true in your country, but I lecture a lot in England to different graduates, in schools of education to which people come from all our universities. Each time I do this, I find a way of asking in an uncolored kind of way: "Would you tell me, please, how many of you have been invited or asked during your university course to engage in some piece of study which was of your own selection, a study in which you were to find your own problem and work on it for a substantial part of two terms, say?" The proportion is very small. These people are going into university and are being taught, and taught, and taught, and much of what they are taught is just as irrelevant to them as Neolithic and Paleolithic were to that small child that my friend saw in the New York school. The teaching is all a process of making people unreal.

So this is the problem that we have—to help people to find their own reality again, to help them affirm their value and experience in the delight and terror of shared uncertainties.

The only thing I have against this conference is one phrase somewhere in the brochure about inventing new ways of relating child and world. I think we must do this, of course, but I think we also have to rediscover old ways. If you read Leonard Williams on "woolly monkeys" and if you look at what these various kinds of monkeys are doing, you will note that the young creature is never "out there" but always within the warm context of grooming; if you look at birds teaching their young to fly—a very, very old process— your realize that we have lost something that is very natural.

Nevertheless, having made this protest, I accept that there is a new discovery that we have to make, and this is something that in our work at the Goldsmiths' Curriculum Lab we have called "collaborative learning." In an era of the kind of uncertainties we face, we have to realize that the concept of an adult who "knows it all" is really something in the past. It is bad luck on us, but we are the first generation that cannot sit there saying, "Right! We know it." In the past, the young might object, protest, and sow wild oats, but they knew that sometime they were going to reach the stage of certainty. It is not like that anymore.

And this is what makes the situation for the teacher so complicated, even for the teacher who has not had this education in unreality. There are many roles the teacher plays in the double give-and-take with the young. He has to be a senior person, he has to be somebody who can guide and help, to be an advisor and a consultant for the young. At the same time, he himself has to be there learning, acknowledging his own daily bankruptcy. He must go in and examine himself and be unsure every day. There has to be this strange mixture of assurance and uncertainty for the teacher.

I would like to tell you briefly a little bit of what we do in our in-service work with teachers and something also about some hopes that we have for pre-service work with teachers for the future. In the Curriculum Laboratory, our year-round progam has three full-time courses. We always have teachers with us for eleven weeks at a time, and these teachers are invited to come and work with us in total mutuality. Any idea of a teacher coming into higher education to be told anything seems to me an unforgivable impertinence on the part of the people providing the "higher education." Because as members of "staff" my colleagues and I represent the permanent aspect of the course, we have a certain concern for the people who join us temporarily—always acknowledging, however, that, if the roles were reversed, they would have the same concern for us. This is the mutuality of respect.

As we go on, we look for small signs of well-being, mental or spiritual if you like, among the people in the courses. This is what it is all about—the signs of people being able to be truthful with themselves, being able to shed some of the defenses which they have learned to build against the world.

That is our main concern. But we are not doing a sensitivity project; we are working on task-based projects, in that we have given ourselves the task of creating policy. The first job we set for ourselves five years ago was to think about policy for secondary education as a whole. Out of this has come an extraordinary energy for radical change among many teachers. It has become a focus of many teachers talking to others about new possibilities—not a university saying "You ought to do this," but teachers thinking and planning together for the betterment of schools. Every term, I think to myself: "Good, it will be marvelous if we work out something better than what we've done. We've got some nice things, but we ought to be improving them." And so we work together in this kind of way—concerned with truth, with finding our own truth, and with finding ourselves as people. People who work together in close-knit groups of this kind come to be very truthful with each other. They make the great discovery we all have to make about ourselves—that in spite of our weaknesses, we are basically acceptable as people.

Above all, the thing that we learn is to work very experientially as we would work with children: we are involved in Nuffield junior science (a very open kind of science); we do a lot of acting together; we go and see schools together; we go and talk with children (disturbed children perhaps); we work together in museums; we work with each other making things. There is always a very strong artistic component in what we do. Especially, we learn the most important thing for experienced teachers—we learn to waste time together, and we learn that wasted time is not wasted. I so much respect those people at the beginning of industrialized society who wanted to break the clocks. Clocks are really irrelevant to time. Time is not about clocks. We, each of us, create our own time. There are moments when we can move quickly and there are moments when we have to withdraw into what Keats called "negative capability." That is what time is really all about. Learning to waste time is one of the most difficult things for teachers to do.

Learning that you are more than your function is also essential. It was said of Tolstoy that he would never, when he was writing, merely say someone was a peasant, a farmer, a cleaner, a plumber, or a teacher. I would never say that either. I would say: "I am a person, and I teach." For a short cut I might say: "I am a teacher." But I do not think of myself as just a teacher. I am just me and you are just you. One of the dangers of teaching is that you tend to dissolve into your role. You very often leave the real part of yourself at home and bring certain bits to school—the historian bit, the biologist bit, the reading-teacher bit—and all that other part of yourself, your own useful self that children so much need to know, is left at home. We split our lives, just as that small boy split his life when he did not understand the difference between younger and older while he was being told about Paleolithic and Neolithic man.

In our unit, we are hoping to do a small-scale experiment with pre-service training for graduates, alongside our in-service work. The values—the mutuality and the concern with personal well-being rather than with the immediate learning process—will remain the same; the problem of the learning process will solve itself. The young people, of course, will need advice, but collaborative planning in the group work will be the experiential basis, governed by concern for the ability to waste time and the recognition of the totality of the person.

One thing that becomes vitally important in pre-service training is the individuality of a student's choice. I would propose, for instance, to have a conference about three months before the students arrive for a one-year course, a conference in which they would be able to tell how they see their course and how they would like to have it. Some of them will be able to work very freely, and others will need a good deal of help and guidance. Why should they all be forced to a degree of freedom that perhaps they are not ready for and might never enjoy? But there would be a very strong element of student decision about what they are going to do and when they are going to do it—even about how long they are going to be in schools and how little. I would like them (though I think this is difficult) to have this kind and degree of freedom whether they are with us at college or are off in the West Riding of Yorkshire seeing some good schools and doing a piece of work up there.

Although young people still need group work, I think there is need for a more individualized kind of learning. When you are dealing with younger people, there is a difference in the kind of relationship that they want to develop with you. The important part of our in-service work—concern with learning to be able to be free about oneself—is not that people say something to me or to one of my colleagues; it is that they are able to say it to the others, to admit their difficulties to each other. But when you are dealing with younger people, there is more of a parental relationship, like a child sorting out the problem of communication with parents. Therefore, in working with younger people, there is more person-to-person contact as complementary to the person-within-a-group element.

For these two aspects of personal relationships, we plan to continue a pre-service course related to the needs of our schools as has been done for the last five years in my college. The schools of the teachers on our in-service courses work on interdisciplinary studies for perhaps fifty percent of the timetable for the younger children (equivalent of sixth to eighth grades). Therefore, the skill and experience of working in an interdisciplinary group of teachers, creating a new curriculum, is something very important to our young teachers. The satisfactory thing we find is that in their practice teaching these young apprentice teachers, who have not developed a separatism they must unlearn, move very readily into working in collaborative groups—not in planning a rigid course for their students, but in planning together how to be available to children working in self-directed inquiry. The school practice that they are involved in is revolutionary. They go out as a group of perhaps five teachers taking over a group of one hundred and fifty students, or ten teachers taking two groups of one hundred and fifty students each, depending on the size of the school. This experience is undoubtedly what the young enjoy and need, and the planning together is their task-based work—not just sensitivity training, which I believe does not have that much effect, but task-based openness.

Finally, in the Lab we are working towards a new kind of collaboration—collaboration with schools. There is a false demarcation line between training institutions and schools. There is the idea that the college of education or university is concerned with the training and education of teachers, and teachers are concerned with the education of children. I do not believe that that is what it ought to be at all. What we must have is a collaboration where it is acknowledged that teachers are profoundly concerned not only just in observing and guiding the work of young students in our schools but also in planning it with the students and with the university; and the university people, who have more time to think about curriculum, should be available to the school as consultants on curriculum. You would therefore have a total mutuality in the relationship between these two bodies of people—the school teachers and the university teachers.

To us, the idea of the school teacher involving himself deeply in the training of teachers is becoming more and more common. The idea of the university teacher as a welcomed consultant, being able to be around in the school, noticing possibilities and having teachers ask you questions about what might be done, seems to me to complete the whole, to complete the sphere within which young people can learn how to teach well. So here is the parallel quality of teacher education with the kind of education you want children to have. A young teacher in training from Northern Ireland once said to me: "Our lecturer keeps on lecturing to us in rows about how to set children into free and autonomous work." And there is the irony, the unreality.

If I might just go back (and be personal again) to that small girl who said, "The journey is long, but I shall come there in peace," I would like to comment on the rewards to me and to my colleagues who have worked in this manner. The gain that I have felt from working with experienced teachers in the free way, and the longing that I have now to work with younger people, show me that there is newness of understanding that one can gain from the young. A young teacher, a student of twenty-four, said to me the other day that he notices a difference even between himself when he was in university and what nineteen-year-olds are like now. There we might have a gap caused by the electronic age. I do not know for sure what the cause is. It may be not having had parents at war—there are many possible causes.

In any case, I now long to learn from the young. This feeling arises from these kinds of shared experiences and from the good, the help, that I have had affirmed to me by the teachers with whom I have worked over the last years.

9. A Shared Search for Values (1967)

This article has something to say to American educators, even though the specific attitudinal differences may not be the same here as in England.

Whatever the accepted values of the various classes or ethnic groups may be in our countries, my line of argument is clear: the school should not seek to impose one traditional viewpoint on all, but should engage in a searching moral inquiry: it should aim at creating a school community which might foreshadow a more appropriate value system for the future.

This demand does indeed present practical difficulties. It often happens, for instance, that affluent white students and members of minority groups come together in "alternative programs" because of a common protest against the value assumptions of the traditional school. But their mood and expectations are often quite different. The suburbanites may have significant problems of apathy and lack of identity which cause them to look for total lack of structure in a place where they can express (and hopefully live through) their aimlessness: "I might make a candle today, but again I might not," as one of them said to me when I asked if he had any plans for the day.

On the other hand, minority students may simply have experienced social injustice beyond measure, and hence have incorporated negative self-concepts; such students may be perfectly content in a conventional school with an outdated curriculum if they can find one in which they meet good order, high expectations, and genuine respect.

As I see it, both situations might have been avoided, or

minimized, if their education had been throughout interactive, diversified, and experiential. Neither group is correct in demanding anything less than a way of life based on those values. In a school where those values live, everyone will be concerned to some degree in recognizing the personal needs of each individual and ensuring that each receives according to those needs. In a "high-synergy" society[1] of this kind, receiving and giving are two aspects of the same actions.

IN A CHANGING SOCIETY the values we live by should be those we discover through the process of living. When the values of a society are agreed and relatively static, and if there are the techniques of social control to promote and enforce them, it is possible to say that values can be transmitted, and the establishment in the young of agreed codes of behavior is seen as an important function of the socialization process, both in homes and in schools. The process can work effectively as long as cultures or subcultures are relatively segregated and introspective. In a divided culture like our own it could work to the satisfaction of the dominant subculture so long as its members did not lose their nerve. Thus middle-class teachers at the turn of the century will have had little doubt that any changes they could effect in working-class children's values were for the better, and Jackson and Marsden[2] indicated that this anthropological myopia lingered on into the grammar school of the 1950s. A change of values might lead imperceptibly to an abandonment of the whole way of life of one's family, but for most the lesson was probably a cruder one: if you want to join the group where the power is, change your accent, adapt your values, and you're on your way; if you don't want to, or feel too deeply rejected by the dominant group even to contemplate trying, then opt out.

The very fact that there is a good deal of questioning in educational literature and among reflective teachers about the proper stance of the middle-class teacher (whether born or bred) towards his working-class clientele is a significant and welcome step down from the pedestal. It reflects a new situation in which people are increasingly coming to realize in their own lives the implications of living in a society that has no certainties. But it is unfortunate that so much of this class-based re-thinking is of an either/or kind.

Teachers tend to take up one of two positions. Either they stand firm for the dominant ethic with its inner-directed, individualistic, work-based and highly goal-oriented. values, which can be semantically recognized by talk of responsibility rather than shared enjoyments, of perseverance or being "stretched" rather than of varied rhythms of work, of the importance of competitiveness (or at any rate its inevitability) rather than of group or gang loyalties; or they take up an antithetical position which one might describe as neo-Hoggartian[3] romanticism, expatiating on the warmth and generosity of the newly discovered working-class product but ignoring the sense of social powerlessness and the stereotyped thinking of those relegated to low classes (and usually to low streams in school).

Failure to broaden the familiar alternatives into options shows that we have not taken to heart the challenge of quite different cultural values, some of them brought to this country by immigrants (whom we tend to fit into our class dispositions, slipping them all too readily into a low-class niche), others to be seen operating in a rich diversity across a narrowing world. Whichever side one chooses, this kind of thinking is stereotyped and provincial. It draws attention away from the facts of our situation which are that neither the middle-class virtues, thrift-based, competitive, exceedingly devoted to postponed gratifications and basically functional rather than personal, nor the values of the "unredeemed"[4] working classes, often rigid and highly authoritarian, grounded in cognitive inflexibility and status-based rather than personal[5], are going to provide an adequate guide for decisions or attitudes in a changing technologically adept world that is geographically unifying but still culturally divided. We shall not keep the human race going by these means.

Teachers who get caught up in one or other of the alternatives are denying themselves the delight *and* obligation of a new role in society, which invites them in collaboration with young people to live towards new values. This changing role is the outcome of the power shift between older and younger generations, which once again derives from our loss of certainties. Neither as parents nor as teachers can we transmit traditional values because we have no authority to turn to which is universally accepted, because many of us cannot accept the methods of social control being used to enforce them, because young people have cottoned on to the credibility gap

between adult practice and precept, because somehow dimly or
clearly each one of us is aware that our own attitudes are changing.
Whether we are ultimately relativists in ethical standpoint or ab-
solutists, we are likely to agree that the only moral rules that people
could live by today would have to be of the most general nature, the
law of love, the kingdom of ends, or something of that rank of
generality.

Our task *and* opportunity, then, is one of adventure in inquiry, not
of regulative transmission: we are involved in a shared search for
values. But once we start this examination the great sea-change occurs. For we find that inevitably we are led to examine human
beings, and human beings are diverse; procrustean beds diminish us
all.

The practical implications for change in the secondary school of
this kind of thinking are too various to enumerate in a note of this
kind, but here are a handful of important ones.

First, the disjunction between the pastoral role of the school and
the subject-matter of the curriculum is healed. As members of a
community of young people and adults inquiring together into
values, political, social, moral, we are bound to examine among
other kinds of evidence the differences between the needs, expectations and attitudes of each member of a group, as they emerge in
discussion, in the arts such as dance or improvised drama, or in
classroom behavior, by which I mean the diverse ways in which people engage in living and working together.

Secondly, this concern with values becomes a requirement of the
curriculum for all pupils, not just for the statutory leaver, or the sixth
form (aged 16-18) for it is the very stuff our lives are made of.

Thirdly, whereas as transmitters we had in controversial matters
to take a conventionally acceptable line, which we might or might
not privately support, or to appear neutral by laboring both sides, we
can now be more overtly ourselves, for we are not claiming to be
right, only to be persons.

Fourthly, we can begin to see the implications of the increasing
evidence that attitudes are the outcomes of personality structure;
and it becomes the first priority of the school to create conditions in
which we can better perceive our pupils. In a freer, more open situation than the class lesson, personality traits can emerge to an extent

that they do not usually in school today except in school journeys or extra-curricular activities. This will enable us to concern ourselves more fully with the long-term development of the personality, to create an environment which will feed the person with the experiences he needs and will help him to share our confidence in him. We shall still say "thus far and no farther" at moments when that is what he most needs to hear, but we shall take awkward phases of development more in our stride, recognizing that an adolescent needs periods of regression and goes through phases when he is simply not able to channel his aggression into activities that are useful for his career or are socially beneficial.

Finally, I would like to quote one of the wisest of the many wise things said to me by experienced teachers on our "courses" in Goldsmiths' College Curriculum Laboratory. As he left, one teacher, now a headmaster, said "All my life I have wanted boys and girls to be what I wanted them to be. Now I want them to be what they *are*." This willingness to, as it were, demoralize oneself, stopping oneself short in acts or attitudes which invade the personal space of the student, is a characteristic of the new mood of teachers today. "Judge not that ye be not judged" is a good pull-up for teachers working with adolescents.

References

1. Ruth Benedict, quoted by A.H. Maslow in *Farther Reaches of Human Nature*, Esalen Institute, 1971, Ch. 14.

2. Brian Jackson and Dennis Marsden, *Education and the Working Class*, Routledge and Kegan Paul, 1962.

3. Richard Hoggart, *The Uses of Literacy*, Chatto, 1967, and Penguin, 1969.

4. R. H. Tawney, *Equality*, Allen and Unwin, 1952, p. 138.

5. Josephine Klein, *Samples from English Cultures*, Routledge and Kegan Paul, 1965.

10. Nesting

I wrote this article for Ideas *(no. 21, December 1971), an issue dedicated to the subject of "Relationships."*

I WAS BROUGHT UP on classical Greek, and all my life I have admired the way the Greek language enabled writers to articulate with great subtlety the relationships they wished to establish between ideas, linking one sentence to the next by a delicate accommodation of connecting particles. One could have an "and" with a little touch of "but," or a "but" strengthened by an "indeed" almost to a full "however." This was a language of persuasion, a marvellous instrument for orators and philosophers who wanted to establish cogent, tightly related linear arguments.

At one time I was able and willing to make cogent, tightly related linear arguments. Today I feel that to do so is too often to do violence to other people. I prefer to be sporadic, fickle, even feckless, knowing in how many ways ideas can flow and come together. So rather than settle down to write a coherent article on relationships—no, let me be honest. I have tried to do just that, several times, and each time the fuse has blown. Perhaps the attempt to encompass wholeness has helped me to understand better what Traherne was saying to us in *Centuries of Meditation*. All space, all time, all matter, all spirit, exist here now. Even to dissect in that way is to maul reality. Being finite we have to focus on this blade of grass, this pain or joy, this moment of truth. We may momentarily glimpse a whole but cannot fully articulate it; my vision will be different from yours, and both will be incomplete.

A blonde friend of mine worked in the BBC during the war and used to sleep in the basement. She woke one night to find a mouse tweaking at her blonde hair. One thing we can do for each other, in mutual respect, is to leave others free to make their own nests from the materials they choose, sometimes exchanging or offering a few more choices.

Here are some white hairs which you are welcome to make use of if they suit your nest. They are falling out anyway.

■ In *The Riddle of the New Testament,* Sir Edwin Hoskyns contrasted the Greek meaning of truth, roughly a correct relationship between the notions in one's mind to a reality outside it, with the Hebrew concept of truth as consistency in action, following a God who keeps his covenant. It takes work to achieve this kind of authenticity, the work of self-examination, suffering, search and action. I was telling Mary Caroline Richards—author of *Centering* (Wesleyan) and a former Visiting Professor at the Curriculum Laboratory —of a young man we both know who had spent several years searching through and discarding a variety of kinds of jobs. "He's fine in himself," I said. "It's just the problem of settling down to the right work." " 'Work,' what do you mean 'work'?" she said. "That search is his work. He's been doing it." Some teachers know that the most important contribution they can make to young people's lives is to support them in the work of self-discovery and self-making, a search which makes it possible to be in this sense truthful in relation to others and oneself.

DARK BIRTH

■ This poem is about authenticity, not primarily about physical blackness. I wrote it out of an experience of my own duplicity. I had spent an evening working with university students from a minority group and had had an uncomfortable itchy feeling around my shoulders that I was somehow being deceptive. Later I had a nightmare about my head being on the block, where it would be revealed that only my public face was black. Of course, it isn't chance that the poem is expressed in terms of physical color, since our relationship to race and color is one of the greatest tests today of authenticity and wholeness. But the sure white men who mock are the empty mechanized people who mock everyone and thereby make the task of becoming authentic so threatening. These mocking voices are inside us as well as in the outside world. To be whole we have to overcome them, and we do this by seeking a living relationship with the dark center of our personal being and with the mysterious darkness beyond us, for both inner and outer darkness nourish and give us form.

> *My body has to learn to be black.*

It's not enough to be black down as far as the neck.
I have to be sure that when they lay my head upon the block
my torso as well as my neck will be purpled and dark
under our red blood.

For with you today I learned a harsh fact that I had never grasped:
I am only half-cast.
The bronze head thrusts in pride and in revolt
but the body's plaster, saintly, friable and soft.

From today I shall teach my body to become black,
I shall look first at my feet so that when I snuck
my toes in at the grating scratch
of sure white men who mock
I shall know: my feet are black.

Then firmly holding my arm I shall gaze at its form
willing it to be bronze and ripple like a gong
reverberating the muscled power of my attack
and I shall be able to say: my arm is black.

And when I put my finger here on my breast
the flesh will be smooth and dark
as a pansy's face that welcomes the sun's blaze
to its embrace.
And I shall touch each breast, and each breast
shall be black.

After this long dark travail is complete
I will come back
to greet you.

The word "snuck" in "Dark Birth" means to grip one's toes in a prehensile fashion. My daughter invented it when she was four or five and was irritated at the idea that "the Romans had made up all the words." She quickly discovered this gap in our vocabulary and filled it. I like this relationship to language, and if I were teaching in school today I would encourage children to invent words. It seems to me as important as accepting words from their home lives. Naming and defining give power, and if our language as well as our spelling is conceived as immutable, we encourage a sense that society is unalterable, a given to which we cannot contribute.

■ From Paolo Freire, *The Pedagogy of the Oppressed* : "Men, . . . because they are aware of themselves and thus of the world— because they are *conscious beings*—exist in a dialectical relationship between the determination of limits and their own freedom. As they separate themselves from the world, which they objectify, as they separate themselves from their own activity, as they locate the seat of their decisions in themselves and in their relations with the world and others, men overcome the situations which limit them . . . Once perceived by men as fetters, as obstacles to their liberation, these situations stand out in relief from the background, revealing their true nature as concrete historical dimensions of a given reality. Men respond to the challenge with actions . . . directed at negating and overcoming, rather than passively accepting, the 'given.' "

■ One of the most satisfactory things to see in a school which practices open access of students (pupils) and teachers, whether it's called IDE or whatever, is that students learn to make such good sense of their environment. They turn to the teacher who has the particular expertise they happen to need, moving to another as a new need develops. But they also do much of their getting on work, planning, sorting evidence, writing up, rehearsing, computing, illustrating and the like, in the place of the teacher whose temperament and style best suits them. Some need a cool, quiet atmosphere; some like it hot, funny and exciting. Teachers don't have to be passive in this: one described himself very well as "enticing" into his room some of the more disturbed children because he had special experience with them.

A young sociologist recently pointed out to me that to discover the meaning of an environment in this way, and thereby to help to shape it, is the precise opposite of *anomie*.

■ We the People—a letter to a teacher from a 7th-grade student (12/13) in California. "Me, the pupil and student of seven different periods, protest against the teachers for unfair work given to us. I have seven different classes and constantly have to remember all kinds of odds and ends to bring with me to class such as paper, pencils and pens, answers and myself. If the student could burden you with work from seven different periods you'd end up by throwing a fit and winning because you're older than me. With me it's either do the work or get a bad grade and that's not fair. Me the student is tired of being pushed around by you the teacher because you the teacher is gonna do all you can to take out on us all of what your teachers took out on you."

■ I wonder if close personal relationships can ever arise out of shared consumption. Does consuming inevitably divide us, not just because we may become miserly or jealous but because consuming, eating, talking, even listening are such private acts? Of course people who create together may often want to restore themselves together also; so a family whose shared work/play is to make a way of life together can be enriched by the ritual of sharing food, travel, amusements, whether it is a family by birth or by affinity. But this is quite different from being consumers who just use the same supermarket.

Before hard-edged institutions went out of fashion a traditional school could perhaps claim that it involved all its members in creating and sustaining its life. Of course, in class the pupils were merely consumers but their desire to share in a creative enterprise was met to some extent by pride in the institution, wearing uniform, playing for the school or cheering on the side-lines, whether the game was athletic or academic. Today our search is to create communities rather than to join institutions, and we want mutuality rather than commensalism.

In this context, innovative schools which simply offer a more and more sophisticated cafeteria of choices are misreading young people's needs. The affluent young in the United States have

lready shown their contempt for private opulence, many of them
opting for communal squalor. I fancy that soon the delight in having
a new range of mini-electives or in outgoing or off-campus education
may well fade also, if all the student is doing is to press an in-
titutional button and receive the course of his choice.

It becomes increasingly clear in my mind that young people need
to feel themselves productive members of society, and we are keeping them for longer and longer as dependents, as infants. The vision
of the collaborative school towards which we have been working in
he Curriculum Laboratory-is very different since it emphasizes self-
directed enquiry, *making* of all kinds including inventive thinking,
and an ethic of mutuality. It remains to be seen whether this is
enough to suffice young people throughout their teens. I suspect
hat advanced societies, needing extended schooling in order to keep
young people off the labour market but increasingly aware that
over-qualification is as miserable a state as under-qualification, are
going to have to find new ways of proving to the young that they are
ruly needed, by relating them to the society outside the schools as
co-creators, not merely as consumers.

There is a close analogy between the collaborative school and
Paolo Freire's work with illiterate adults in Brazil. One model of
education of the poor and oppressed is that there is a ready-made
culture which the educator enables these outsiders to join. The other
s that if you enable the oppressed to become conscious you enable
hem to share in the creation of a new culture, which would not have
been possible without their presence. This is comparable to what the
collaborative learning of older and young people in a school
signifies. The essential point is not that the teacher acquires new information in the process of learning alongside the student, or dis-
covers new connections within a systematic world-vision, though he
may well do both of these things. The point is that despite all the
differences in age and experience, in roles and responsibilities,
tudents and teachers work together to create and re-create a community of learners.

"Last week someone came to give a slide lecture on ancient
Greece, and I suddenly realised that somewhere out there there is a
place where geography and history and art all belong together. And

then I realised that we'd never be given the time to find it." (5th former—15-year-old—in London.)

■ A Canadian friend of mine was visiting a middle school where some of the 12-year-olds were working on an enquiry. One dejected girl was copying a picture of a submarine. "Are you enjoying what you're doing?" "No." "Why are you doing it?" "Well, we're doing transport, you see, and my group got the sea and I got submarines." The following term I visited the same classes, which were now doing a study of different countries. I found a girl making a folder about Siamese cats. Yes, she was enjoying it. Even so, why was she doing it? "Well, we're doing Canadian life, and you see on this chart— look, I'll show you—we thought up all the things about Canadian life we could find out about, and that's my part there, do you see? Pets." Neither was what one could call vintage IDE, but the difference was significant. Every student I spoke with volunteered to show me on his or her chart the place of the individual work in the plan. Each child's place in the scheme of things had been agreed and the agreement or contract made visible. This occasion made visible to me for the first time the full importance of something I had often talked about, that we have to re-learn the art of seeing ideas and relationships between ideas. In so much schooling the making of pic- tures is seen as light relief in a long lesson (think of all those crayon drawings of Harold with an arrow through his head), and although there is plenty of three-dimensional material about to work with its relevance is usually seen as confined to spatial or quantitative relationships. One rarely sees the visualising of processes of thought, the visible charting of relationships, the visual communication of ideas to others. In working with younger pupils who are not ready for formal operations this is a stinging failure. But seeing ideas and connections isn't something we should think of growing out of. There is massive evidence, of which the double helix is the most spectacular recent example, of the importance of seeing in the work of the greatest creative thinkers.

■ Ever since I read the article by Kenneth Beittel and Robert Burkhart on strategies of art students in Elliot Eisner's *Readings in Art Education*, I have been haunted by the idea that we ought to make much better use in IDE/M of their findings as they apply to more general areas of learning. The strategies were identifed in relation to still life drawings but seemed to indicate personal differences of approach that went beyond this formal task in art. The authors distinguished the "Academic student" . . . "a technician who concentrates on competency" from two other groups, whom they called "Spontaneous" and "Divergent." Spontaneous students are basically concerned with problem-solving: they sketch out their problem on broad lines, and they exploit errors for their good purposes, whereas the Divergent student "is concerned with precision and clarity at any point and with every element," and "he completes one part at a time, and it has to work." "In Divergent work complexity is progressive, and discovery through elaboration and enrichment is the objective. Spontaneous students begin with wholeness; their objective is to give increasing vitality to the whole through suggestive progressive interactions." "The one tends to focus on problems and the other tends to keep problems open," so they can be mutually supportive.

I fancy that if we were to look at students' styles of learning through this lens we could understand their processes and difficulties much better. I feel also that the study contains a reminder that too often we think of open enquiries in the broad problem-solving mode of the "spontaneous" artist. The kind of enquiry which works gradually through detailed evidence towards an unknown whole may be more subtle and ultimately more original. To suggest that we always know what the problem is before we start to work on it is quite false.

■ Close your eyes and visualise your job, what you do, how it relates to other people.

There is no key, but there may be a cage if you visualised relationships in the form of horizontal and vertical lines, the cage of a time-table, for instance, or seeing school or L.E.A. in terms of authority lines running vertically and of horizontal status lines. Among answers I've had which I have specially enjoyed: "I see myself as twisting like a snake, but supple, not evil"; "I see myself as part of a field of forces"; "I see my work as a dance, different partners, different sets, different rhythms, different moods."

■ When I was younger we used to see the main problem of social change in terms of timing: which comes first, a change of heart or a change of organisation? Today the problem seems to be a dilemma of scale: does the energy spent on civil rights for minorities (ethnic groups, students, women . . .) drain it from coping with the massive internal and external injustice of our nations? Each group trying to defeat its own sources of oppression seems divided from others, whose oppression is experienced as different. The oppressed do not see the connection, so the energy cannot become confluent.

■ In a recent article I wrote that unless we learn to live together better we shall be destroyed by our technological proficiency, and this must be a central concern of education. I didn't labor the point because I thought it so familiar an idea that warfare, pollution, poverty from overpopulation, were jointly products of our technological skill and of our insensitivenss to the effects of this skill. The editor wanted to cut out this section. "I don't see the connection," he said. "There's the technological problem and we have the know-how to deal with that. But the real problem, the problem the schools should be dealing with is how we can live better together. That's quite a different matter."

■ "This book belongs to Sam Black, Form 3, White Junior School, North St., Southton, Middlesex, England, Great Britain, Europe, the Earth, the Solar System, the Universe."

■ From T.C. McLuhan's collection of Indian sayings and writings, *Touch the Earth, a Self-Portrait of Indian Existence*: "I had learned many English words and could recite part of the Ten Commandments. I knew how to sleep on a bed, pray to Jesus, comb my hair, eat with a knife and fork, and use a toilet . . . I had also learned that a person thinks with his head instead of his heart."
(Sun Chief, Hopi Indian, of his education in white men's ways.)

■ One of our visitors to the Curriculum Laboratory some years ago wrote a minute when she returned to Whitehall: "At the Laboratory, they write poems to one another. Here we write minutes."

■ Of all our tasks perhaps the most important is the re-association of the sensibility, healing the split between thinking and feeling which T.S. Eliot noted in the seventeenth century. I would be satisfied if children could be conscious in the classroom. How can we hope that we or they will get on with our work of being true, authentic, if people are made to pretend that unless the lesson is about art or literature their feelings are irrelevant to their learning? One day perhaps we should settle down to list and categorise ways in which feeling and thought are slashed, pinpointed, their wholeness destroyed in the conventional school. There's the notion, for instance, that art is about feeling, math about thinking; there is the destructive aggression of the teacher who speaks about "training the mind" but conveys in every gesture his contempt for the person whose mind it is; there is the attentive mask. I have actually seen programmes of objectives for a unit of work which specify (for a hundred or more unique thinking/feeling human systems) two affective and two cognitive behavioural outcomes, and when I have described the two aspects of open access, the turning to the teacher whose skills you want and the settling down with the teacher whose temperament suits you, many people have said, Ah yes, the cognitive and the affective needs are being met, respectively.

■ Excerpt from a letter to a friend of mine from an acquaintance of hers: "My wife and I feel that we are on the *cutting edge* of the affective movement." Good Lord, deliver us.

■ The good *is* enemy of the best. The search for a medical cure may be postponed by the discovery of a palliative. In education also to think within too small a system postpones true reform. I see the whole curriculum development movement of the '60s as palliative rather than curative, and as the materials created by one curriculum research group after another come off the line they may well postpone more fundamental reform for the best part of the '70s. Of course the teaching of various subject disciplines requires reform, and teachers need new ideas and kinds of help. But working on these elements without a radical reconsideration of the curriculum as a whole is to take a consumer's way out. In terms of the fourfold curriculum, these projects are useful for autonomous studies and special interests; they have little or nothing to offer to inter-disciplinary studies or to the diagnosis and meeting of individual needs, being too narrow for the one and too general for the other.

The truth is that one can't arrive at a reconsideration of any system by a reshaping of elements. The whole is more than the sum of its parts: it includes the relationships between those parts. We shouldn't be thinking of joining together elements in a curriculum into a bundle of activities. We have to think of a whole system and of sub-systems within it, and this is so whether we are thinking of students' very diverse systems of experiences or of the curricular system offered by a school.

Similarly the curriculum is not an element in a bundle of behaviors of a school. It is thoroughly dangerous to think about curriculum except in relation to the total system of attitudes, ways of grouping students, structure of relationships (whether, in Durk-heim's sense, mechanical or organic), relationship to the wider community. So many people think of curriculum change as if it were simply slotting in a different cassette. The machine works as before, but you opt for colour instead of black and white, or for a tape recording from the Curriculum Laboratory instead of one from the grammar school up the road.

■ I find it helpful to remember the distinction between an individual in a mass and a person in a society.

■ If your aim is to conquer, you do well to divide. If you want to create, you have to glimpse a whole, even if it is pretty fuzzy to begin with, and this is true whether your process of articulation is "spontaneous," "divergent" or both, in Beittel and Burkhart's sense.

■ The Curriculum Laboratory has stood for a change of paradigm: the concept of a collegiate centre of learning, one which defines itself by what it does, not by any building it may use; of the small risk-taking group (pupils, teachers, both) working comfortably as part of a flexible organism; of the respect for the diversity of all persons involved in the daily making of the school, the reassociation of the sensibility, the emphasis on relative strengths, teachers' central concern with getting to understand better the personal styles of students, the need for open and for narrowly demarcated studies, the emphasis on mutual help, the emphasis on the arts, the insistence on working in fields of personal concern to students, the importance of learning to want to go on learning, the refusal to make arbitrary divisions between school and community, between streams—all these are mutually sustaining sub-systems in a totality which we have glimpsed. You can start wherever you are, and each school will make a different nest, emphasising some of the straws, discarding others because something better has turned up, making a new whole according to its needs and its strengths. In the long run I don't think anything less than a total change of paradigm will suffice, but we are likely to see people making do with palliatives for as long as they possibly can.

■.Again from *Touch the Earth*:
"The man who sat on the ground in his tipi meditating on life and its meaning, accepting the kinship of all creatures and acknowledging unity with the universe of things, was infusing into his being the true essence of civilisation."
(Chief Luther Standing Bear.)

■ How many ways can we find to describe the relationship of a student and a teacher? We are warned by ethologists that we are witnessing a contact between two members of a dangerous and endangered species, who may have neither the instinctual responses nor the intuitive or generalising flexibility to cope with each other very well; anthropologists have taught us to think in terms of acculturation, of behaviors chosen largely unconsciously because alternative ways of behaving are not recognised; social psychologists have much to tell us in terms of the dynamics of interpersonal and intergroup relations and of role theory; we may see the learning as an instance of operant conditioning (usually and mistakenly conceived as a one-way process) or as one person sharing an opportunity for an "Aha" with another; we may speculate on the pair's neuroses; sociologically we are likely to be looking out for class or caste differentials or studying the institutional framework within which socialisation is taking place; some people will see a meeting between a Libra, say, and a Taurus; we are learning to think in terms of the interplay between two energy systems, of which the energy may be confluent or one may drain the other. It seems only rarely that we pause to think of the relationship as the touching of two spiritual beings who for a time are to journey together. I wonder if any of our relationships will prosper until that vision is restored.

■ Finally, and throughout, E. E. Cummings' poem:
"Seeker of truth
follow no path
all paths lead where
truth is here."

Part III

Passport for the Journey

This section consists of papers and articles I wrote while working as director of the Curriculum Laboratory at the University of London's Goldsmiths' College from 1965 to 1970. It would be good to be able to describe those years and to explain fully the debt I owe to my colleagues there and to the members of the Pilot Courses, excellent head teachers and teachers with whom we worked. But that would take more space than I have here. Instead, I hope that some of the achievements and the feeling-tone of the Lab—our shared commitment to justice for all children, our sense of scope and adventure, our conviction that we were getting to the heart of many educational problems, our care for one another—comes through in these pieces. These courses provided me with a passport for my subsequent educational journey.

The first two descriptive pieces are, of course, quite dissimilar in style and intention. The first was written for the journal *Forum* immediately after the first Pilot Course; this course led the way for all the others although some of the later ones were no less significant.°
The second is a paper which I wrote as a member of a small group of people responsible for some well-known innovations in higher education in England; my paper concerned the education of teachers, the others concerned that of engineers, architects, doctors, and so on. After I left England the group designed a schema which we all followed in preparing descriptions of our work. This explains

---

° M.C. Richards, in *The Crossing Point* (Wesleyan University Press, 1973), gives a full and perceptive study of the seventh course, for which she was our visiting professor.

the format and specific headings I used. The chairman and editor, Dr. K. G. Collier, Principal of the College of the Venerable Bede, encouraged us not to avoid sensitive issues, but to try to pioneer a kind of research in which the writer offers his own interpretation of events yet seeks to go beyond his personal feelings towards those events. We sought, that is, to be subjective, yet dispassionate.

Much of the material in this piece is specific to an English situation, but it may be interesting for people in the United States to have a picture of some of the activity of the Department of Education and Science (DES), the counterpart of the U.S. Office of Education, and of the workings of an English college. Beyond this, the values and life of the Lab, and some of the opportunities and problems it encountered, are quite relevant to people working in in-service programs in America.

The Lab has been described to me in the United States as "the Number One teachers' center" in England. There is enough truth in the compliment for me to be tempted to accept it. But it is more important to acknowledge that it worked out of a different base, the well-established initiative of the DES to support full-time professional courses to which experienced teachers are seconded on full pay during term-time. Courses of this kind have been an important element in English educational change and deserve attention in the United States.

11. The School and Social Change
(1965)

EINSTEIN, WE ARE TOLD, never ceased to be surprised by the obvious. In a period of radical scientific enquiry and technological change we should look equally to the quality of our educational questions. Secondary education today is under pressure from consumers (namely, parents and employers, not adolescents). To them educational aims are obvious enough: they want a larger supply of familiar preparations, labelled "A" or "O" or even "RRR."

Meanwhile as teachers we have accepted a determinist framework of assumptions within which good answers are possible, but not good questions. Some of our questions are poor because they accept false dilemmas, as when we declare for or against examinations as if no other kind of appraisal were conceivable. Others, especially those emphasising educational organisation to the exclusion of content, are too narrow. Most damaging are those that beg other more fundamental questions. We grow increasingly realistic in preparing children for adult life but forget to prepare them to improve it; or we make admirable proposals for better subject teaching, and fail to question the design of the whole curriculum. The predicament of the Newsom Committee was significant. Required to answer an ill-conceived question, it rightly attacked one underlying assumption, the fixed pool of ability. But two others lie unchallenged, that our criteria for estimating "ability" are adequate and the education of our "more able" children satisfactory. Hence in the teeth of studies in creativity over the past decade, which indicate the need to encourage problem-solving behaviour, we continue to grade children by their capacity to perform conventional tasks (future ploys for computers) and contine plans for an outgoing, problem-solving, education to those we designate as failures.

It is clearly the professional duty of teachers to seek creative alternatives to outworn responses, and to ask questions more fundamental than those which engage us today. For this task two conditions are necessary. Experienced teachers must have time and opportunity to withdraw from school to confer at length on educational policy, and they must be able to call on the co-operation of their colleagues in Colleges and Institutes of Education. This the Department of Education and Science has helped to promote, as an outcome of the Newsom Report, by sponsoring one-term full-time courses for teachers which provide an unprecedented opportunity for such a fundamental reappraisal.

A PILOT COURSE

The first Pilot Course, for 27 experienced teachers, took place at Goldsmiths' last spring, and I have been asked to record some personal impressions of it. No one would wish to claim that it was a success, for that has a retrospective finality, but those who took part believe that it was a fruitful beginning. Out of it have arisen new proposals already being tried out in schools. This immediate result is due to the foresight of certain L.E.As.—Essex and Middlesex together notably seconded seven leading head teachers—and of the schools which released heads, deputies and senior staff well able to advise their colleagues on their return. On our side, Goldsmiths' gladly offered its facilities, as well as contacts with many schools, colleges and members of allied professions.

From the outset, courses were planned as working conferences, each of which would produce an informal report for the guidance of its successors and useful to colleagues and authorities. Planning the first plunge was not easy. Candidates had made it clear to the Warden and myself that an exegesis of current educational proposals would not do at all. Many had echoed the head teacher who said, 'I welcome the Newsom Report. Much of it could have been written about my school. But I am still not satisfied.' Our belief that we needed an international perspective was confirmed, and with it our gratitude to Professor G. D. Phillips of Boston University, who had offered to spend his sabbatical leave acting as co-tutor. By providing a cosmonaut's overview of our problems, he greatly helped us to find solutions appropriate to English needs.

PROBLEM-SOLVING

Dedicated ourselves to problem-solving in education, we offered our teacher colleagues the most fundamental and urgent problem we could formulate. What is the role of the school in a period of rapid social and cultural change? Apart from a brief survey of theories of socio-cultural change the first fortnight was freed from lectures so that members could discuss this problem, in small or large groups as they preferred. No process could have been more exacting, but as we ranged over familiar areas of concern—streaming, middle-class *mores*, working-class disadvantages, relations with parents, problems of fourth year leavers—we began to place them in the context of larger questions. Recent studies show little awareness of the gathering momentum of change. Crowther's demographic information is invaluable, but a need for flexibility among employees is hardly the full democratic answer. Should not schools do more to mediate change? Is induction into yesterday's certainties appropriate today? How can we help pupils to break through our latter-day passivity, so that as adults they may transform mere change into social progress?

The answer must lie in a comprehensive reappraisal of the curriculum and relationships of the secondary school. We proceeded to a strenuous four-week study of two interwoven themes, an enquiry into different kinds of curriculum (based on subjects, interests, topics, themes) and lectures by specialists describing the character, scope and limitations of their disciplines and discussing their potential contribution to the curriculum.

This was the basic design of the first six weeks, but there were other activities. Most secondary teachers are deprived of the creative arts from their early teens, yet how can one understand their value for children except by experiencing them for oneself? Every member took part in a weekly "art practical," and most found them a source of great personal enjoyment. So also, I think, was the series of lectures by members of other professions concerned, like ourselves, with the future, such as architects, planners, designers. Then there were lectures by allies in the field of mental health, from one of which sprang a request for regular group work with a distinguished social psychiatrist. All these, together with our continuing discussions and occasional visits to schools, kept us sane and contributed to a growing feeling of confidence.

During the final five weeks, which had not been time-tabled at all, the majority chose to continue work on curricular problems. But two heads undertook a survey of methods of appraising children. This period of consultation, consolidation and further study seemed to us all to be essential.

The immediate outcome of the conference was the sixty-page First Pilot Course Report, written co-operatively at excessive speed. (See Chapter 13.)

RESULTS AND PERSPECTIVES

While it will take time for the long-term influence of the course to emerge, some effects are already evident. Nearly all the schools involved are planning some modifications. At least eleven will start off their first-year entry this autumn in unstreamed groups, spending the morning with teams of teachers on a year-long theme, the afternoons being devoted to subjects which require progressive development or where integration would be forced and unnatural. Plans vary greatly, as they should, but all assume flexible group work and many turn on the theme of man's increasing power to understand and control his environment—an encouraging start to a child's secondary education.

Incidentally, Goldsmiths' is to profit by a new co-operation with nearby schools working on such thematic studies. These are accepting second-year students who will spend their second practice working as teams with teams of teachers. This should provide invaluable experience of satisfactory teaching, and we hope that, by planning beforehand with their specialist tutors, students may make a useful contribution to study of the school's chosen theme.

A series of pilot courses has been planned for this year when the visiting professor will be an American from the South, an expert in appraisal and integration. The autumn course is concerned especially with problems of appraisal and self-appraisal of children, and continuing study of the curriculum will be biased in this direction. In the spring, we turn to problems of social handicap and the school's role in social integration. In the summer, we look at the changing balance of leisure and work and its implications for the curriculum. We hope that these courses will be supportive, for the themes are those requested by our colleagues in schools.

We invite new requests for the future.

12. The University of London Goldsmiths' College Curriculum Laboratory*

I wrote this paper in the United States during the early autumn of 1971, having asked for a second year's leave of absence to undertake my study for the Ford Foundation. It was already clear that I was unlikely to return to Goldsmiths'. The Lab was closed at the end of the 1971-72 academic year, although when I wrote I was not certain that this would happen. The courses, originally set up as a pilot scheme by the DES in 1965, had well outlived their expected period of existence.

Much of the innovative work carried out by the Lab has been incorporated in College courses, and the journal Ideas, *initiated by the Lab, continues to be published by the College under its original editor, Leslie A. Smith. I am told that requests for speeches and workshops on the Fourfold Curriculum and Interdisciplinary Enquiry continue. And many schools are on the move, including far more than those represented by members of the courses. Change at the secondary level cannot match the scale of developments in "open education" at the primary level, which have been officially sponsored for four decades, but as is the way with innovations in England the work of the Courses has been accepted into the bloodstream. Even when the source of change is not known or deliberately (and quite properly) not acknowledged, the influence of the Lab continues, and proposals which eight years ago seemed to many people to be preposterous are now commonplace, even among those who do not accept them. This in England is an important phase in the process of integrating an unfamiliar idea.*

* A version of this paper also appears in K.G. Collier, ed., *Innovation in Higher Education*, NFER Publishing Company, Windsor, England: 1974.

A. CONTEXT OF INNOVATORY SCHEME

(1) **Institution:** The University of London Goldsmiths' College is a complex institution. Until the late 1960s it had for many years consisted of three separate schools: the College of Education, with much the largest body of full-time staff and students, the Goldsmiths' School of Art, and the Department of Adult Studies, which serves large numbers of part-time students in S.E. London.

A new structure was then created in which each of these schools became a Department of the College as a whole. At this time the inner structure of the College of Education (now known as the Department of Arts, Science and Education) became more fully articulated through the creation of four faculties.

The Curriculum Laboratory was set up originally in 1964-65 as a Department of Special Courses within the Faculty of Education, being renamed Curriculum Laboratory two years later (and alternatively referred to here as the Unit). From the outset it could call on the assistance of members of all the faculties and also contributed to the work of the Education Faculty. Later on, its staff also engaged in very fruitful exchanges with the former College of Art and with members of the Department of Adult Studies, which by this time was moving into full-time professional and undergraduate courses with a basis in the behavioral sciences. These exchanges were necessarily informal, since the sources of funding of the three constituent Departments of the College were different.

The relationships of the Department of Arts, Science and Education to the London University Institute of Education are atypical. It is funded directly by the Department of Education and Science (DES) and governed by a Delegacy of the University of London. For many years it had complete autonomy in planning and examining its Teachers' Certificate; and the student body is unusual in that about one-third of the students are taking degree courses followed by a post-graduate training course in education.

(2) **Structure of Institution:** In 1964-65, before the publication of the Weaver Report on their government, colleges of education tended to be closer to schools than to universities in their power structure, decisionmaking being mainly vested in the principal rather than in a council of senior members. Even though a principal might choose to work through consultation and shared planning, he

was the source of most decisions. In Goldsmiths' College an academic board had been well-established for many years, but much still depended on the willingness of the warden, as principal of the whole complex, to welcome and support innovation. The strong personal support given by the warden was therefore essential to the Unit's early development. However great the gains in making an institution more democratic or, more precisely, in moving over to a system of management by a council of appointed elders, there has also been value in the supportive leaderships of authoritative individuals with the power and purpose to sponsor innovation.

(3) **Climate of Opinion in Institution:** During the early stages of the Unit's existence the mood of Goldsmiths' was optimistic and expansive. The College was in the middle of a period of rapid increase in student numbers and hence in staff. It had now mastered the severe problems created by the change in the balance of training from secondary to primary in 1961. In rapid succession there followed the regaining of internal status in the University of London for the College's degree courses, which had been lost after the war; the extension of the College's undergraduate work; the creation of a new Postgraduate Teachers' Certificate to supplement the PGCE of the University of London Institute; the setting up of a well-funded TV unit; and the prior planning required for setting up the new B. Ed. degree. Although the work was strenuous and time-absorbing for people already bearing a very heavy teaching load, the College was on an upward sweep. In this climate a small new Unit could be generously provided with staff and general funding, and was likely to be left to develop its ideas with a good deal of autonomy.

The Special Courses Unit had two aspects which lent favour to it in the eyes of the College of Education as a whole, First, it arose from an invitation by the DES to renew and develop the College's long-standing interest in secondary education, which had been adversely affected by the new emphasis on preparing primary teachers. Secondly, it made possible a new way of improving the interaction of the College with schools, always a matter of deepest concern to colleges of education.

(4) **Factors External to Institution**

Educational Reform: From the late 1950s the nation undertook a substantial review of its educational provision, issuing in a series of reports (Crowther, Newsom, Robbins, Plowden) which in their different ways greatly affected colleges of education. It was the decision to raise the school leaving age to 16, recommended by the Crowther and Newsom Reports, which brought the unit into existence.

Expansion of In-service Education: The implementation of educational reforms required the expansion of in-service education for teachers. The setting up of the Special Courses Unit was the outcome of a direct request to the College by the DES that it should run a one-term pilot course for teachers in connection with the raising of the school leaving age, then planned for 1970. If this course was successful others would follow at Goldsmiths' and elsewhere; and this in fact occurred.

The invitation was part of a general move of the DES to extend in-service courses for experienced teachers. In subsequent years increasing emphasis was laid on teachers obtaining qualifications beyond the Teachers' Certificate or initial degree course. This change of emphasis had an adverse effect on the numbers seconded to shorter courses which provided no qualifications and were concerned with the professional competence of teachers rather than with their further academic advance. Expressions of interest in the Units courses and requests for application forms remained fairly stable at least until 1970—the writer was not able to check thereafter —but the numbers seconded were seriously reduced and thereby the justification for its staffing was reduced also. The common explanation by Local Education Authorities (LEAs) and schools was that sparing a teacher for one term only is disruptive (and for this reason in-service units were asked to experiment with other designs) and that teachers applying for courses leading to qualifications should have priority. This latter point of view needs very serious consideration: the bonding of promotion to qualifications has disadvantages, and those who attend courses mainly to improve themselves as teachers have a great deal to offer to the profession.

Liaison with the DES: Relationships with the branch handling in-service courses were extremely satisfactory. It was generous, for instance, in permitting a shift in content. The DES's original proposal concerned the education of older secondary pupils "of average and less than average ability," accepting the narrow terms of reference laid on the Newsom Committee. The courses early decided that it was essential to reconsider secondary education as a whole, and by agreement the limits were removed, to be replaced by courses with changing emphases. Secondly, the limitation of secondary schooling was removed when several LEAs asked the Unit to handle the problem of the new 9-13 middle schools. There was similar collaboration about course format. Since one-term courses created difficulties for schools and LEAs, the Curriculum Laboratory was asked to undertake courses for one day weekly thoughout the year. The staff proposed a compromise, which it operated for two years, whereby each course came in for three weeks at the beginning and end of the session, so that the members could become a working group with some mutual trust and at the end had time to bring their ideas together fruitfully. The staff of the Laboratory found that the one-term design was preferable, since the members were able to forget their anxieties and responsibilities as teachers and heads, and the DES permitted a return to the one-term pattern from 1969-70 onwards. (It is quite possible that for another kind of course, in which the school experience of members was more similar, and which could therefore be concerned effectively with immediate day-by-day practice in the classroom, the day-a-week design might be very satisfactory.)

Thus so long as the Laboratory could be seen simply as an in-service unit, relationships with the DES departments were flexible and accommodating; and in general, apart from occasional informal pressures, the tradition of academic freedom was scrupulously observed even though the policies proposed by the Unit's courses were highly innovative—indeed, to some people, radical in the extreme. The difficulties experienced by the Unit arose only in so far as it wished to extend its functions beyond pilot in-service courses and to set up a pilot unit of a new kind providing a consultative service, undertaking research relevant to its policies, and producing experimental curriculum materials. It was this new undertaking which the term Curriculum Laboratory was intended to describe. This development was not formally sanctioned, and in fact after its initial period as a *pilot scheme* had come to an end, the additional staffing originally provided by the DES was withdrawn. Although the College was generous in supporting the new Curriculum Laboratory from within its own normal resources, the Unit remained tiny (effectively four people at most) and quite inadequately provided with staff and funds to meet the insistent demands made on it by LEAs, schools, pre-service and in-service institutions, and the overseas educators who thronged to visit it. The problem of an innovative unit requiring to grow beyond its original role is doubtless not uncommon: it is of its very nature that its new vision will create needs which could not have been foreseen.

Educational Retrenchment: At the end of the decade, educational expansion was followed by retrenchment. This had a dual impact on the Curriculum Laboratory, first through the decision to postpone the raising of the school leaving age to 1972-3, which took pressure off seconding LEAs, and more seriously through severe cuts in teacher education. Retrenchment in teacher education meant that colleges of education necessarily became more inward-looking, concerned more with the "bread and butter" task of training young teachers than with a new vision of teacher education as a whole. The staff of the Curriculum Laboratory had supposed throughout that their expanded role had been formally sanctioned, and this misapprehension aggravated their distress under the pressures of retrenchment, since it became easy to remove staff and funding which they had thought to be theirs by right but which turned out to be privileges that could no longer be provided.

It was particularly unfortunate that the new strengthening of academic boards and the articulation of a new structure of standing committees were immediately followed by severe retrenchment, for it meant that the first task of the new committees was to cut costs drastically. When the signal next turns to "go," the colleges will have a well-developed system of government but no experience of shared responsibility for growth. Since the next "go" is likely to concern in-service, it is also regrettable that the Curriculum Laboratory was an early casualty of retrenchment, since it was working towards a new concept of interaction of schools and colleges which could have given useful indications for the future.

B. OBJECTIVES OF THE SCHEME

Problem Tackled; Scope of Scheme: The Unit was not set up with the idea of being an innovation in higher education. It was to concern itself with innovation in schools, and even the innovation envisaged in schools was not expected to be based on original thinking. The Unit was simply asked to run a course for experienced teachers which would discuss, disseminate, and help to implement the proposals of the Newsom Report, published 18 months earlier.

As an essay in higher education the Unit was initially innovative only in the way its staff chose to work with the members of the courses: they early decided that a course for head teachers and other experienced colleagues must be a working conference of equals. In so doing they challenged an assumption made all too often, that those who work in universities and colleges are in a position of authority towards those who work in schools. Thus they provided an entirely exceptional opportunity for teachers to meet together at length, away from everyday preoccupations, and to think seriously about their role in a changing society, about their pupils, about the curriculum and relationships of their schools. Their express purpose was to be to formulate an educational policy which should lead to change in schools. The staff and course members were involved in a continuing process of enquiry. They shared a deep dissatisfaction with schools as they are (even those they thought the best schools); they rapidly threw aside their mandate of considering only the problems of young school leavers and decided that school was damaging also to the academically competent; they refused to limit their thinking to 13- to 16-year olds, arguing that the early years of secondary schooling must be totally re-thought; they were shocked by the divisive practices of schools; they believed that much of the curriculum was trivial. From this rejection of the known, they came gradually to envisage a quite different kind of education. In effect, they emerged with a more searching and fundamental reappraisal of secondary schooling than had been made by any other individual group in the country.

The conclusions to which the first course was driven seemed so extraordinary, they pointed to changes in schooling so fundamental, that its members felt they could not return to their colleagues or their seconding LEAs without preparing the ground—and this despite the fact that most of the 27 course members, a third of them head teachers, had been seconded specifically because they had already gone beyond the norm in meeting the needs of young school leavers. "The Newsom Report could have been written about my school, but I'm still dissatisfied" had been an opinion frequently expressed. It was therefore decided towards the end of the first course to hold a day conference at which its members' views could be presented, and also to produce a written report. In this way another innovation came into being, the idea that each course could concern itself with a special problem, on which it would report. The reports of the first seven courses were published by the Laboratory, and were an important means of diffusion of teachers' ideas to other teachers. Two other minor innovations are perhaps significant: the teachers were known always as "course members" and never as "students," and the separate identity of each course was acknowledged by the practice of numbering them as course 1, 2, 3, and so on.

(2) **Underlying Values or Criteria by Which the Scheme Was Judged to Be an Improvement:** The specific aim of the unit was the practical one of effecting reform in schools, and this was clearly established at the outset. The underlying values were revealed more gradually in the course of the work. As the Unit's policies for educational reform became more clearly delineated, the parallelism between these policies for schools and its own practices became evident. The Unit argued that young people should have the opportunity as part of their curriculum to make open enquiries in areas pertinent to them, drawing on the help of the specialists they need; that group work rather than the class lesson should be the norm; that the arts should be seen as of central importance; that pupils' concern with their own inner development should be respected and their diversity welcomed and encouraged within a climate of mutuality. This was the stuff of the courses also.

This similarity between the values implicit in the courses and those explicitly stated in the proposals for school reform is not a coincidence. Both are the expression of the same value system, a passionate belief that education should, and can, evolve through a deep consideration of the needs of the students and staff and of the opportunities presented by staff, students, resources, and the broader environment, rather than by having innovations imposed by external pressure, overt or covert.

Retrospectively, it would be possible to assign behavioural objectives to the Unit's work. One could ask, for instance, whether the members of the courses emerged with this kind of attitude, whether they went out competent to undertake such ventures, whether they found themselves better able to accept and enjoy opportunities for change in their schools. One could then argue that since the answers are on the whole positive (see page 181) the objectives of the courses had been achieved.

The historical truth cannot readily be encapsulated in an input-output model of this kind. The experience of those partaking in the work was not of finding means to foreknown ends but of glimpsing in blurred outlines an embracing theory of how people might work and learn together, of these outlines gradually being mapped in closer and closer detail, of relationships between seemingly disparate notions suddenly becoming clear.

With techniques of educational engineering in the ascendant to-day, this distinction between the clarity of retrospective analysis and the confusion of the creative process seems in the light of the Curriculum Laboratory's experience to be extremely significant.

C. MEANS OF BRINGING ABOUT THE INNOVATION CONCERNED

(1) **Source of the Decision to Proceed:** It will be recalled that there were two phases:

(a) Setting up the Special Courses Unit in 1964-65. This decision was made by the warden with the approval of the College Delegacy, at the invitation of the DES, with the Academic Board being consulted and kept informed of developments.

(b) Extending the Unit and renaming it the Curriculum Laboratory in 1966-67. This was proposed to the warden and registrar by the staff in the summer of 1966 and agreed within the College.

(2) **Methods Used in Innovatory Scheme:** In setting up the first course the Warden invited a member of the Education Department, who had previously been in charge of Secondary Education and had later been Academic Head of Postgraduate Courses, to be organiser of special courses; this was the author of the present paper. An American visiting professor was appointed to work with her. A small committee was then set up within the Department of Education to

help them plan this pilot course. Members of specialist departments were consulted and asked what contributions they could make. The responsibility for running the courses was left in the hands of the two members of staff concerned. Since course members came from outside the College, it was not possible to consult them as a group, but the courses were discussed during interviews. Later it became a regular practice to invite applicants to visit the Unit together in the forerunning term, and there to make known their special interests. Selection of course members for the first course was made by the Warden together with the two full-time members of the Unit; subsequently it was made within the Unit.

The staff developed their methods of working with the courses quite intuitively. It was only after a time as they came to realise that the courses were unusual and that people wanted descriptions of them that they began to analyze their special character; the best way of characterising them seemed to be that they consisted of exploratory, task-based, unstructured group work. They differed in style from most courses in that they involved collaborative learning of which the outcome was not foreknown. They were thus as far as possible unstructured, there being no regular pattern of weekly or daily meeting unless this happened to be convenient; the only exception was also the only compulsory element of the course, a weekly involvement in some form of creative or expressive art, and this was a fixed point in the week only because the unit was dependent on the generosity of the art, design, drama, and movement departments. In certain of the later courses which were especially concerned with expressive and practical aspects of education, both extra space and more flexible staffing were obtained, with very beneficial results from which other courses could have profited. For the rest, arrangements were made in advance only when it was necessary in order to secure a speaker with expertise relevant to the task in hand, to arrange a significant visit or to plan extended work outside the College. The staff quite often made prior arrangements for a few days' practical work at the beginning of a course, working in a museum, for instance, or with an expert on elementary science, in order to break away from the habit of extended conversation; on the other hand, sometimes the first days were left totally free for talk until everyone became desperately aware of the limits of discussion and thankfully went to look at pictures, to examine the learning potential of the environment, to work in the arts, and to settle down to the discipline of inquiry. In the early stages of a course the hope was that visits to schools or elsewhere would be communal activities for all the participants, since differences of personal preconceptions are revealed most quickly by this means and become open to examination; later on, smaller search parties would go out, and others could evaluate and interpret their reports because by this time people were well known to each other. The general policy was that the area of investigation of a course should be known beforehand, the parameters provisionally established in the early stages of working together, while the course itself should evolve through the shared planning of staff and course members.

The staff were of course concerned with the personal well-being and relationships of the course members. Lest this seem an impertinence towards respected colleagues they kept aware that in other circumstances the roles might have been reversed, and also that often the other course members were seen as more helpful than they were themselves. They were pleased to notice that people for the most part became more relaxed, more open, more ready to trust others and self, less harried by time and duty, less divided by status, funnier, more salty, more natural, braver. Similarly they found that as the courses proceeded they seemed themselves to be changing in ways which they felt to be valuable. Since they could not have foreseen the direction of these changes, they were not tempted to specify precise behavioural outcomes of the course for anyone else.

The process was by no means free of anxiety. Course members moved into phases of distrust and disaffection from which some certainly had not emerged by the time they left; and the staff likewise often felt inadequate, fearing each time that this current course would not solve its problems, personal or professional. That is the usual pain of any creative process. American researchers have recently suggested that the school classroom should be observed in terms of drama. Many visitors commented on the poetry, the aesthetic quality, the feeling-tone, of the Laboratory. That was perhaps the key to its successes and to its failures, but only a regular observer could have interpreted the drama, and none was available. (The staff made an informal approach in 1967 to experts in observation of human relations, but did not have the research funds to put the proposal into effect.)

(3) **Personnel Involved:** The number of staff varied, from two in the first course (1964-65), to five during 1967-70, to two in 1971-72. From 1964-65 to 1967-68 inclusive, American professors were invited to work with the Unit, usually for one year, and their international viewpoint contributed greatly to the courses. For the first course on middle schools a lecturer from the junior department worked with the unit. On one occasion a head teacher joined the staff for a term. When the staff was five, the Unit provided help in other parts of the College roughly equivalent to one person's time, so that the members available were effectively four. This arrangement was made partly to strengthen ties with the other departments and partly with the idea of involving five people in the collaborative thinking of the Unit. The sharp decline in staff numbers clearly reflects the new retrenchment policy.

The Unit met with a serious problem of salaries and promotion. A small innovative unit must consist of people worthy of promotion, but their claims may not seem strong in comparison with those of people carrying greater administrative loads.

From the setting up of the Curriculum Laboratory until the staff was greatly diminished, the roles of three staff members were differentiated, one being overall director, one having charge of the courses, and one being invited to join the Unit to look after its consultative services. Within the Unit these special responsibilities were honoured, but the aim was one of shared planning and mutual support. It was usual to have two people in turn involved closely in each course, the others working peripherally and concentrating on other tasks. This plan was satisfactory for two reasons: First, it was found that the interplay of two members of staff was valuable in the courses. Secondly, the strain of full-time continuing involvement in unstructured work is considerable, and this flexibility enabled the staff to enjoy a welcome rhythm of engagement in the courses and withdrawal into other activities, such as advice to schools and the diffusion of the Unit's ideas. There was sufficient work for a five-day (or six-day) week to be the expected norm. To many members of a College staff, battened down by strict bureaucratic assignation of roles and precise time-tabling, the staff's variety of work must have seemed over-privileged, but it was through mutual adjustment to the varying personal needs of colleagues that the pace of continuing innovation and enterprise was made possible.

(4) **Financial Aspects:** The Goldsmiths' Department of Arts, Science and Education (i.e., the College of Education) is directly funded by the DES.

(5) **Modification of Methods during Course of Innovation:** When a small group of people work closely together, modification of methods seems to arise not from a decision to improve a product but from a need to make the best use of each person's potential. This was one source of change in the courses. A further source of modification was the areas of investigation on which the courses worked: an inter-professional course concerned with home and school inevitably took a different shape from one which considered how best the resources of studio and laboratory could be exploited in interdisciplinary studies. The shared statements of policy issued during the first two or three years reflected the sense of untrammelled exploration that informed the courses, but they also became an unplanned source of change. Members of the later courses tended to work on day-to-day problems along these guidelines; if they were found restrictive they were, of course, readily questioned.

Thus apart from those initiating new work on middle schools, the courses in recent years have tended to be more fragmented into small groups pursuing separate purposes, or have concentrated more deeply on members' personal understanding of their role as teachers, or again have worked on practical problems within an agreed curricular design. In the last two years (1970-1972) the staff, now reduced to a minimum, have been seeking to integrate more closely with the College as a whole, which should be a fruitful development.

D. EVALUATION OF SCHEME

Judgment of Degree of Success or Failure

Practical Objectives: It is difficult to assess the success of the Unit in achieving its practical objectives as already outlined, and it is beyond the scope of this study to examine its impact in any detail. However, there are some indications of the interest aroused among teachers and other educators which are worth recording. These are:

(i) Publications. The reports issued by the members of the first six courses have already been referred to. These were originally published between 1965 and 1967. In 1967 the Director of Consultative Services of the Laboratory started a new publication, *Ideas*, with the object of meeting in print some of the requests for personal advice with which the Unit was flooded. Twenty-one issues have been published and the total sale has topped 66,000 copies. The publication department is self-supporting.

(ii) Requests for information received from LEAs, colleges of education, and university departments of education, teachers' conferences, etc. There was a constant flow of such requests, a good proportion of which the staff managed to satisfy while it was fully staffed.

(iii) Consultation. From its inception, the Unit was under pressure to advise schools. The invitations came at first from past course members, but with the widespread diffusion of its ideas, requests soon came from innovative schools in many parts of the country. Throughout, the staff were at pains to limit the role of a consultant, distinguishing it from that of Inspectors and Advisors. The consultant has no rights: "You don't have to ask us; we do try to help, and you are free to ignore what we say" was a summary of the relationship offered. Moreover, in the role of consultant one does not aim to convert but only to help schools with practical problems of implementing the policies one represents, and that only if they are already interested in them.

The unit was successful in discovering a need for consultations but not in meeting it. The basic staff, effectively four people at most, was quite inadequate to meet the requests received, and schools had no funds with which to recompense the College for its services. (They could not even pay travel costs to the school, so that frequently a head would travel to the Laboratory with a group of teachers— at much greater expense.) The notion of consultation, so well established elsewhere, seems hardly to have touched the consciousness of English educators. Yet there is a greater hunger among pace-setting teachers for advice from innovative thinkers and others with special knowledge and skills, and it is the contention of the Unit (stated in detail in its evidence to the Parliamentary Commission on Teacher Education in February 1970) that colleges will not make their full contribution to educational reform unless the concept of in-service training is extended to include ready access to consultative services as well as the usual provision of courses and workshops.

Interaction with Teachers: It is probably true to say that the Curriculum Laboratory has done a good deal to improve the self-esteem of teachers who want to see their profession engage in fundamental reform. The staff presented themselves as agents of teachers and collaborators with them, not as instructors. Again one of the privileges of in-service work is the number of friends one makes among teachers in schools, and this interaction cannot fail to be advantageous, as is any development which narrows the gap between colleges and schools.

The Unit may fairly be questioned about its decision not to work very closely with any individual school. Detailed observations were carried out in two schools and visits made to many others, but the Unit ran no project with selected schools of the kind which Schools Council research groups undertake. There were various reasons for this omission: for instance, that most of the teachers with authoritative positions with whom the Unit might have collaborated came from some distance; and that the staff hesitated to take any action that might reduce the autonomy of its school colleagues. But the main cause was that members were overwhelmed with widespread demands for information and help. On the whole, the instinct to choose diffusion rather than intensity was probably a wise one in the circumstances; in any case it is difficult to see how it could have been avoided.

One development which could have been of great importance in developing a fruitful relationship with schools was proposed but came to nothing. The Curriculum Laboratory was anxious to work with a postgraduate group within the framework of the Goldsmiths' Postgraduate Teachers' Certificate on a research study in which it would have collaborated very closely with a small number of like-minded schools. The simple pattern of collaboration proposed is perhaps worth recording: it was one of mutual consultation, in which teachers in the schools would be fully involved in the preparation of students while receiving in return advice and help on the school curriculum.

Relationships within Goldsmiths' College: In a large institution, close relations are achieved by working on common problems;

wishing well is not enough. The Unit had many well-wishers in the College but probably failed to capitalise on their good will because it was overwhelmed by the demands made on it in the field. Its focus of attention as an outward-looking unit was different from theirs. Other factors also perhaps contributed to some degree of isolation of the Unit within the College. It may be that its staff were too apt to call on the expertise of the many people outside the College who had become deeply interested in their work, instead of looking to talents nearer home. Possibly also the tendency among many outside observers to speak of the Unit's educational thinking as "the Goldsmiths' point of view" led to some mistrust among colleagues who held a different educational philosophy. In effect it may be that the Unit, by recognizing the importance of the pressing calls made on their services from outside the College, and being willing to respond to them, allowed too little time and energy to the task of keeping colleagues informed and gaining support within the College.

One innovation in pre-service education arose directly from the Laboratory's work and was created through excellent collaboration with colleagues in the College. From the beginning, the courses recommended changes in teacher education to prepare young teachers for the open interdisciplinary enquiry which was an important feature of the Laboratory's proposals for schools. As a result in 1966-67, after preliminary experiments, a new Junior-Secondary course was established, which included many innovations. Perhaps the most important was that of teaching practise being undertaken by teams of students working on interdisciplinary lines and taking over a substantial part of the time-table for a hundred or more pupils. The teams usually consisted of four or five students working for four or five weeks in their second and third years. The idea of group practices of this kind was specifically related to the grouping of teachers for Interdisciplinary Enquiry in the practice schools, and the College development was made possible largely through the cooperation of schools with which the Laboratory was on friendly terms.

Evaluation of the Courses by Course Members: In 1969, Professor James B. Macdonald of the University of Wisconsin in Milwaukee made a study of the reactions of a random sample (19.7%) of former course members, which he presented to the American Educational

Research Association in March 1971. Among other findings, he noted that 27 of the 38 planned or did carry out some curriculum revision. He found too that "dramatic personal changes were also perceived by approximately one-third of the participants," in the direction of "more confidence," "unlocking their selves," or simply of a felt "difference," unspecified. About 50% approved of the unstructured nature of the courses, 50% were disturbed by it; but among these quite a number recorded satisfactory changes in themselves, though they did not appear to have connected them with the freedom provided by the courses. He referred also to "a feeling-tone and inter-personal climate which is a positive justification in and of itself. There is an immanent value in its working which goes beyond the transcendent values of later program and curriculum changes in the schools." He pointed out the limitation of funds in contrast with funding often occurring in the United States for activities with much less potential. Professor Macdonald summarized the results of his survey and his own observations as a visiting professor as follows:

"1. That Goldsmiths' College Curriculum Laboratory has been a highly successful (though limited) enterprise.

2. That it provides insight into the possibilities of in-service education in terms of its unique elements, i.e., an ideology, generality, flexibility, group interaction and collaborative learning, and a professional support system beyond the specific schools of the participants."

SUMMARY

It is difficult to assess the degree of success or failure of an innovation which was short-lived but which had and continues to have an influence far beyond the expectations of those who set it up and engaged in it. In the case of this innovation it is particularly difficult to disentangle sociological principles of general application from the historical circumstances of this one unit; what might the situation of the Curriculum Laboratory be now, for instance, had the College not been under the pressure of a general retrenchment? Nevertheless, it is possible to draw some tentative generalisations from the rise and decline of the Laboratory.

First, from the point of view of its clientele, the teachers and head teachers who attended the courses and those others all over the country who read its material and invited its help, the success of the Laboratory made it clear that there is a need for a new and far more dynamic relationship between colleagues in different fields of the educational system. By establishing a situation of collaborative learning between people teaching at university and school level, the Laboratory was able to draw on the immense inventive energies of good school teachers.

Secondly, the fact that a unit proves its worth and even proves that it is needed does not ensure its survival. It may well come into existence in an expansive situation; if cold winds blow too soon, it will be hard put to survive even if its work is widely respected.

Third, if it turns out that a unit is meeting a need which had not been previously recognized (and for which it had not therefore been originally designed), its hold on life is particularly weak. Secondary sources of funding then become extremely important. There was never any question that the Laboratory had far more opportunities for developmental work in the field than it was able to undertake; the problem was how it could be funded once it went beyond its original task of running one-term courses. In the rather inflexible situation of English educational funding no answer was forthcoming.

Fourth, the problem presented by a unit growing beyond its original function is particularly difficult for a large institution which has to continue with its normal work and to give opportunities to other inventive groups: such a unit is likely to be seen as demanding, disturbing, and perhaps even a threat to the smooth and just running of the whole. This concern with institutional harmony then runs counter to the increasing involvement of the unit, whose members see ever more clearly the potential of their work and the new directions which it ought to take, and who become restless if their scope does not increase in proportion to their vision.

Fifth, the fact that the innovative unit brings kudos to the institution may hinder rather than help good relationships. Other members like to be the source of their own kudos or to feel that it is earned by the institution as a whole. Institutional loyalty is a powerful emotion, and when the innovators are more loyal to a vision than to an institution, this difference of viewpoint can be a further source of friction.

Finally, to ask for a safe life within an institutional structure and also for a continuing opportunity to innovate is to ask for the improbable. This will continue to be so until over the years new, more collective kinds of grouping come into being to replace the present bureaucratic structure of higher education, or (in this instance) until moneys are so disposed that a group which is respected and needed can pay its own way through the services it provides. In the meantime, many innovative groups must see themselves as expendable. They blossom and they fade, and those who have taken part in them move on, enriched by their shared experiences, to new places where new tasks await them.

All these interpretations have some truth in the history of the Goldsmiths' College Curriculum Laboratory. Doubtless there are other interpretations also.

13. Three from the Pilot Course Reports

During 1965 to 1967, the Laboratory published six short books (of some 50 pages each) containing the reports of the first seven pilot courses. At that stage in its development the reports were the main way the Lab's work was communicated to teachers and other educators; thousands of copies have been sold by the College to interested teachers and educators.[1] In retrospect, writing and circulating such reports seems a natural and inevitable way of behaving, but when one pauses to consider, it is actually very unusual for an education course at a university to publish its findings to the world.

In planning the first course, I had always thought it would be good to record our viewpoints so that they could be made available to the Department of Education and Science, and to members of subsequent courses. But the First Report, which set the fashion and custom for later courses, was written in a very different mood from any I had anticipated, a mood of urgency and need. The 27 teachers and head teachers who for 11 weeks had been closeted together, and with Gene Phillips of Boston University and myself, had come up with proposals for revising secondary education from top to bottom which seemed so powerful and so radical in their implications that they felt no one would believe what they said when they returned home, perhaps least of all themselves, unless they had something written down to point to and quote. Gene Phillips had already urged us, as part of our strategy of change, to have a final conference, to which we invited colleagues and administrators from the course members' home ground, as well as a variety of people from the DES and the Schools Council.

I have never been more angry than when one senior administrator at the conference, in which course members gave cogently argued and eloquent witness to their beliefs, said in unmasked surprise, "Who ever would have thought teachers could have expressed themselves so well?" The reports certainly drew some of their impact from the fact that they were written by teachers for teachers— and for the most part were equally cogent and eloquent. This did not preclude their fellow teachers on the permanent staff of the Laboratory from contributing to them, but of course our stuff like everyone else's had to be examined and passed or altered by the course as a whole. I contributed several sections anonymously to the reports of the courses which I was now most involved with. Here I include only two forewords and a preface which I contributed "in my own write."

I have made only a few minor alterations and omissions. Some phrases are added in square brackets to guide American readers unfamiliar with English educational terms. For convenience I have equated English "forms" with American "grades," say, fourth year with ninth grade; but it should be remembered that students in English maintained schools stay with their age group. The nearest English equivalent of the grade was the standard, which was given up a long time ago.

1. Foreword to
The Role of the School in a Changing Society:
First Pilot Course for Experienced Teachers (1965)

An Education Bill of Rights for Adolescents[2]

1. "Man makes and remakes his culture." Those not equipped in schools to share in this process are in a new sense disfranchised. Our legal safeguards and the vote do not suffice today. The school owes it to all adolescents to introduce them to the new physical sciences, the developing social and behavioural sciences, the new arts. There is a danger of a new serfhood as the development of an elite culture gathers momentum.

2. Everyone today moves into an unimaginably changing future. Benevolent paternalism, inside or outside school, is irrelevant to young people's needs today, when each has to learn to make wise

decisions for himself as well as contributing to a social consensus. This requires mental health based on self-knowledge and a capacity to identify with others without rigid conformity; an intelligible integrated view of the world; and rich feelings towards it.

3. The school can create this life for children only by giving them experience of it. If it is to promote change, it must change itself.

4. Today's fragmented time-table presents the pupil with an experience of reality as incoherent as a political map. We should recreate the school day, bearing in mind the following considerations:

a. To understand the significance and application of key concepts of our culture is far more important than acquiring factual information.

b. Much of the information accorded to adolescents in school is quite irrevelant to their needs and interests.

c. They welcome the opportunity to examine problems that deserve attention. These must not be simply topics: at this age they need to study topics in the context of a major theme.

d. A problem-solving approach is vital. By using the social and natural sciences, mathematics and language, the arts in cooperative enquiries, adolescents will learn to appreciate them.

e. Every adolescent has a right to share in these integrated studies. They are not a sop for the 4th or 5th year [9th and 10th grade] "failures," but should occupy some half of the day from the first year onwards.

5. Selection and streaming according to meagre kinds of assessment gives social experience that is anti-social. It denies adolesecents the opportunity to find themselves in relation to a wide diversity of persons. It also wastes talent, since many accept and fulfill the pessimistic predictions of adults.

6. Far more research is needed into the interests, personality, social and intellectual development of our adolescents. At present we shall work largely in the dark in planning a five-year cumulative curriculum.

7. When we have adequate means of appraising children and schools, the examination will be seem to be as outmoded as the blunderbuss. New techniques must be developed to assess powers of

problem-solving, decision-making, and creativity. Mode 3 CSE°
offers hope in this direction, if not rigidly interpreted.

8. The changing needs of adolescents today demand new roles and
hence new skills of teachers. This should influence teacher education
in the future. There is also a need for far more in-service courses, including policy-making conferences such as this Pilot Course.

2. THE CURRICULUM
Foreword to
The Raising of the School-Leaving Age:
Second Pilot Course for Experienced Teachers (1965)

Interdisciplinary Enquiry and Creative Learning

The first Pilot Course urged the need for thematic studies based
on a problem-solving approach as a basis for a five-year integrated
curriculum [for grades 6 through 10]. It is perhaps not surprising, in
the context of English secondary schooling with its bias towards instruction, that on the second course, we have found it necessary to
build up a new vocabulary which will, we hope, identify un-
mistakably the kind of curriculum which they and we intend. This
becomes the more urgent as talk of "integration of the curriculum"
becomes more fashionable. This seems to mean as a rule no more
than a pre-arranged *coordination* of syllabuses sometimes worked at
even within the usual short subject periods. This is no doubt a
creative and enjoyable ploy for teachers, and is a step forward from
the complete isolation of subjects. At times "integration" refers to
activities which status-conscious specialists would not wish to adopt
as their own and it can then be an outcome of a kind of contempt for
"the less able." In many people's minds, "integration" refers to an
intellectual mish-mash which they associate in particular with the
unfortunate attempts to combine history and geography into social
studies in the 1950s. We hope in this section to dissociate ourselves
from all these points of view.

° A public examination at age 16 in which syllabus and method of examining are
proposed by teachers for their own class, with quality control being maintained
through a system of moderation by other teachers appointed by the Regional Examination Board.

We stand for a policy unique in English education. The essence of our work is the belief that if people are to live well in a creative, flexible society the human gift of enquiry and exploration must be fostered throughout school and later life, and that it is the special feature of a democratic society that all its aspects are open to investigation by all its members. Our first pillar is therefore *Enquiry*, enquiry which is active in process and often leads to action. Secondly we believe that once one starts to enquire into and attempt to solve fundamental problems, the barriers between subjects, which seem formidable when they are dividing up a fixed body of knowledge, seem less relevant, and the work necessarily becomes *Interdisciplinary*: we have to use a variety of disciplines in formulating the problem, creating hypotheses as to its solution, working on and communicating our findings. It is no accident that in the knowledge explosion it is in the areas between subjects that the great advances are being made, and it does no service to learners at any level to suggest that subject boundaries are important when they cease to be convenient. On the other hand it does them no service either to suggest that the great disciplines which the human mind has created are trivial; on the contrary, as pupils move out of childhood and are co-opted into the adult world they need the chance to become aware of some of the key concepts, the great general ideas that have emerged in these disciplines and to understand, by using them, the theoretical structures which embody these ideas. Our concern can therefore be identified as being with *Interdisciplinary Enquiry in the Secondary School*, which we shorten into *IDE*.

The fact that we work in secondary schools presents us with organisational problems if we are to make possible a new and creative use of specialisms. The more advanced kinds of thinking that become possible in adolescence remind us that we are at work on a new problem and that simple extension of primary methods into the secondary school will not be adequate.

On the other hand, we need the constant reminders of primary school experience that individual children learn as they are ready and through their interests. It is this lesson that we have tried to incorporate in our concept of *Creative Learning*.

Much of the best thinking in education recently has been in terms of creativity, which as against the instructional model of education has stressed the need to encourage problem-recognition, original ideas and so on. The emphasis on creativity derives directly from the prevailing international competition in inventiveness. It packs a useful economic punch for those of us who are battering on the doors of ivory castles, but too often it betrays its origin by its emphasis on products—original ideas or objects. In this it reflects all too accurately a society which manages the instrumental aspects of life much better than the expressive. In speaking of "creative learning" we draw attention to learning as a creative act in which the learner evolves the coding system through which he interprets his experience and makes it available to himself. This code *is* the essential person, and by creating it he is creating himself. In our dialogue with our pupils we are midwives at the self-creation of persons, not the creation of products.

Self-creation through the arts is at the very heart of our thinking about creative learning, and we see its relations to IDE as manifold. There will be times when the arts are used consciously to communicate and thereby to explore more deeply and personally the findings of other studies or the feelings of anger, delight and so on which these findings have aroused. But we are not given to the heresy of social realism and the subjection of the arts to commonly understood social purposes. Writing, dance, pottery and the rest are ways in which pupils can express, discover and order many areas of concern and enjoyment which have little or nothing to do with their enquiries in IDE. Some of these arise from the material of the arts itself. Sometimes the arts will illuminate IDE, sometimes they will initiate it. Sometimes they will be quite independent. The relationship will vary from time to time and from person to person.

3. Preface to
New Roles for the Learner:
Report of the Fifth Pilot Course for Experienced Teachers (1967)

This fifth Pilot Course Report reverts to a theme touched on in the first (which proposed an "Education Bill of Rights for Adolescents"). The members of this course have been articulating the changing role of the learner in school that follows from (and in turn demands) a new role of the school in a changing society.

People sometimes have said to us that there have been many other "progressive" or liberating movements in education before the one that derives from the Pilot Courses at Goldsmiths'. If these have flourished for a while only to die away, why should this one root? I believe that is has a better chance because it is the outcome of collaboration of teachers across a whole range of schools with others in a College of Education and also because I have seen how as each course tackles the whole problem afresh and in addition moves on to examine some aspect in far greater detail, the whole style of schooling proposed stands up to this continuous analysis and appraisal by very experienced professionals, and is strengthened and enriched by it.

Another reason for believing that we are in the pioneering stages of a movement of lasting significance is that we recognise that we cannot allow it to fail. The stakes are too high, higher than they have ever been. If adults throughout the mechanised world do not over the next few years ensure that in adolescence the young learn to live in a society based in mutual trust and self-trust, we condemn the human race to living—if it survives at all—in the interstices of an authoritarian bureaucracy. "Goodness of fit" will become more than ever "fitting into society" (as if society were something other than the persons composing it) and we shall have less and less hope of designing a way of life flexible enough to fit our changing human needs. If the human race ends with two Frankensteins (or more) moving inexorably into the last phases of a war game we have programmed them to play, it will be because at each daily level of choice we have not been determinedly and simply human. Dehumanising is all around us. In schools it takes the form of requiring the young to channel their irreproachable aggression into patterns of competition and contempt, in which it becomes a requirement of self-satisfaction to have others that one is better than, or a reassurance that one exists at all to know oneself despicable. We have to move on from the disastrous introversion of "cogito, ergo sum" to the confident communality of "tu es, ergo sumus," finding our assurance in our own being through living in a system of mutual empathy.

Teachers rightly tend not to think in national terms, but if internationally this country has a new contribution to make, may it not be through showing a way of using school time to invite the young, in so far as we are able, to build with us collaboratively a kind of schooling that is based on sensitivity, suppleness and equality of esteem for persons? If we can together with the young invent an education based on collaboration, flexibility, exploration, making, openness to experience of persons and things, we shall be helping them to become the kinds of persons who will expect such humanness of opportunity for others and themselves in the long future. Already there are educators and teachers in other nations who are beginning to interest themselves in our work, and this because they recognise the courage of their conviction of experienced teachers who go beyond the now-ness of so much educational thinking. A teacher bounded by the present is living in the past. And the teachers in all countries who are cowed and tied by outmoded concepts such as "coverage" of an inevitably obsolescent curriculum, of training people for jobs, of training functionaries rather than encouraging self-direction— these teachers are living in the past while the world moves on. For those of us working to create a kind of schooling such as the Reports envisage to describe ourselves as some of those all over the world who live in the future as well as the present may sound grandiose, but it is all very simple (that doesn't necessarily mean easy) and resolves itself into clusters of tiny choices in which each time we replace judging by observing, using by being with, telling by doing with, worrying ourselves by consulting others, ordering by advising, obeying by contributing, shouting by listening, envying by greeting. This goes for all the relationships in the school. It's for this reason that we declare our purpose to be *person-centred* schools, not child-centred, seeking mutuality of relations in which the fulfilment and personal development of the teacher is part of what Edwin Mason has called the "giving, taking and sharing" of school life.

References

1. Those interested in the policies and historical impact of the six Pilot Course Reports may like to know they are still available. Requests for order forms giving full details should be sent to the Editor, *Ideas*, University of London Goldsmiths' College, London S.E. 14.
2. The idea of the Bill was proposed by W.J. Preece, M.B.E.

14. Four from Ideas *

Ideas is the creation of Leslie Smith, who was appointed in 1966 to look after the Consultative Services of the Lab. The first issue came out in February 1967. The Lab was already nearly drowning in a tide of requests for speakers and active help in schools, but unfortunately the idea of a nonregional consultative service based at a college or university—or, for that matter, an independent enterprise of the kind familiar in the United States—had no British precedent. Ideas was intended to give some practical help to those whom we could not serve more directly. It had a further value also: whereas the main source of energy and new thinking had at first been the Courses and had been expressed through the Course Reports, it was by now important to find a way of reporting on the many changes which were taking place in schools. These changes began as a direct result of the activities of course members, but increasingly they also occurred as an outcome of the Reports and of the many conferences and workshops at which the staff of the Lab and past course members were asked to speak. For this section, I have chosen four articles which I published between May 1968 and March 1970. All of them post-date Young Lives At Stake.

Dialogue, Disciplines, Objectives (1968)

WHAT IS YOUR IMAGE of educational process? Are you drawn to a mustard seed analogy, where the small beginning explodes into growth beyond what could have been precisely foreseen, or to an

---

* *Ideas* is available in North America from APS Publications, Inc., 150 Fifth Avenue, New York, N.Y. 10011.

analogy of logistical planning, patiently designed to get the troops and their supplies from one fixed point to another on a pre-planned route? Years ago, Whitehead[1] drew a distinction between the historical periods that were given to Speculation (concerned with the future, inventive) and periods that were concerned with Scholarship (retrospective, priestly, formalised). A modern technological society is of its nature speculative, and a major task of its school system (even from the point of economic survival, quite apart from any other hopes one might have of lives fully lived) is to help the young to live inventively, to move at ease in uncertainty and to collaborate in effecting change. Yet there are many trends in our educational thinking today that are better suited to the age of Scholarship, for they assume the necessity of fixed reference points, usually arrived at by looking at the agreed standards of a while ago, screwing them up a few notches, and aiming to get more young people to achieve them.

Mustard seed education is not a happy accident. It demands professional skill and forethought and a flexible relationship with children's thinking that is no less taxing than logistical planning. For it can prosper only if the seed is one that generates genuine involvement, if the processes are significant to teachers and pupils, and if the school is sufficiently free to draw on the fund of imaginative opportunism of everyone concerned.

The phase of work which Jessica James describes in this issue of *Ideas* met these requirements. The hopes she had for students were generous and important, for she wanted to enrich the quality of their response to the environment; and she chose as a starting-point a symbol of archetypal significance, water, and in particular the silent stillness of a lake. (Seonaid Robertson, in *Rosegarden and Labyrinth*, identified other symbols with the same capacity to engage concentrated attention and hence to foster creative work.) Secondly, the work involved three fundamental processes of human living. Enquiry and Making we have talked about often enough; this study was based also on a recognition of what what I call "Dialogue," the non-purposive, non-manipulative awareness of things, creatures, or people, akin to what Einstein called "wonder." This is incidentally a requirement of all creative enterprise, although we do not have to justify it by its products.

Those of us who have seen her film will recall the alternation between the quiet, seemingly aimless visits to the lake and the vigorous enquiry and creative work that arose from them. Beyond that, the enterprise demonstrated the attractiveness of collaborative learning, for it smoothed away distinctions between teachers and pupils and between children from the infant school and adolescents. (One day, when someone asks "Why on earth did they segregate young people into these tight little age-groups?" what answer will be given?) Finally, although there was plenty of pre-planning it was of a kind to *facilitate* the venture, not to limit it or manipulate it towards pre-ordained ends. The result was a happening that was highly inventive, vastly enjoyable, involved a great deal of learning, and was serendipitous, for it clearly went on picking up good ideas far beyond what could be pre-planned.

Secondary schooling today requires a fundamental shift towards this kind of education, and towards the flexible and imaginative dialogue between pupils and teachers that the *Nuffield Junior Science Project*[2] so admirably analyses (Teachers' Guides 1 and 2, especially the latter part of volume 2). This will be a first step towards an education for adolescents that is based on a full understanding of recent research studies.

Our proposals in the Curriculum Laboratory are an advance, not a throwback to older "progressive" movements such as a thirty-ish Deweyism or the Engish social work of the 'forties which Denis Lawton referred to in *Ideas* No. 4, admirable as was much of their understanding of how people might live and work together. Quite apart from the filtering through into modern thinking about curriculum of existentialist thinking, and now more recently of new insights from ethological and biological studies, between the curriculum thinkers of those days and ourselves lie the vigorous psychological and sociological researches of the 'fifties, a period which in retrospect emerges as being extraordinarily fecund in important studies.

There are at least five major developments of that time that need to be acknowledged in schools today which were unknown or not fully established even 15 or 20 years ago:

1. The final demolition of the "capacity" or fixed I.Q. theory,

together with an acknowledgement of the effect of environment on intelligent behavior. (Closely allied to this for my immediate purposes, although of course having broader implications, is the sociologist's revelation of the disadvantages of children whose home environments do not give them access to the values and experiences of the dominant middle-class culture of the school.)

2. The "creativity" studies, which sought to identify dimensions of human behaviour that we had keen awareness of but which had been masked by I.Q. and standardised attainment tests, and by most conventional academic curriculum with the didactic teaching methods that involves. It is satisfactory, although not surprising, that the Schools Council's Project on Applied Science and Technology is already confident that "from the work being done in our project schools . . . a whole type of ability is being uncovered and developed through teaching based on immediately relevant application of academic subject matter and an extension of the range of creative opportunities." Creative behaviours are not, of course, limited to applied studies of this kind, and we look to similar developments elsewhere in the curriculum as well, but this report is a sharp reminder of the harm we have done (again in economic as well as more fundamental human terms) by undervaluing *Making* in our schools.

3. Piaget's continuing and fundamental studies of cognitive development. These are perhaps potentially the greatest contribution of the mid-century to the well-being of young people in schools. Already our youngest ones are benefiting since it is no longer excusable to treat them as performing monkeys, who are required to perform computational tricks without understanding what they are doing. It will be a good day when we can say that the implications of his findings about concrete and formal operations have been fully absorbed into secondary schools—or even, for that matter, his reminder that concepts are comprehended only when the appropriate stage of cognitive growth has been reached and in appropriate affective circumstances, a reminder which might well trip up some of the adherents of the "concept-box" approach to secondary education.

4. The work on the nature of the intellectual disciplines, which is largely associated with Jerome Bruner and Philip Phenix.

5. The setting up of a "Taxonomy of Educational Objectives" by Benjamin Bloom and his colleagues.

The Fourfold Curriculum and the emphasis on the processes of Enquiry, Making, and Dialogue, represent, among other things, an attempt to meet the full challenge of the first three groups of studies listed. In this article, I am more concerned with the work on disciplines and the notion of educational objectives. For the first three, being based on careful observations of human behavior, can work only to the advantage of children in schools. The last two, being more abstract armchair analyses, can be useful if they are interpreted in the light of the other three; taken out of that context they may well be damaging.

The studies of the nature of disciplines are in no sense an intellectual breakthrough, but they have merit in that they draw the attention of people who are comparatively unreflective about their subjects to the exploratory, creative and necessarily tentative nature of human systems of thought. They are a reminder that we ought to look at "subjects" not as subject-*matter* but as *ways of behaving*. A discipline is a tool for interpreting experience. Its findings are not inevitable and given, but are relative to the input of those using it, who select from the continuum of experience certain aspects of the environment which they want to study, and select also the theories, concepts and forms of communication they will use to manipulate the selected data. Subject-matter is subjective matter. (In terms of games theory, a historian and a biochemist have decided to play different games, with different roles, rituals, rules, and languages.) Discussion of the nature of their disciplines should be given greater prominence than it is in the education of teachers, who in England are not usually disposed to reflect about their activities unless accepted traditions are actively challenged. We learned this three years ago when we first invited specialists to talk to our first Pilot Course on the contributions of their disciplines to the curriculum, an invitation which they interpreted as a call to talk about method.

The danger of thinking about the structure of disciplines lies in the word *structure*, which is too often envisaged not as an organic structure of mutually supportive theories and their constituent concepts, but as a piece of architecture which will fall flat on its face (or should one say on its elevation?) if it is not built up in a brick-by-brick order. Bruner has recently come out on the side of Speculation as against Scholarly dogmatism by declaring *(Toward a Theory of*

Instruction, Harvard, 1966): " . . . structure must always be related to the status and gifts of the learner. Viewed in this way, the optimum structure of a body of knowledge is not absolute but relative."

Provided we remember that different learners will approach any system with diverse needs, expectations, perceptions of their problems, actual problems to solve, and levels of competence in conceptualisation and in the kinds of communication required, reflection on the nature of disciplines is valuable; and the active character of disciplines is fully acknowledged in our notions of interdisciplinary and intradisciplinary studies, as against proposals for integration or segregation of subject matter in the curriculum. On the other hand, teachers should not overplay this hand: this is an age that sprouts new and important disciplines, and in secondary schools the range of important disciplines that can be made available to the young is sadly limited. And many teachers are still subject-*matter* specialists rather than students of *disciplines*.

A major task of the next few years is to liberate subject disciplines from the fixed linear approaches involved in much standard syllabus construction, and to see how far education of an exploratory, creative kind can enable the young to find personal routes along which they can pass more speedily and with greater assurance than any common route can provide, because the context of their learning (their investigation or their invention) has meaning for them.

When we turn to thinking about *objectives* in education the terrain is confused because there are unacknowledged differences between the English and American usage of the word. The result is that if one expresses doubt as to the value of working towards objectives (in the American sense) it seems to the English as if one is inviting teachers to work in a totally unpurposeful way, and perhaps thereby harking back to the flabbiness of some "progressive" work of the past. When English curriculum workers speak of objectives they often mean simply general aims, or intentions. Thus the admirable Technology Project states as its overall objective "to help all children to get to grips with technology as a major influence in society, and, as a result, to make their lives more effective and satisfying," and also lists a number of manpower objectives with which it is concerned. But to those who have been *au fait* for some years with American thinking (as formulated in the Taxonomies of Dr. Bloom and his colleagues), objectives mean something very much narrower. The essential characteristic of objectives in this sense is that they are operational, are geared to a careful but fixed analysis of cognitive and affective behaviours, and that planning towards them involves by definition finding a technique for evaluating whether or not they have been achieved. This narrower usage having been so well-established internationally for well over a decade I would strongly recommend that in England we accept it, and for the broader term substitute *aims* or *purposes* or even *hopes*, which properly acknoweldge the autonomy of the pupil, who may or may not fulfil our hopes for him.

Once this semantic confusion is tidied up it becomes proper to ask people involved in some of the important curriculum developments which usage they are employing in recommending teachers to identify their objectives before proceeding with any piece of work. If they mean aims and purposes, then what they are saying (to my mind rightly) is that teachers should undertake the fundamental study of the character of their discipline and of its contribution to the curriculum that I have referred to earlier. In this sense I might state, for instance (and I should like to argue this case one day), that one of the objectives of science teaching for "non-scientists" (that is one of my hopes for them as members of a scientific society) is that they should be aware that we live in a post-Newtonian world and should have some access, in however primitive, external, and necessarily descriptive a form, to such concepts as relativity or complementarity. I would experiment with the offers I made to young people over the years of schooling in accordance with this hope. But I would also do so in full awareness of the learner's individual processes of learning and growth. I would still see the curriculum as something like an adventure playground, or if that does not sound sufficiently serious, as Piccadilly tube station, with different actors in the scene using different entrances and exits, in the process of taking their own diverse routes.

This is very different from any kind of thinking which uses the word in the technical American sense and identifies behavioral objectives *of a piece of work* and sees them as common to all pupils engaged in it, as for instance the influential UNESCO Report on Curriculum (1956) recommends. That is a concept that can have a place only when education is seen as a logistical exercise. It sets aside all the work of the creativity studies and of Piaget, and Bruner's (later) recognition of the relative nature of the system of disciplines.

We certainly do not want at this stage in English curriculum reform to get caught up in a fashion which is already past its prime, and for good reason; and I cannot help feeling guilty for having introduced the Taxonomy to many teachers in England, some of whom, and these the most sensitive and imaginative, have found themselves seriously inhibited by it. Nevertheless, I believe that to know about the work is part of the professional equipment of teachers today, and as long as the honeymoon does not last too long and the commitment to it is not total, it can be valuable to teachers who are trying to break away from unexamined assumptions about traditional syllabuses. If they study the first volume of the Taxonomy they cannot fail to profit by the important distinction that emerges between the lower and higher mental processes, and they will become aware how much work in schools is at the humblest level of factual recall.

However, if we take seriously the "individual differences" we all talk about so much, thinking about objectives in this American sense *must* be thinking about the different objectives that are appropriate to each individual child. If teachers find it helpful to study the taxonomy so as to have a better checklist of possible cognitive behaviours to look out for, or to add to their vocabulary for recognising diverse cognitive styles; if they take the young into their confidence by proposing targets which they might be aiming at; if, above all, it is used as an additional means whereby a group of teachers can identify *relative strengths* of different children and so ensure them an adequate experience of personal success in their school work, then it can do little but good. On the other hand, if it is part of an educational processing which requires similar objectives of totally different children, and if it limits teachers' experiments to what they know they will be able to evaluate afterwards, then it can do nothing but harm.

A taxonomy sounds very well, but whole children cannot set in a taxonomy. In practice, too often, for what goes on when people work to behavioural objectives (American style), *taxidermy* is nearer the mark.

Childhood Towards Adolescence:
The Middle Years (1968)

THE TROUBLE WITH CLICHES is that we come to believe them. One of the accepted cliches of English education is that we have a superb model for primary education, but although there are a handful of L.E.A.'s which can claim to have a large number of excellent schools there has been far too little development in theory or practice since the 1931 Hadow recommendations. The chapter on Curriculum in Plowden is a good example of perfunctory and hence retrospective (if not reactionary) thinking. In fact, one of the main weaknesses of this report, which is in many respects admirable, is that the implications of the growth of educational sociology since the Second World War are acknowledged in the research and in the attitudes expressed towards school-home relationships, but have not filtered through into the thinking about curriculum or the nature of the school community. The relationships of adults with young people in a changing society and the changing ways and kinds of learning that are possible and appropriate today—these are not seriously reconsidered.

To cliche add question-begging and you are in real trouble. It is becoming a cliche to say that the choice of the best age of transfer from primary to secondary school is a major educational problem for all nations. Let us not be so naive as to leap in and join those who ask this question. For to ask what is the best age for transfer is to beg the more fundamental question: is there *any* good age for transfer?

I have seen no convincing argument, developmental or sociological, to justify the assumption that transfer is a good thing. Hadow started it all, I suppose, in 1926, blatantly rationalising what was clearly an administratively convenient break (since it neatly chopped the elementary school in half, and in the countryside made good use of the I.C. engine) by referring in phraseology that twangs the heartstrings to the rising tide of adolescence—at 11! A remarkably prophetic Report, one must declare, for now forty years on the secular trend to earlier puberty has begun to catch up with its premonitions, and there *are* quite a lot of children who are around puberty at around 11 plus. But today our brows are furrowed by other problems, ones associated with comprehensive education, with the use of buildings, the supply of teachers, with developing hardware; so now we are busy rationalising these and finding splendid arguments for postponing transfer to 12, 13, 14.

Each L.E.A. pays our money and takes its choice of the system which enables it to operate its schools efficiently and economically. And why not? This is sensible behaviour, so long as we do not pretend to ourselves that there is something in the slow and gradual process from one culturally established institution (childhood) through another one very much of our time and place (adolescence), that justifies any slashing of the individual person's growth.

Once admit frankly that the basis for decision is administrative and we are free to recognise that since it seems beyond the dreams of possibility to have all-age schools in this country our most important task is not to decide on age of transfer but to defeat the damage it can do. Then our whole panoply of schools, Junior Schools, Middle Schools, Secondary Schools, High Schools, Junior High Schools, Senior High Schools and the rest—whatever their title, all may free themselves from preconceptions about having a special character as institutions and be more ready to look together at pupils in their genuine diversity of individual interests, talents, cognitive styles, characteristic ways of behaving, sources of enjoyment, emotional difficulties, temperamental tendencies, learning problems, relative strengths.

We may hope then that teachers together will find all kinds of ways of making their schools more porous. As Barbara Mogford makes clear, once you allow a school to become an open community it becomes open not only horizontally, as it were, to the surrounding community but also vertically, so that far more mixing up of age groups within schools, between schools and with other institutions becomes quite natural. Jessica James in *Ideas* 5 gave an excellent example of this cooperation between schools, and she has since moved on to other experiments on which we hope she will write later on. John Jones in *Ideas* 3 described cooperative ventures within a school, and chronological mixing within school is of course fundamental to two cells of the Fourfold Curriculum (remedial or Clinic and special interests or Orbit) which are by definition intended for open access. We suspect that vertical grouping will become more common in IDE/M and autonomous studies also, and are moving towards proposals for resources for this in the early years of secondary school and up to 16. There are valuable moves also towards closer cooperation with Further Education, which open up the scope of schools.

Furthermore, schools undertaking in their first or second years an interdisciplinary enquiry into Growing Up (see Pilot Course Report No. 2) are finding not only that it is an area of investigation which invites important contributions from all the disciplines represented in schools, but also that it has led to the study of younger children at work and hence to collaboration with infant and junior schools. Similarly this appears in special courses for Young School Leavers in quite a number of schools.

In terms of a growth in understanding of self and others, this kind of collaborative learning and friendship among young people of different chronological age is an important adaptation to a completely new cultural situation in which *most* young people are brought up in nuclear families which are small in size and very close in age, so that their experience of human behaviour is much more limited than it would have been in an extended family or even in a larger or more widely spaced nuclear one. Young people today need more opportunities, not fewer, to be with those younger and older than themselves, and for some the dependence on a teenager or the dependence of an infant or the shared enjoyment with people whose age helps them to see things differently can be something they very much need and greatly appreciate.

But this kind of experience has valuable academic side-effects for teachers and students in secondary schools, when they see how advanced and complex good infant and junior work can be. I do not personally like the didactic undertones of Jerome Bruner's often quoted remark that in principle anything can be taught to any child of any age, but there is little doubt that much of our schooling is repetitive and Parkinsonian. Younger children who are allowed to learn in ways they appreciate and are at home with often delve more deeply, scour more broadly and report more competently than many secondary pupils are trusted to do. Robert Oppenheimer has suggested that we could all learn from them for another reason: "There are children playing in the streets who could solve some of my top physics problems, because they have modes of sensory perception that I lost long ago."

This is not to say that all is so well with our junior schools as idle cliche suggests, and it is worth considering the possibility that the thinking of radical secondary teachers may have something to contribute there. The important thing is to make common cause, and the opportunity has been given to us with the ending of 11-plus examinations. Too many primary schools are still engaged in preparing the young for a test that no longer demands this sacrifice, and have not woken up to their new freedom; nor does it seem that they would know how to use it. The acceptance of a notion that transfer to secondary education has some educational significance is partly to blame for this, since it makes us all think of children as being pupils at the top or bottom of an institution, of finishing one course and moving towards another. We should be thinking of them as persons who are in or approaching puberty, who are coming to be able to work in terms of complex concrete operations though not as a rule ready for formal operations except occasionally and at their own demand, who need experience not only of enjoying a rich educational environment but themselves enriching and changing it, whose differences in developmental age make for fruitful variations in interests—and so on, not as top juniors or bottom secondaries, or even middle middle-schoolers.

When it comes to brass tacks we know very little about 10- to 13-year-olds. Whether the cause of our ignorance is this tendency to think in terms of institutions rather than of persons, or something in the behaviour of the young people themselves, or the very complexity of Piaget's kind of observations at this age, or a combination of these with other causes which other people could suggest, the facts are clear: we know far too little about these transitional years from childhood to full adolescence.

Being Enquiring,
Enquiry and Enquiries (1969)

I HAVE TO ADMIT that we came to use the term "enquiry" without any great forethought. In the second Pilot Course, we were aware of an urgent need to find words which would identify our proposals. The first course had spoken of "thematic studies with a problem-solving approach." But we found that many people noticed the idea of a theme but ignored the problem-solving. Themes all too easily break down into topics, and topics into assignments—no questions asked by pupils, no problems seen by them as deserving their attention. We had spoken also of "integrated studies," but we began to realize that this would give us some strange bedfellows. We would have welcomed partnership with people workng on "integrated days" in primary schools, where that means that a teacher is working as one of an interdisciplinary team or is a one-teacher team in his own right, sometimes helping children to look at data as an artist might, sometimes seeing their scientific implications, and so on. But we found ourselves in poorer company that that. People were beginning to talk of integration as something special for "the Newsom child"—more talented children, it was suggested, could integrate what they learned without help. Integrated studies were appropriate to the lower orders in the lower streams, and included, it seemed, activities ranging from peculiarly spine-free social studies to "decorating the D.S. [Home Economics] flat quite delightfully" (doubtless through the integration of emulsion and water, an apt metaphor for much that is offered to the statutory leaver).

It was evident that we must try to describe our thoroughly vertebrate proposals in words which would distinguish them from these kinds of goings-on. "Interdisciplinary" was easy enough, since it is an established term, and its use made it clear that we were not speaking of an LCD of subject matter but of complex collaborative studies. The noun was more difficult to choose, and I proposed it only because I had been working with students for some time on what we called group enquiries. Although we didn't know that IDE would become so popular as it has, and the choice was perhaps more casual than it should have been, I think it has served rather well. Its value turns out to be the number of connotations that the word "enquiry" embraces, for it has a number of different meanings, with all of which we are concerned, and it is useful to use a broad linking term.

Nevertheless, we have been at fault, I think, in not identifying before now the uses we make of the term enquiry. It is true that I have tried to identify different "styles of enquiry." But beyond that I would like to distinguish between three different connotations. These are enquiry as *being enquiring*, a disposition to behave in a certain way, *enquiry* as *process*, and *enquiries* as *investigations*, or phases of work in a school curriculum. In this article I shall concentrate on the first two meanings.

1. *Being enquiring.* In this connotation, enquiry is a stance towards the world which is at the opposite pole from apathy. It is a tendency to ask questions, to examine and seek to explain experiences, to explore new possibilities of interpreting data or of possible action. This disposition to enquire is a human tendency clearly visible in babies, surely essential to the competent human animal (quite apart from any higher pretensions we may have); together with our tendencies to creativeness and awareness which I have called Making and Dialogue, it is an essential aspect of a human being's involvement in living. But it is a disposition all too easily conditioned out of children by parents, by the mass media, by the familiarity of repetitive circumstances—and (alas) by many teachers, although it is one of their main tasks to foster it.

2. *Enquiry as process.* Schooling often destroys or disastrously diminishes the disposition to be enquiring because the nature of knowledge is quite simply misunderstood; teachers who see their task as introducing the young to a body of knowledge see knowledge as a collection, or at best a system, of assertions. But to know is not to be informed of other people's assertions, as R. G. Collingwood pointed out many years ago:

A crude empiricism imagines that knowledge is composed wholly of assertions: that to know and to assert are identical. But it is only when the knower looks back over his shoulder at the road he has travelled, that he identifies knowledge with assertion. Knowledge as a past fact, as something dead and done with—knowledge by the time it gets into encyclopedias and text-books —does consist of assertion, and those who treat it as an affair of encyclopedias and text-books may be forgiven for thinking that it is assertion and nothing else. But those who look upon it as an affair of discovery and exploration have never fallen into that error. *People who are acquainted with knowledge at first hand have always known that assertions are only answers to questions.* (My italics, C.J.) So Plato described true knowledge as 'dialectic', the interplay of question and answer in the soul's dialogue with itself; so Bacon pointed out once for all that the scientist's real work was to interrogate nature, to put her, if need be, to the torture as a reluctant witness;

so Kant mildly remarked that the test of the intelligent man was to know what questions to ask; and the same truth has lately dawned on the astonished gaze of the pragmatists.[3]

I have italicised the sentence which by its unobtrusive qualification "knowledge at first hand" domesticates Collingwood's paradox. It is true that we can memorise other people's assertions, but that does not give us "knowledge at first hand," or "personal knowledge." It is possible to argue that some people are too young or too stupid or come from too inferior a sub-culture to be allowed to acquire knowledge as it is known by the more privileged; and there are of course many societies which have maintained this stance. I do not think that many teachers would maintain it (and in any case I have not the space to argue about it here). It is also a perfectly tenable proposition that not all that a child learns needs to be personal knowledge—and I would certainly agree that within a curriculum in which the process of enquiry is respected it is perfectly reasonable for children to cut some corners by acquiring data which they can't fully appreciate but which they know they need, perhaps for some process of *making*. But I don't think this is the reason for so much teaching being presented in the form of assertion. Much more often it is because teachers are themselves ignorant of "knowledge at first hand," having themselves had so much experience of being asserted at. They see knowledge as property to be handed on and so they find it difficult to introduce children to the process and satisfactions of enquiry.

The relationship of assertion to questioning must be fully understood if we are not to replace Whitehead's "merely well-informed man . . . the most useless bore on God's earth" by the intellectual rubberneck or the lepidopterist who has not acquired a net. Again, Collingwood is illuminating:

Questioning is the cutting edge of knowledge; assertion is the dead weight behind the edge that gives it driving force. Questions undirected by positive information, random questions, cut nothing; they fall in the void and yield no knowledge.

It is here that the contemporary concern with introducing children to the structure of a discipline has relevance. For this should be seen as introducing them to the system of question-and-answer which a discipline is, whether it is the discipline of a science or of an art-form. Emphasis on subject disciplines reminds us, that is, that it is not much good having a disposition to ask questions if you have not developed skill in asking them, in making likely guesses as to good answers, testing the guesses, modifying them and finally reaching assertions which one can use because one has understood the need for them and can tentatively accept them.

When knowledge is seen as question-cum-answer, two contemporary proposals for curriculum design appear in a different light. First, the idea of a concept-based curriculum, where that is seen as "teaching a concept,"is shown up as trivial. It is certainly legitimate at times to take a concept which children think they fully understand and to muddy the waters. For instance, if children are sure they know what a family is, it can be valuable to introduce them to very different kinds of family structure from those they know about. But even here it is better to help them to find a stick to muddy the waters with themselves, by intruding materials or experiences which invite questions that will lead them on to understand the functions of families and the great variety of ways in which these can be fulfilled. Of course they may not take up the invitation, having other questions to engage them, which will lead them to a grasp of concepts which they independently find they need. Both these approaches are fundamentally different from instructing children in the meaning of a word, which is what concept-based teaching often amounts to, and must inevitably amount to if it is not enquiry-based. For a concept is a summarised assertion, part of a theory arrived at through stringent enquiry. To understand a summarised assertion in such a way that it is part of one's intellectual tool-kit requires that one has seen the need for it.

Secondly, it looks as if a good deal of the argument between proponents of a "process-based" curriculum (as outlined by a number of American educators) and defenders of our traditional "knowledge-based" curriculum has arisen because of a narrow and mistaken view of the nature of knowledge. If you emphasise the element of assertion without acknowledging the process of enquiry through which assertions are arrived at and made one's own, then of course the two types of curricula are very different. But if you see the knowledge as question-and-answer the difference fades.

To ask for an enquiry-based curriculum is not the same as to emphasise critical thinking, as that is usually intended, although John Passmore's term "critico-creative" thinking would apply to it very well.[4] In far too much of our academic education at all levels young people are taught to criticise other people's assertions (theories or arguments) without having been engaged in the process of questioning out of which the assertions arose. Quite often training in critical thinking is an education in impertinence. Students are invited to sharpen their wits on the life-works of others without any understanding of the problems that the inventive thinker was facing. Young people need to have ample opportunities to experience the hazards of serious enquiry, to understand the history of their mistakes and achievements, and in that context to be creatively critical. Moreover, an enquiry-based education, unlike some approaches to critical thinking, is not exploitative. Professor Peters has protested with justification that "disciplines like history or literature are debased and distorted if they are used consciously to inculcate 'critical thinking'."[5] To take part in a process of historical or literary enquiry is not to distort a discipline but to engage it and to do so much more authentically than many pupils or students are invited to do, who learn in a critical but not a creative way.

Sex and Unisex (1970)

This was the lead article to Ideas *#15 and it therefore refers to a number of other articles in that issue.*

CRAFT for the boys and Home Economics for the girls; Commerce for the girls and Engineering for the boys. This has been the traditional form of differentiation between the education of boys and girls. Intellectual interests could be expected to be shared, and few were seriously concerned as to whether the poetry taught in the class lesson, or the style of history studied, was or even could be equally appropriate for girls and boys of the same age, but of very different levels of social and sexual maturity. Yet it is just as tenable to suggest that the practical interests could be shared while lines of interest in literature, social studies and the discussion of personal problems and of public events might well show considerable variations between the sexes, at least in adolescence.

In the past it has been adults who laid down the interests which it was acceptable for boys and girls to evince. And the distinction between "girls' subjects" and "boys' subjects" followed the adult pattern, whereby the roles of men and women in family life and in employment were sharply differentiated except perhaps in shop-keeping and in certain highly verbal professions into which a few women might infiltrate. The development of a more open curriculum in which children are given far more choice of activities than in the secondary schools of the past happens to coincide with a time when differentiation of role between men and women is becoming blurred. There is the move towards "democratic marriage," for instance, with young couples having shared interests and responsibilities; there is the growth in the relative importance of secondary and tertiary employment which require verbal skills rather than physical strength; and this, together with the growth of automation within heavy industry, the mechanization of agriculture and even withdrawal from East of Suez and all that stands for, continues to demonstrate that the specifically masculine opportunities for physical prowess and for adventure are coming to an end. Not suprisingly we have Unisex.

In thinking about opportunities for young people in schools to follow their bent, it seems that two things will be important to look out for. One is to make sure that the stereotypes of a previous generation do not narrow the scope of either boys or girls. The second is to ask ourselves whether there is still a place for some differentiation of learning as part of the process whereby in mid-adolescence the young come to identify with their own sex; or is this becoming less important as more and more aspects of life are shared?

As to the first question, quite a lot of evidence is becoming available, even if it is simply of a descriptive kind. Mervyn Turvey's article gives good examples of a tendency of some boys and girls to trespass on territory previously allocated to the opposite sex, and to feel very much at home there. Knowing about this issue of *Ideas* I have been listening out for similar examples. There is plenty of evidence that boys very much enjoy needlework or embroidery. According to Michael Rose of Carisbrooke School this is not only true of older boys, whom Edna Beaken of Romford Comprehensive

School and others like her have welcomed to the D.S. [Home Economics] rooms and helped them to make their gear. It is true of eleven-year-olds also, and this in spite of children's knowledge from their parents of the traditional expectations of secondary schools. The trend of boys towards cookery is perhaps less strong—only a proper survey could enable one to say—but at least it does seem that where the offer is made to them, they begin nowadays to feel free to learn cooking without going through any rigmarole of ostensibly applying for a career in catering, a subterfuge which some have resorted ·to in the past.

The crossover from the other side is equally evident. Girls are beginning to find their way into the woodwork and metalwork shops. (I am glad to say there are three women students in the main Craft [Industrial Arts] course at Goldsmiths'.) I have heard Tom Gannon describe the work of a nine-year-old girl in his Middle School at Grimethorpe, who successfully went off and did some creative turning on a lathe. And I have more than once witnessed how girls can become absorbed in woodwork, even though it has often happened just because of shortage of staff on the D.S. side. I remember one Head telling me he has never seen second-year secondary [7th grade] girls so absorbed as when they had to take woodwork for want of a cookery teacher. They chose first to make (surprise, surprise?) a huge communal totem pole. I must say it has taken a long time for the message to come through that girls like working with resistant materials and becoming competent handymen. Thirty years ago it was considered an electrifying novelty to sponsor "handymen" courses for girls in the A.T.S. [women in the army], yet why should young women face life as apprentice sorceresses, waiting for their husbands to come home and cope with the malevolence of domestic machinery? It has been noticeable with members of our courses that the women teachers have quite often chosen to work for an afternoon a week with wood or metal, sometimes leaving the men behind writing poetry.

A further side benefit of promoting crossover is that it reduces a narrowly vocational attitude towards, for instance, commercial and motor mechanics' courses. It is possible for young people to learn these skills without making firm decisions about jobs in a school where it is quite usual for boys to learn typing and girls to work on car engines. Both are useful additions to the competence of both men and women.

The crossover of some pupils, although of course not all, is pretty clear. It is relatively easy for co-educational schools to cope with, but is seems to require some new thinking about the provision of practical facilities in single-sex schools.

There is one point on which we would welcome comment from schools. One teacher, working in a very open way with first-year secondary children [6th grade], believes that by eleven, boys are more "inventive" in craft than girls, in the sense of identifying more practical problems to work on and solving them rather ingeniously. Yet the evidence of the work sent to Edward de Bono, as reported in *Where*, shows no difference in the inventiveness and quality of "lateral thinking" between younger boys and girls: the plans are equally original from 6-year-olds, for instance, the girls' work merely tending to be tidier. If there is this incongruity between the age groups, what happens? The question is an important one, for it adds another dimension to one that perplexes many people working in the 9- to 11-year-old group who find more imitativeness and less individuality both in practical problem-solving work and in expressive arts than earlier childhood would have led them to expect. If there is this greater conformity, what happens?

Another kind of crossover which is relevant has been the interest of boys as well as girls in the study of early childhood, not only in fourth-year work [ninth grade], but in the first years. When I first suggested that "growing up" might be a worthwhile area of investigation for children in their earlier years in secondary school, I had in mind the idea of confirming their sense that they were all right in terms of physical development—a point which Dr. Marshall underlined in my interview with him. I thought also that they would be thinking a good deal, as I believe younger children probably would, about "growing up in other lands." But as it turns out, interest seems to have centred on the young child, and beyond that on the processes of conception and birth. At Southfields School, Gravesend, it was a small mixed group of boys and girls which started with a quite mundane study on furnishing a house, arrived at the nursery and discovered they didn't know how to furnish it. So, back to the study of young children, to visit them in day nurseries and study their early education. At this school it was the boys who constructed a womb containing a foetus; at Fairlop school this was the same interest of a group of girls, though they happened to use collage. What is interesting here, I think, is the concern with basic life processes, and the fact that children can find their own way through to sex education, reaching it through a care for the young human creature. These examples arose in IDE in the first year onwards, not simply among young school leavers [9th and 10th grades], when teachers might expect to interest girls at least in early childhood as part of a "preparation for life."

So much for the first question. There is a trend towards more crossover than the traditional divisions of the secondary school would lead one to expect. The second question is much more difficult but must at least be mentioned. With the old clear demarcations it was the practical subjects which gave some of the most important opportunities for identifying with one's own sex. It is extraordinary to think that the Home Economics and Craft teachers have often been rather low in the caste system of secondary schools, when many have contributed so much to young people's growth in maturity just because with concentration on practical work personal problems could be referred to casually and usefully. Both have often been splendidly avuncular or parent-like. The difficult question is this. Is growing up becoming today so much a shared experience that boys and girls no longer need these times in school to be studying with their own sex? Or does the need remain, and in that case should we be thinking or creating opportunities in the school day which can be concerned with differences of outlook and expectation between the sexes rather than similarities? And would these opportunities need to be formal, or would some blocked periods for work of an IDE type in the third to sixth years [8th through 12th grade] provide the necessary conditions? Bearing in mind the emphasis of Derek Miller, following Erik Erikson and others, on the importance of the 14- to 18-year-old age range for establishing personal identity, this is the kind of question which will be facing teachers planning for RSLA [Raising of the School Leaving Age to 16] or already at work with the new (and old) sixth forms [Juniors, Seniors]. Again, even quite short reports would be most useful.

These are questions of curriculum in the simplest sense. Joan

Maizels' article draws attention to another very important difference between boys and girls, which she identified in her study of young school leavers in employment in Willesden. She suggests that one of the ways in which our educational system incidentally supports some of the more depressing aspects of the labour market is that young people find it such a pleasure to leave some schools that any job is welcome. But it seems that it is the boys, rather than the girls, who have lost heart. The girls don't like school. The boys don't mind it so much but aren't "brainy enough." It is interesting to debate how one might explain this difference. It is in line with a study made by Professor Musgrove some years ago which showed that the role conflict (anxiety and dissatisfaction with self) expressed by young people was highest among grammar school [selective] boys, lowest among secondary modern school [non-selective] girls. The simplest explanation is to tie it up with the close association for working-class men of job status with masculine prestige. The girls have, after all, a second life-chance in marriage and family life.

If the privatisation of life continues, as described by F. Zweig in *The Affluent Worker*, and people find more of their satisfaction in their private lives and less in their public roles, it may be that boys will be better protected against the destructiveness which so damages their self esteem. But I don't really believe this. The new schools must create a caucus race in which all are prized and no one learns to feel inadequate. No lesser revolution will do.

References

1. A. N. Whitehead, *Science and the Modern World*, Macmillan, 1926.
2. *Nuffield Junior Science*, Glasgow, Collins Educational, 1967; New York, Agathon Press, 1972.
3. R. G. Collingwood, *Speculum Mentis, or The Map of Knowledge*, Oxford University Press, 1924, pp. 76 ff.
4. John Passmore, "On Teaching to Be Critical," in A. S. Peters, ed., *The Concept of Education*, Routledge and Kegan Paul, 1966, p. 201.
5. A. S. Peters, *Education as Initiation*, Evans Bros., 1963.

15. The Open Curriculum

This article was published in the University of London Institute of Education Bulletin (new series no. 19, Autumn term, 1969), which was devoted to a consideration of the concept of integrated studies in schools. (The Bulletin has now been replaced by London Education Review.) Through its title, the article may have had an importance in American education which I did not expect and would not have wished, for the term "open curriculum" was picked up by an American visitor to England and brought back as a way of distinguishing the informal tradition of English primary schools from the American "free school" movement. "Open education" is not a term used in England, and I have never much cared for it, so I was relieved when I re-read the article in preparing this book to find that it clearly distinguishes "open" and "closed" aspects of a well-balanced curriculum. This distinction is a central feature of the Fourfold Curriculum to which the article refers.

I have often pointed out that the values of the Fourfold Curriculum obtain in elementary education no less than in middle or high school education. If you look at the classrooms of good English primary teachers, or their counterparts in this country, you will notice that at times children work in an interconnective fashion, which I describe here as "open" and had earlier described as IDE (Interdisciplinary Enquiry) or IDM (Interdisciplinary Making); at times they work more narrowly—in math, say, or in scientific observation and experiment, or in music; at times they have special coaching or special additional opportunities because of their individual needs; and at other times they wheel away in a flight of special interest. In the larger middle or secondary school, with its more complex specialist staff and more elaborate facilities, it is

215

usually necessary to formalize these distinctions to a greater extent than in a self-contained classroom or open corridor. The truth remains, however, that good elementary teaching is as varied in style and intention as these more formal secondary arrangements. If the term "open education" is to be used, it is best equated (to quote the article) not with "a totally open curriculum . . . multi-disciplinary at all times," but with "a flexible interplay between open and closed work."

Perhaps, too, a word of explanation about the meaning of "integrated studies" in English secondary education would be helpful. They are not the same as the primary school's "integrated day" but are the integration of subject-matter by teachers who agree to cover a broad syllabus together, on an "I'll teach this if you'll teach that" basis. They do no harm, but as a basic diet they lack two essential qualities: first, that of student inquiry and initiative; second (as I argue in this article), a sound epistemology. I discussed this question also in Young Lives At Stake *(pp. 132 ff).*

I AM NOT AT ALL SURE that I am a suitable person to contribute to a collection of essays on integrated studies. Such references as I have made to them have been pejorative. I greatly respect some excellent work that takes place in primary schools under that name or as the "integrated day." But I think they have chosen a dangerous description. "Integration," whether it is used of individuals, societies, or curricula, can indicate a synthesis too cheaply bought. I suspect the "integrated personality" of being a pretty dull dog, one who denies the divergent and challenging aspects of himself in an attempt to match some ego-ideal of unruffled maturity. And the ideal of an integrated society suggests to me a world fit for ball-bearings to roll in, in which the spiky ineluctable conflicts of belief, personality and interests which differentiate us are not acknowledged and welcomed but are smoothed away or hypocritically ignored, often for administrative convenience or in lazy support of the status quo. Integration is not the same as de-segregation. It implies blending rather than collaboration. It is an arithmetic rather than an algebra.

So it is with curriculum. The integrated day as Brown and Precious describe it is admirable:

As the child works he is involved with learning as an integrated unit coping perhaps with a foray into mathematics, science, geography, art or English in a short space of time.[1]

But although integration to them means "easy transition between areas of learning," which they recognize as different, it can too often mean that people think it vaguely immoral to suggest that there are fundamental differences between the subject disciplines. Such people speak of "breaking down the artificial barriers between subjects." Then the result can all too easily be waffle, for the barriers between one subject and another are not artificial; they are its necessary limitations.

The urge to combine is very strong in schools today. I have even met foreign-language specialists who feel guilty because they just do not see how they can join the heavenly choir of scientists, artists, historians and so on (although some do make valuable links). With this pressure of fashion on them, it is very important that teachers' concepts of disciplines should be sound. A historian, a geographer and a biologist looking over the same gate will view the scene through different intellectual lenses: what they select to notice will be different, and they will interpret it differently because the explanatory theories they bring to bear on it are different. They cannot integrate or blend these insights, but experts in different disciplines can contribute to a shared problem, whether this is a pure or applied study, and whether the task is seen as understanding of process, as making practical decisions or as formulating value-judgements.

The scale of human problems is so great and the amount of knowledge so vast and so rapidly changing that it is not surprising that individuals can no longer scan data adequately in isolation, or evaluate the importance to them of different items; hence the increasing number of interdisciplinary teams in research. In a team, each member has a far greater hope of achieving a comprehensive view of a problem. Sometimes, perhaps, one or other of them will have a flash of understanding of the whole, akin to Mozart's experience of hearing a newly composed symphony all in one instant of time. I do not know if this is so. But I am convinced that for most of us, most of the time, learning on a broad front demands constant acknowledgement of the differences between the disciplines we use. In the educational process this should become increasingly explicit in middle, secondary and higher education, although in ordinary conversation our capacity to make use of concepts from different disciplines (and thus by implication of the theories which they summarize) often masks their different origins.

It is possible, of course, to group the disciplines. I do not personally use Professor Hirst's term "forms of knowledge,"[2] partly because I think it may give rise to an idea of knowing as passive (as against Professor L.A. Reid's "ways of knowledge"[3] or Philip H. Phenix's[4] "realms of meaning"), but mainly because I think his concern with sets may draw attention away from the important differences between neighbouring disciplines. It is certainly useful, for instance, for young people to discover that theology is no longer the queen of the sciences; but they need also quite early to come to terms with the different levels of scepticism required by the different sciences, the kinds of evidence each will accept or has to make do with.

Although I am convinced that the interdisciplinary concept as proposed by the Goldsmiths' College Curriculum Laboratory, and described in our publications, is epistemologically superior to that of integration, there are practical difficulties about talking of interdisciplinary studies in schools. One rather trivial one is that I sometimes think we have overdone talk about disciplines: too many people seem to see them not as necessary limitations of human knowledge but as a source of virtue. Some lock themselves in "the logic of my discipline" as if it were a chastity belt, despite the fact that even intradisciplinary work can at its best be remarkably unchaste. How many logics, for instance, has the English teacher, who is at times one of the school's linguistic specialists, at times a cultural historian, at times an art critic, at times an artist, and at his best a human being who uses all these tools as he needs them? The other difficulty, although also merely tactical, is more serious: a difference of names may divide Interdisciplinary Enquiry in the secondary schools from the best work in the primary schools of which it should be a development. Nathan Isaacs said, ". . . it is imperative that the teacher must not only be able to recognize when a child is studying mathematics, or science, or history, but that he must also be aware of what constitutes *good* mathematics, *good* science, and *good* history." It is one thing to say that the good infant teacher is encouraging integrated studies, but pretty pompous to describe her as a one-woman interdisciplinary team, although that is precisely what she is.

I certainly would not want to abandon the term IDE (Interdisciplinary Enquiry), which was chosen because it is accurate and self-explanatory, although I later had to add IDM or Making, to describe the full range of interdisciplinary studies. But at times it might be wiser to speak simply of *open* and *closed* aspects of the curriculum. A totally open curriculum would be multi-disciplinary at all times; a totally closed one would be like that of the traditional secondary school. The "fourfold curriculum" which we propose is at times open, at times closed to meet the different requirements of learners, at times closed because of differences in what is to be learned—the aspect we call "autonomous studies." This is the time when the demarcation lines between disciplines are used to exclude all data not immediately relevant, when the musician or biologist or mathematician ignores all aspects of the environment except what can be encompassed in music, biology or mathematics.

Until recently I have thought of autonomous studies as given over to separate subject-disciplines separately studied. It seems now that even here some desegregation or gregariousness is developing. Sometimes this may be for lack of a range of specialized staff: in the middle school, for instance, a group of prospective heads working with us this year came to feel they would need two kinds of scientists (if technology is a science, not a humanity), one a biologist, one with a technical bias, both able to draw readily on the chemistry and physics they needed. But it seems to happen in secondary schools also: some non-IDE times are seen as opportunities to work with teachers who have allied interests, e.g. in the humanities or in the arts and crafts (including English, drama and movement).

At the moment there is a sharp division between IDE and autonomous studies in secondary schools, sharper than its equivalent in junior schools, partly because change has deliberately been gradual, partly because of the organizational problems, which are much greater in larger schools with more specialized staff and equipment. It seems, though, that once schools introduce an element of blocked time into the school day, more adaptable planning becomes possible, and this trend may increase if specialists find children better able to grasp their subjects as short sharp spurs growing out of IDE than in the usual two periods a week to which English secondary education is so strangely addicted. I see a flexible interplay between open and closed work as the basis of education right through at least to the first degree.

There remains the fundamental question of values. Why should there be open or interdisciplinary studies? A proper regard for clear conceptualization should not enslave us to an either-or. To use the language of integration for a moment, I have heard teachers bullyragged (not in this Institute, by the way) to state whether they were seeking what was called integration in the mind of the child, integration of subject-matter, or integration of the school staff, as if it were greedy to want all three. As I see it, a good paradigm of educational practice should include a satisfactory model of how, a child learns, how the aspects of his learning are intrinsically interrelated, and what the social system should be within which he learns—and similarly with the teacher and his teaching. Three birds killed with one stone make a good meal. We should know what we are eating and why, but we shouldn't be forced to choose, or even to assert priorities.

From the point of view of the social system of the school, the opening of the curriculum is arrived at by small groups of teachers working in collaboration, once a child is old enough to work with several teachers rather than needing the security of one all-comprehending adult. In this way the balance of power in a school is gradually modified. In order to become effective, teachers' groups become non-hierarchical: on what grounds can even the most distinguished head of a department claim authority over even the youngest teacher who represents another specialism? And as the situation frees them to become more inventive, and requires it of them, the Head is free to move from initiating policies and seeing them through to supporting and encouraging the initiative of his colleagues. Initially in a transitional period through this staff collaboration, increasingly in the relationships developing with children and between children, the school can become within the limits created by compulsory schooling, a model of an open society.

In terms of the unifying experience of the child, an open curriculum allows him to explore widely, to have access to different kinds of resources (including teachers' expertise) as he needs them, using the most appropriate discipline to formulate his problem and express his findings. Thereby he can begin to create his own well-planned conceptual map. He is able also to work to his own rhythm of involvement and withdrawal.. A first-year secondary girl [age 11-12] described recently on television how "horrid" it had been in primary school having teachers always saying "Do this, Do that." Now she sometimes worked hard, sometimes seemed to laze, but always made up for lost time (she had transferred from a rigid primary school to one working in IDE).

An open curriculum also transcends the false division between thinking and feeling which a school crudely demonstrates by distinctions between hard and soft subjects. Children, like pioneer mathematicians, delight in the rightness and inevitability of good mathematics, and this can be expressed as an art form. And certainly studies of human beings, their creations, their environment and the creatures they share it with engage our feelings and should be allowed to. I saw recently a good example of the scope IDE gives to use both the correct impersonal language of science and the powerful personal statement of the arts, and also to use enactive, iconic and symbolic representation, as required.[5] A group of thirteen-year-old girls was studying early childhood as part of a study of human growth. They had played with and observed young children, they had considered moral problems associated with child-birth and child-rearing, they had made precise scientific statements, in their own formulation, of the process of conception—and one had made marvellous embroidered collages of conception and the development of the embryo. It might have been poetry or music or dance, for all the arts share the power to summarize experience yet leave its full significance hidden, open to acquire new meanings. Here was something a good primary school would recognize as integrated studies, in the careful sense of making a whole while acknowledging diversity.

Finally, as to the intrinsic interrelatedness of what is learned: at the Curriculum Laboratory it has always been the enquiry or making which is fundamental, the interdisciplinary character of the work secondary, but inevitable once free-ranging work is permitted. As to the basis of studies, we have to admit to having learned as we went along. We talked at first of thematic studies, and this was sometimes seen as working within the framework of a concept which apparently had significance in several different disciplines, even though the common use was necessarily only analogous. I prefer to think of broad areas of investigation, in which children and teachers, perhaps after an initial "starter" which may or may not be planned by teachers, work together to formulate questions to be asked, problems to be solved, decisions to be made, hypotheses to be tested. Elsewhere I have suggested a distinction between exploration, experiment and explanation.[6] I suspect that younger children will be involved mainly in exploration, but that as they grow into mid-adolescence they will increasingly be concerned with explaining to themselves the complex interrelated phenomena of personal and public life.

Our proposals have sometimes been parodied as concessions to the trivial passing interests of young people. Occasionally triviality is all that they are able to muster. Very often, however, their grasp of priorities is more sober than that of some of their elders, not excluding their teachers, and McLuhan's crack about the level of information outside the school making going to school a waste of time is often all too true also. Our concern has been that the young should learn to deal skillfully with complex data, but more important still that as members of a jeopardized species they should learn to think and feel both broadly and with precision about themselves and their fellows. In particular, exponents of IDE stress that social studies should not be isolated from the natural sciences, the arts and technical studies. How can you understand about lunar man if you exclude a study of his creations, his origins and his physical make-up? And what hope have we that lunar man, who is also man the polluter and destroyer, will survive unless the young of the species are invited by their elders to take a long, hard, but compassionate look at him?

References

1. Mary Brown and Norman Precious, *The Integrated Day in the Primary School*, London, Ward Lock Educational, 1968; New York, Agathon Press, 1969.
2. Paul H. Hirst, "Liberal Education and the Nature of Knowledge," in R.D. Archambault, ed., *Philosophical Analysis and Education*, Routledge & Kegan Paul, 1965.
3. Louis A. Reid, *Ways of Knowledge and Experience*, Allen and Unwin, 1961.
4. Philip H. Phenix, *Realms of Meaning*, McGraw-Hill, 1964.
5. Jerome Bruner, *Toward a Theory of Instruction*, Harvard University Press, 1966.
6. Charity James, *Young Lives at Stake*, Agathon Press, 1972, pp. 100-104.

16. Changing the Curriculum

*In 1970, the centenary of the introduction of compulsory educa-
tion in England and Wales, the Council for Educational Advance invited Brian MacArthur, then education correspondent of the London Times, to edit a collection of papers about future developments
in English education. The book is called* New Horizons in Education. *Mine was the main contribution on curriculum, which accounts
for the fact that I did not have to confine myself to secondary education, as I so often do. The papers were intended to be·forward-
looking but not to delve into the immediate controversies of the day.
I think the paper gives a fair picture of the broad general agreements
to be found among leading English educators in this decade, as well
as making some more personal comments on current trends in
English education.*

THE GREEKS HAD A WORD for what I most fear for English education.
The word is *hypoulic* and it means that although on the surface a
body looks healthy, underneath.there is a festering sore. The ways in
which an image of a healthy educational system can be presented
are already familiar: comprehensive education, plenty of
educational technology, more young people qualified for more
places in tertiary education. All these are part of the minimum
decencies of education in a modern society. Add to them smaller
classes and adequate support for teachers, both in salary and in
assistance, and the picture could be very presentable. But our education will be hypoulic if we do not admit to the deep wounds society
inflicts on young people through its schools.

The most obvious wound, and the best documented, is caused by the social divisiveness of schooling. The slum schools described by both Newsom and Plowden are its pustules. But this is not yet the hypoulic condition: their disadvantages are overt, almost brashly displayed. There are other schools which are newly-built and elegant where the sore festers unseen. The distinguished expert on prisons who recently described some city secondary schools to me as "just like little prisons" was not referring simply to mouldering three-deckers, some of which are the homes of thriving egalitarian schools. You can be a pupil in a plate-glass house and still learn the essential social lesson of an elitist curriculum. It runs, "You don't seem to us, your teachers, to be much good at anything. Therefore you aren't much good," or worse still, "Therefore we expect you to be good-for-nothing. You have very little place in our scheme of things. You don't belong."

To be good at something in a competitive system can only mean that in a rank order you stand higher than others. The only thing you can be good at without others having to be bad at it is being yourself. But in the "little prisons," being good at being yourself, following your own bent, developing confidence, self-respect, and thereby a trust in others—this is not part of the curriculum.

The children who feel themselves extruded and drop out of the life and work of a divisive school are mainly from the working-class families. The middle-class has its safety net of parental support, insistence on perseverance, and being in every sense of good address. Some working-class children are robust by temperament and have firmly opted out of the value system of the school: "I've been waiting to leave since I was five." But as the importance of school in establishing one's place in the adult pecking-order becomes more and more obvious, parents of all classes are increasingly anxious to play the labour market, and we can expect more "school failures" to feel worthless and inadequate and so to continue to provide job-fodder for our less savoury employers. Others respond to the implicit violence of the institution by personal violence, and may well continue in that style in adult life, especially if this confirms their experience of violence at home.

When we believed in the capacity theory of intelligence, the belief that intelligence was fixed and innate, teachers could be thought of as licensed academic bartenders, making sure that the pints went into the pint-pots and so on down the line. We now have widespread authentic evidence of the extent to which teachers' expectations affect children's learning. It follows today that education can no longer be thought of as socially or politically neutral. The teacher who writes off the "bottom band" of a comprehensive entry is not just lacking in human sympathy, any more than is the head who gives poor teachers to low streams, or bleeds the staffing ratio of the younger children to ensure an expensive system of options for his sixth forms. Both represent a force in the profound struggle of our time. By their self-fulfilling prophesies, effected through their expectations in the classroom and through the priorities in the school's total curriculum, they contribute to our meritocratic oligarchy. They ensure too that between the elite and the rejected there lies a no-man's land which is occupied by displaced beings.

The opposite force is represented by a different kind of schooling, in which schools do not try to judge children by preconceived norms but help them all to become confident in developing their own strengths and in communicating with each other and their teachers. In this way they acquire the many intellectual and practical skills which it is convenient to have in the modern world—because they find they need them. It is encouraging that some of the most imaginative and innovative schools are in run-down city areas. Their existence disproves, for this country at least, the appalling argument being put forward by some pressure groups in North America that deprived children cannot make use of a free and open kind of schooling.

The other sore is just as much in need of cleansing, but it is so familiar that we do not notice it and barely have to hide it from ourselves. It is part of the hypoulic condition to ignore the damage that we do to children who are thought of as academically successful. In making a case for public education, one line of argument is that it is an instrument of personal aspiration which a welfare state owes to its members. The Crowther Report pointed out that it is also an important aspect of a nation's capital investment. What is less often noted is that it is the means whereby the old see to it that they can control the young.

If religion could be accused of being at one time the opium of the people, ensuring that the have-nots would not make demands upon the haves, education in a secular society all too easily becomes the heroin which adults prescribe to the young, making quite sure that they will not have the creative energy to improve on the system they inherit.

We have a traditional education which stresses accuracy in the performance of set tasks, requires classes of thirty or more vastly different children to perform the same tasks, makes much classwork a guessing game in which the teacher alone knows the right answers —and in this kind of teaching there are always right and wrong answers—and through its examinations lays down fixed standards to be reached, scaring mid-adolescents and young adults by the way it ritualises a series of extremely dubious assessment procedures. This is not the way to help young people to face the vast problems of an endangered and divided species, nor the way to enable them to arrive at a noble and equitable social order. It isn't even the way to get British business to flourish. Nobody in their right senses would invent it now. The trouble is that all successful adults have undergone it, and it is difficult to break out of a mould which we have come to think of as the proper human form.

The poison in the social system is powerful and will take time to heal. Over the coming years many strong social and cultural pressures may make the wounds more ugly. But looking back at the past decade it is possible to see encouraging improvements within our schools. It is becoming clear to many people that changes of organisation, however well-intended, are not enough. Comprehensive education and unstreaming are a beginning, but they have to be matched by fundamental changes in the curriculum and relationships of the school.

The 1960s were a period of unprecedented activity in reforming the curriculum. At their most radical the new curricula are based on the dynamic interrelationship of several vitally important perceptions about people. First, human beings have different concerns and different strategies of learning; teachers' careful observation of younger children and the researches on individual differences are beginning to bear fruit. Second, in learning, one cannot distinguish what one learns from how one learns it: the method is the content. This is one cause of the rapidly increasing support for enquiry-based learning. Third, the curriculum is obsolete, and always will be. The knowledge explosion requires a far more rapid infiltration of new modes of adult thought than has been dreamed of in the past. Fourth, people don't need the incentives of fear or competition in order to learn. These can be replaced by the dynamic collaboration of small groups developing ideas new to them, and by the acknowledgment of individual concerns in the curriculum. Finally, learning to want to go on learning happens only when children are in a setting where they feel at home.

It is fair to say that there is a broad consensus on these lines which, finds expression in the work of forward-looking teachers in schools and is strongly supported by the general run of findings of Schools Council projects. It is an accepted target of primary education, and is finding its way into the secondary schools too. The sources of these developments are varied. Probably the most important of all is the confident practice of the infant school, from which all other educational institutions have much to learn. But credit goes also to the scientists, who initiated the first major reconsideration of their curriculum. Another stimulus to invention has been the proposal to raise the school leaving age. The first excursions in this field tended to assume that secondary schools were satisfactory and that changes were needed for the young school leavers only because "non-examination pupils" were in some way lacking, and could not cope with a normal education. I look back with pride to January 1965, when the first Goldsmiths' College Pilot Course for experienced secondary teachers decided that the secondary education of all children needed radical re-thinking, and particularly in the first two years. It no longer seems a startling point of view, and, in fact, these years are a centre of concern in curriculum development today.

To say that there is some measure of agreement is not to say that there are no differences of emphasis. Some teachers who want to make their teaching seem more relevant to children are developing integrated studies, but do not welcome the concept of enquiry, so in secondary schools they end up with a carefully constructed form of team instruction. Others believe in enquiry, but see no need to combine; they do not acknowledge the thesis of primary education and of Interdisciplinary Enquiry in secondary schools, that at least part of the curriculum should be open, allowing children large blocks of time in which to track their own enquiries (which in secondary school means drawing on the help of a group of subject specialists). Other teachers, perhaps under the influence of Paul Hirst's analysis of different "forms of knowledge," are satisfied with partial integration and aim at a core curriculum of a 1950-ish style involving general science, combined social studies and undifferentiated arts. There are also serious questions as to the degree to which the various subject disciplines need to be learned sequentially; some people see some disciplines as intrinsically sequential.

To those active in the arena of curriculum development, these are very different positions and the subject of vigorous controversy. But they run along a recognisable continuum. The similarity is clear when they are contrasted with the bells and cells and formal class-teaching methods of our previous model of curriculum, which are still the established practice of some junior and most secondary schools. They are very different also from some recent developments in the United States towards individually prescribed instruction. These acknowledge individual differences, but only in the rate and order in which assignments are studied. They barely acknowledge enquiry, except in the spuriously cheerful style of "Let's find out" in which some programmes are written. They assume a fixed body of knowledge. They ignore the importance of human intercourse and group process: each child learns alone. This is a highly appropriate preparation for a functionary in a large bureaucracy. It is a training in conformity and the isolation of the individual. All our attempts, in contrast, can be fairly seen as early fumblings towards a person-centered participating society.

So far, quite good, but we should do better. I can only pick out four aspects of curriculum which at present seem to be generally un-dervalued. First, enquiry is acknowledged but the child's inven-tiveness seems to be less welcome, particularly when it is construc-tive and technical. Probably two different aspects of our traditional culture are at work here. One is the lingering tendency to roman-ticise the younger child and to try to fight against our man-made en-vironment. It is marvellous to discover the natural world, to look after plants and living creatures; also to enjoy natural beauties when there are any around. But there is a place for making and tinkering as well as for discovering and responding. Is it not better for children to be confidently urban than nostalgically sub-rural? In secondary schools the obstacles to inventiveness are different. They arise from the Platonic, aristocratic notions of the superiority of "pure" or "theoretical" studies over practical and applied, a superiority which is strongly reinforced by the internal caste system of many school staffs. Over and above this, most teachers are victims of an education which has taught them to think in words or perhaps figures, but not through diagrams or three-dimensional models. The value of what Bruner calls *enactive* and *iconic* representations, explanations to oneself or others by physical action or by images, is readily acknowledged for infants, but there is a tendency to think that the ability to manipulate more abstract symbols is an unqualified gain. Many adults have lost a very helpful tool for inventive thinking, and do not see its value. The result is not only a weakening of practical invention, but a loss of effectiveness in other kinds of problem-solving.

Secondly, there is a danger of schools becoming too much concerned with products at the expense of process. The school where the walls are plastered with pictures from the latest project is not necessarily aiding the internal growth of the child. An occasional show-piece raises the spirits, and there is great satisfaction in working with one's fellows towards a completion. But it may be much more important for a child to learn to survive through confusion, to take false steps and not quite know how to retrace them, to get completely stuck for a while, to move sideways and re-group his ideas, than to produce a splendidly competent piece of work. What matters is that children learn to formulate questions which have meaning for them, make guesses, follow hunches, test evidence, and find the best ways of coping with the kinds of problems they meet and recognise. This slow internalised process is hard to evaluate, and a show of products gives something of the same comfort to some teachers of younger children as good examination results do for their colleagues higher up the age-range. Education which emphasises process more than product often looks untidy. But real hard thinking is untidy, and work of this kind is far harder both for teachers and children than the pre-packed project or the pre-digested syllabus.

A third element, the move towards a more "outgoing" curriculum, is well canvassed and is important. Its importance is not primarily the immediate value to the pupil but its significance in the community as a whole. The calls for more environmental studies, more and earlier studies of the world of work, more visits and more assignments to day nurseries and so on, more community work, more residential courses away from home—these are not just ways of keeping young people occupied or making their education more "realistic." They should be seen alongside the trend to involve parents more deeply in their children's education, and to open the school's resources and even classes to the community; they are parallel also to plans for linking courses between schools and Further Education, which give people access to more advanced equipment and specialist staffing while still at school. It then becomes clear that they are part of a long-term, almost unconscious process of re-plotting our social institutions, a process which affects family life and the work-place as well as education.

These trends to break down the isolation of the school signal the beginning of the end of compulsory education as it has been understood in the past hundred years. Very shortly, the community will be building data banks which adults and children will share. These ought to be paralleled by an outcrop of arts centres and workshops clustering round working artists, actors and craftsmen. Grown-ups are coming to expect continuing re-training for jobs, and for many this will run alongside continuing personal education through mass media and many kinds of courses. The idea of a fixed period of once-for-all education in a place set apart from the rest of the world will probably come to seem very strange indeed.

Education should become more outward-looking, and we can be quite sure that it will. It is even more important that it should become more inward-looking, and this is less certain, because it is more difficult. Our curriculum should be far more openly concerned with people, their needs, their difficulties, their conflicts. The school is already on its way which is concerned with process more than product and which offers a broadly diversified environment in which each child can discover his own relative strengths, his own sources of enjoyment and what he can best give to his fellows and needs to receive from them. But learning to feel our feelings and communicate them is in part a skill to be acquired. Emotionally speaking most of us are limited by a restricted code in a quite special sense. In static societies, when the range of accepted behaviour is predictable and familiar, the ability to express one's own feelings and read those of others was probably less essential than it is now. Today, when young people can try on such a great range of personas, they are in danger of losing themselves behind them because there is so little opportunity for truthful communication. It is a traditional task of literature to make possible a deeper study of human beings. The arts, while being much more than media for self-discovery, make perhaps the most important contribution to it. There is a place, too, for role-playing and psychological games and studies; and where a teacher is at home with unstructured discussions they are rewarding.

Even more fundamental is the general openness and truthfulness of a school. Basil Bernstein, describing the difficulties of working-class children meeting the middle-class assumptions about language, has said recently that if the teacher is always having to say "Say it again, dear; I didn't understand you," then in the end the child may say nothing. This is precisely the situation of many children, adolescents and teachers faced with the impersonal propriety of their schools. A sunny school is not a truthful place. Men have dark thoughts, hopes, fears and hates. So have children. Yet in the earlier years of schooling the required mood is sometimes happy-happy, and children are asked to connive with their teachers in a game of "let's pretend," acting together a primal innocence that never was, a game of which the conventions permit only certain kinds of "naughtiness." It must be tempting for teachers of younger children to escape from facing personal difficulties by creating an atmosphere of energetic cheerfulness. Teachers of adolescents have succeeded all too well in denying access to the darker uncertainties of adolescence by demands for academic rigour which culminate in the spurious catharsis of the public examination. In each of us the wound festers. We can begin to heal it only if we admit that it is there. Then and then only, hope can be authentic.

To those who share the viewpoint of this chapter one can say that the expectation for the first ten years of schooling (3 to 13) is not unsatisfactory. After that age, it is to be hoped that the presence of grown men and women of 16 in compulsory education will nudge even the most repressive secondary schools towards a serious curriculum for the statutory leaver, which will be diversified, will meet their personal needs as they see them, and will be concerned with questions of fundamental human importance. But a bigger proportion of young people than ever before will be coming within the control of the universities. On present showing, it is unlikely that in the near future universities will become sensitive to the needs of undergraduates. By implication, the prognosis for the curriculum of mid-adolescents who have hopes for higher education seems unpromising.

17. Flexible Grouping in Secondary Schools (1970)

"Flexible Grouping in Secondary Schools" was written as a contribution to a Penguin Education Special, Education for Democracy *edited by David Rubenstein and Colin Stoneman, whose purpose was to provide an answer to the first Black Paper on education. The Black Papers were documents extremely critical of developments which in the United States would be called "open education." They were widely circulated free of charge in a well-printed format. Many of us who had been working in elementary and secondary schools towards nonstreaming, greater respect for children, and improved curricula were grateful to Mr. Rubenstein, a historian from the United States, and Mr. Stoneman, a chemist, both young lecturers at the University of Hull, for giving us an opportunity to make a united statement which should be constructive, rather than responding to spleen with spleen. This article contains the clearest description in the book of the Fourfold Curriculum, which I refer to often in other sections.*

THE CHILDREN NOW IN OUR SCHOOLS may be present at the final extinction of mankind. An educational system cannot solve the problems of a society, far less of a species, but it can at least be appropriate to the context in which young people are growing up. The context today is a horizon of immense danger, on the one hand, and seemingly limitless human development on the other; in contrast, everyday life seems to offer few deep-felt satisfactions, and this is in part because we have not learned to be satisfied with ourselves. Adolescents need an education which they sense to be in accord with their own idealism and despair, because it acknowledges the profound seriousness of the human situation, the tenuousness of our hold on life, the inadequacy of many of our social prescriptions. This does not mean, of course, that it has to be doom-ridden; if it deals in truth, it can be often warm, light-hearted and funny.

The new radical reforms in primary and secondary education are sometimes represented as arising simply from observing children and working with them. They should be seen also as the outcome of a thorough-going reappraisal not only of our context but also of human nature. In particular, they bring into the schools a modern understanding of the character of human knowledge, the sources of human behaviour and the problems of human societies.

First, we have to recognize that we are an exploratory, creative, problem-solving species, whose best and most assured statements are necessarily contingent, speculative and partial. Today's facts, like today's norms, may well be tomorrow's errors. Knowledge is an activity, not a commodity. On the other hand, information, which is a commodity, is no longer a scarce one. It follows, therefore, both from the true nature of knowledge and from the present overwhelming quantity of information, that children should spend little time memorizing facts. Rather they should learn to scan and evaluate complex data.

Again, the attempt to separate thinking from feeling has been a disastrous failure: it is the whole person who learns and acts. From this, two changes follow, apparently disparate but closely interconnected. The first is that the expressive and creative arts become central to the curriculum rather than outlets for feeling only and so in some way inferior to the hard core of academic learning. But beyond this, the importance of the child's involvement in his work comes to be acknowledged. It is not true that provided you learn it does not matter how you feel about what and how you learn, since in large measure it is those feelings which determine what kind of person you become.

Finally, the reform represents a vision of the school as a society grounded in the primacy of persons. This may sound facile, but I believe that a new understanding is involved, not a return to rank individualism nor a synthetic sweetness which denies the need of human beings for truthful conflict, and indeed the frequent tiresomeness—and worse—of human behavior. The point is that equality alone is seen to be insufficient. It has become little more than a quantitative concept which was mounted to avert exploitation and has failed to do so. In the context of human jeopardy, the stress should be not on mere equality but on diversity. Men are born diverse, and everywhere are under pressure to become the same; only the local moulds are different, and often mutually exculsive. By welcoming the fact that people are different, have different pulses, talents, growth rates, physical build, interests, sexual ambitions, temptations, temperaments, even physical scales of perception, we have some hope of countering the in-built tendency of all modern large-scale organizations to quantify and depersonalize, which is one of the greatest threats to survival. More means worse only if it means more of the same.

In the new developments, flexible grouping of children and reform of curriculum are inextricably interwoven. Simply to un-stream children and then teach them the old curriculum meets none of the requirements of our situation; nor is it enough to attempt a new curriculum while maintaining the same techniques. The class lesson, for instance, which attempts to keep thirty or forty children on the same hard tack, is extremely wasteful as a technique of com-munication. True, occasionally a teacher's magic may keep a whole class enthralled, and he should not be deprived of occasions to exer-cise his magic, nor they to enjoy it. But the normal basis of work becomes the small group or "cluster" of less than half a dozen, or the individual who is happy for the time being to work on his own. The teacher's activities are varied, demanding and interesting. He is a partner in formulating problems and hypotheses for resolving them, he gives access to resources or experiences which are needed, he ex-plains the nature of evidence, he sorts out learning difficulties and at times he provides straightforward exposition where this is needed. All this can be done without denying the learner's need for autonomy in inquiry and problem-solving.

With younger children, flexible grouping is relatively straight-forward, but as they move to secondary schools, with specialist teachers, larger numbers and more sophisticated equipment, more complex planning is needed. The proposals which follow are the out-come of long-term consideration at the Goldsmiths' College Curriculum Laboratory by heads and other experienced teachers in conjunction with the permanent members of the unit, and are being used as a basis of innovation by a number of schools.

The aim is a mosaic, not a melting-pot. Adolescents need to be able to follow their own bent; they also have much to contribute to and gain from common enterprises. We have formulated a fourfold foundation of study based on the nature of the subject matter and the special requirements of the individual. First, we think young people should have the opportunity to work in an open situation, devoting themselves to problems of some complexity. This we call Interdisciplinary Enquiry (IDE), indicating by the name that the basic activity is enquiry (in the broadest sense of questioning, identifying problems, seeking explanations), and that study of major human problems will be meagre unless it draws on the resources of many disciplines, including the natural sciences and the creative arts. Young people work in "clusters" for up to half the time-table, perhaps five forms blocked together with five teachers from different fields. Secondly, they need at times to work within the accepted limits of a discipline, and this will be in a group of the usual class size with the usual single teacher. There is also a growing tendency for teachers in allied disciplines to collaborate in something broader than their own subject but narrower than IDE, so they are already moving away from a rigid interpretation of a four-fold curriculum.

The two other bases for bringing children together are quite different, for they are not concerned with the content of study but rather with the varying requirements of individuals. Children have special interests which cannot always be met in IDE or in the ordinary study of a subject. They may need to go into the same material in greater depth, or they may want more out-of-the-way provision. Acknowledgement of special interests is vitally important in adolescence and should not be side-tracked into extra-curricular events; it may be particularly important for children with a very specialized talent, but it has value for others also. For practical reasons of staffing, but also as a matter of policy, we propose that groups sharing special interests should cross age lines, as this broadens young people's social experience and their chance to learn from one another.

The same is true of the fourth aspect of the curriculum. Here the criterion is the learner's special needs: a child is blocked in something he wants or needs to do by some lack in his education. He needs coaching. Sometimes a group will be similar to a remedial set in a conventional school, but more successful children have special needs too, sometimes at a high level of work, and are held back by lack of diagnosis and special help. It is really extraordinary how little this has been recognized in secondary schools, especially when one considers how many children are ill, change schools or go through bad patches in learning and then want to catch up. It is here that the use of programming and technical aids, closely related to the diagnosis of individual difficulties, will probably be most fruitful.

These four bases for grouping might be called the macrocosmic aspects of flexible grouping in a diversified curriculum. Diversity is also the essence of IDE, for it is in the open, free-wheeling work of IDE that one begins to see how narrow has been our concept of "mixed ability." Many clusters are based on friendship or shared interests, but there are times when the teacher can propose other constructive groupings. Negative mixed ability grouping, a refusal to divide children, is a refusal to do harm; but we need more positive concepts, and it should be a growing part of a teacher's skill and understanding to develop them, with the help of research.

Already Roda Amaria and her colleagues at the National Centre for Programmed Learning have shown that at quite ordinary tasks the best results are achieved when children of different I.Q. and appropriate personality are paired. Liam Hudson has shown the advantage given in our traditional education to the "convergent" thinker, who is happiest doing what he has been told. Some modern searchers for talent invert the rank order and cherish only the child who can produce plenty of ideas of his own. This isn't just to change victims; it is surely to miss the whole point. In IDE young people can be engaged in very complex studies, perhaps looking at the biological and cultural aspects of growing up; or at the local environment, how it has changed, is changing and ought to be improved; or at human survival and the balance of nature; or at the influence of technological change on employment; or at love and hate; or at themselves as individuals and as a group; or at any other of a vast range of important questions which are open to them and their teachers. For this they need not only a variety of disciplines but a variety of dispositions. There is a place for the technically or intellectually inventive, for the person who can clothe an idea with examples or test it effectively, for the scholarly ferret, for someone who just feels there's something wrong somewhere but can't put his finger on it, for those who can contribute a clear analysis of data and for others who more readily make direct personal statements in the arts. Young people who would otherwise be in a low stream can give a great deal; indeed their insights are often more penetrating than those of the academic sprinter. In this microcosm of an open society all can be welcomed as they are, without any limits being set to what they might become.

New developments of this kind in secondary schools are in their infancy. They should not be treated as dogma, but they do deserve to be allowed their early difficulties and growing pains. One should not be sanguine that this will be granted them. Reforms with such radical implications for society disturb and anger many people, for they run counter to an elderly regime with intellectual and economic assumptions which belong to the past There are those, too, who think one can bring secondary education up to date by more superficial means, offering social justice in the form of more examinations for more children, adding some visual aids, a soupcon of team teaching because it "helps the teacher to put on a better performance," and some social education for those who have been tested and found wanting—any coherent study of the human situation being viewed as a waste of good learning time for those who expect later to manage our affairs. Patching of this kind may seem to get our education into the twentieth century. It will not help us to survive into the twenty-first.

Index

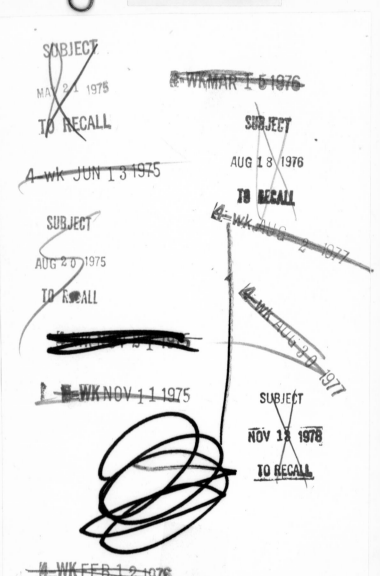